| | DATE DUE | | |
|---|---|---|---|
| | | | |
| | | | |
| | | | |
| | | | |
| | | | |
| | | | |
| | | | |
| | | | |
| | | | |
| | | | |
| | | | |

# THE
# INTERNET
# BUBBLE

**REVISED EDITION**

# THE INSIDE STORY ON WHY IT BURST

—AND WHAT YOU CAN DO
TO PROFIT NOW

# THE
# INTERNET
# BUBBLE

## REVISED EDITION

**ANTHONY B. PERKINS**

**MICHAEL C. PERKINS**

HarperBusiness
*An Imprint of* HarperCollins*Publishers*

HarperCollins books may be purchased for educational, business, or sales promotional use. For information please write: Special Markets Department, HarperCollins Publishers, Inc., 10 East 53rd Street, New York, NY 10022.

REVISED EDITION

*Designed by Elliott Beard*

Library of Congress Cataloging-in-Publication Data

Perkins, Anthony B.
    The Internet bubble : the inside story on why it burst—and what you can do to profit now / Anthony B. Perkins, Michael C. Perkins.—Rev. ed.
        p.  cm.
    Includes bibliographical references and index.
    ISBN 0-06-664001-6
    1. Internet industry—Finance.   2. Online information services industry—Finance.
I. Perkins, Michael C.   II. Title.

HD9696.8.A2 P45   2001
025.06'332—dc21                                                            2001024129

01   02   03   04   05   ❖/RRD   10   9   8   7   6   5   4   3   2   1

*To Julie and Kristin, the sunshine of my life.*
*—AP*
*To Alex and Claire, with love and affection.*
*—MP*

# CONTENTS

# PROLOGUE: **PLAYING THE INTERNET IPO GAME**

*J*eff Bezos is a smart guy. He graduated summa cum laude from Princeton in 1986 with a double major in electrical engineering and computer science. But Bezos isn't just a nerd; he's ambitious and he likes to sell stuff. That's why he founded Amazon.com.

In 1994, while doing a stint on Wall Street as a hedge fund manager at D. E. Shaw, Bezos sat down and made a list of twenty things he thought he could sell online. He felt books had potential because with more than 3 million English book titles in print, even the largest chain stores like Barnes & Noble and Borders could carry only 150,000 at a time. "It was clear that computers and the Internet could be uniquely applied to organize, present, and sell the entire stock in a way that a physical store or mail-order catalogue couldn't possibly imagine," Bezos explains.

Bezos chucked his job and pin-striped suits, packed up, and moved west. His destiny was to return to his computer-geek roots, immerse himself in the Internet, and become a multibillionaire along the way. So with classic entrepreneurial drive and passion, Bezos raised money—$1.3 million from family, friends, and others—built up the infrastructure over a year's time, and then launched Amazon in July of 1995.

After bootstrapping his company for several months, Bezos realized that to take Amazon to the next level he'd need more money and some help recruiting a top management team. It was time to get a professional venture capitalist on board. Bezos was in a good position to fetch a high valuation for Amazon's first professional venture capital round because he had real revenues and a significant customer list to show to venture investors. "We joked at the time that we would have to change our voice-mail system to say, 'If you are a customer, press one. If you are a venture capitalist, press two,' " he recalls. His must-have choice was John Doerr, the premier venture capitalist with one of the top firms, Kleiner Perkins Caufield & Byers (KP). But as it turned out, Doerr wasn't one of the investors ringing Amazon's phone.

Bezos is not one to leave things to chance. Instead of waiting around to hear from John Doerr, Bezos called him. Bezos said that given Kleiner Perkins's reputation in the Internet space, they should at least talk. Doerr agreed and was on a plane and in Seattle the next day.

Bezos wanted to split the deal between Kleiner Perkins and two other venture capital firms, Hummer Winblad and General Atlantic Partners, but Doerr preferred not. "He argued that if Kleiner Perkins owned the whole round, their partners could justify giving the company their full attention," says Bezos. This request seemed reasonable given that Amazon was selling only 15 percent of the company for an $8 million first-round investment. Before Amazon had even deposited KP's check, John Doerr got to work helping CEO Bezos fill out his management team with experienced professionals from both the software and retail business worlds.

In spite of this boost, several months later Amazon was still operating at a significant loss. Meanwhile, brick-and-mortar booksellers like Barnes & Noble had started to take notice of the online opportunity. Bezos was deeply paranoid that they might storm his market and put him out of business. To hold them off, he needed a financial war chest fast. In the old days, Bezos would have gone back to the venture capitalists for more money, but this would mean selling stock at a low valuation and surrendering more of his ownership in the company, something he definitely didn't want to do.

Fortunately for Bezos, he was building his company at the beginning of the Internet boom era, when the public market was hungry to buy any new stock, as long as it had a *.com* in its name. By taking advantage of pent-up investor demand and spinning some of the company's stock into the public market, Bezos could fill his war chest with cash at a much higher stock price than the venture capitalists would pay. Not only that, the IPO would also provide an ideal opportunity to make a huge public relations splash about Amazon's market leadership. In John Doerr's words, it was time for Amazon to "put the puck on the ice" and raise as much money as possible to invest in scale and snatch the first-mover advantage.

Unfortunately, Bezos's timing couldn't have been worse. Amazon's IPO plans bumped right into the Internet market's winter 1997 mini-correction.

But Bezos did have an ace or two in the hole. He'd teamed up with a couple of aggressive investment bankers—the legendary Frank Quattrone and his longtime sidekick, Bill Brady. Both bankers were eager to do the Amazon deal. Recalls Quattrone, "We saw Amazon as a wave rider—as a business that would benefit from the Internet regardless of who the technology winners were."

Quattrone had something to prove, too. In April 1996 he and several executives had bolted from Morgan Stanley, where they had built a technology practice that was the most dominant in the industry. Now they were opening up a rival office for Deutsche Morgan Grenfell (DMG) in Menlo Park, and a marquee deal like Amazon would be a great way to best his old employer, as well as his longtime archrival Goldman Sachs. "We told Amazon we would go through a brick wall to get their deal done," says Quattrone.

Quattrone and Brady were seasoned enough to see an advantage in the slow market for Internet stocks—it would mean having less competition when telling the Amazon story to the big institutional stock buyers like Fidelity. And as they hit the road with Bezos selling "The Earth's Biggest Bookstore" to institutional investors all over the country, the company's deal book filled with interested investors.

But how much to charge for the stock? Amazon's original S–1 filing proposed $13 per share, but the huge demand for Amazon's stock created a last-minute debate between bankers and management over whether the company should go out at $17 versus $18 per share. Given that Amazon proposed to sell 3 million shares at its IPO, the decision between choosing $18 instead of $17 meant a difference of stuffing an additional $3 million into the company's coffers.

When Bezos, Quattrone, and Brady met in New York in March 1997, they were joined on the phone by John Doerr and Scott Cook, an Amazon board member and cofounder of Intuit, maker of the financial software package Quicken. The haggling started right away. Bezos had no doubt about the best price; he wanted to go out at $18 per share. Quattrone and Brady were more cautious; they recommended $17 per share, thinking they could sell the stock more easily to the institutional buyers. "The safe thing was to price it at $16," says Quattrone. "Seventeen dollars would have been bold, and $18 would have been incredibly aggressive."

Meanwhile, Doerr and Cook played devil's advocates, challenging Bezos on his motives. "It wasn't easy to articulate the benefits of a $17-per-share price, but it was easy to articulate the benefits of $18," Bezos asserts. So $18 per share it was.

By the time the Amazon team went on the road to sell the stock in May 1997, the Internet stock market was ticking upward. Without ever having made a dime of profit, the company raised $54 million in its public stock offering. Amazon was valued at a whopping $475 million. As usual, Bezos's shrewdness paid off, as he and his family retained 41 percent of the company stock. John Doerr and Kleiner Perkins kept a little over 14 percent.

But Amazon's stock value didn't soar to a billion dollars like that of the many Internet IPOs that would follow. "The stock initially popped to $29 per share," says Quattrone. "But it came under pressure because Barnes & Noble sued them and a lot of people were shorting the stock; the price actually came down to the issue price." For the company's next infusion of cash, Amazon skipped the equity route and instead hired DMG to raise another $75 million in debt financing from a group of banks.

By the summer of 1998, with more than 600 employees and heavy investments being pumped into advertising, promotion, and more technology, Amazon had lost $27.6 million on sales of $147.8 million. Still paranoid about the competition, Bezos decided to float a high-yield debt/junk bond financing to raise an additional $325 million. This move had an extra advantage for the Bezos family, who still owned a commanding percentage of the company, by avoiding the dilution that an equity offering would have posed.

This time around, though, Bezos turned down DMG's plan to do the deal in favor of Quattrone's former employer, Morgan Stanley. Bezos clearly had visions of grandeur. Even though Amazon's stock was hovering around the overvalued price of $90 per share, the junk bond was a gamble that in three years the stock would be closer to $300 per share, a rise of more than 233 percent. This would allow the company to refinance the debt in a second offering sometime in the future at a much more attractive stock price. "Placing our debt was all about flexibility," explains Bezos. "You can't predict what some of the opportunities might be and how much cash they might require."

By the end of 2001 Amazon was continuing to finance its negative operating cash flow by borrowing money. Its $2 billion in long-term debt accounted for 99 percent of its total capitalization.

"Originally we were hoping to build a small, profitable company," says Bezos. "And of course what we've done is build a large, unprofitable company."

On the way to building his "large, unprofitable" company, Bezos expanded his dream beyond selling books. For holiday season 2000, Amazon offered its 17 million customers in 150 countries millions of distinct items: DVDs, videos, toys, electronics, software, video games and home improvement products. Ultimately this helped make Amazon the largest e-tailing company, accounting for about 11 percent of all goods sold online in the fourth quarter of 2000 as it rung up sales of $972 million. At the same time, Amazon also posted losses of $545 million in the same quarter, bringing its net loss for all of 2000 to a total of $1.4 billion. One result was that after the holiday season, Amazon closed two of its operation centers and laid off 1,300 people (15 percent of its workforce).

A year before Bezos dreamed up Amazon, a different story was unfolding in Silicon Valley. In the summer of 1993, Jerry Yang and

David Filo should have been working on their doctoral theses in computer science, but surfing the Net was a lot more fun. Their Ph.D. adviser was out of the country on a sabbatical, so what the hell.

Hanging out night and day in a cramped, stuffy office trailer on the Stanford campus, Yang and Filo put together a catalogue of Internet sites. At first it was for their personal reference, but it gradually evolved into *David and Jerry's Guide to the World Wide Web.* Soon, hundreds, then thousands of Web surfers were accessing their guide. In a spirit of whimsy and refreshing self-effacement, Yang and Filo called their growing service Yahoo.

Like the Homebrew personal computer phenomenon of almost twenty years earlier, Yahoo was an organic, grassroots movement that only gradually evolved into a business enterprise. But when they realized they might have a commercial opportunity on their hands, Yang and Filo slapped together a business plan and began shopping it around to venture capitalists. The partners at Kleiner Perkins wanted them to merge with another budding online service they had already funded, Excite. Yahoo also got offers from America Online and Netscape to sell out for stock and come join those companies as employees. But Yang and Filo, wanting to remain independent, declined.

Eventually, they hooked up with venture capitalist Michael Moritz of Sequoia Capital, a first-tier firm that had built a pioneering image by seed-funding companies such as Apple and Cisco. A charming Oxford graduate with a British accent and a ready smile, Moritz had joined Sequoia in 1986 after serving as a business reporter for *Time* magazine, and he'd been looking for a big hit ever since.

Sequoia decided to invest $1 million in Yahoo (*"Give* is not a verb we use at Sequoia," says Moritz) and helped them recruit a stellar management team. With seasoned chief executive Tim Koogle and chief operations officer Jeff Mallett on board, Yang and Filo could now call themselves Chief Yahoos.

In the fall of 1995, Yahoo was running out of cash, so they raised $4 million from Reuters and Softbank.

Within a few months, Yahoo's online traffic had doubled, they had signed up more than eighty advertisers, and they ran live news feeds from Reuters. Most amazing of all, Yahoo was making a profit—an unprecedented feat for a company started during the early Internet boom.

These developments were not lost on Softbank. Its president, Masayoshi Son, came to Silicon Valley to see Yahoo in their off-campus digs, a dumpy out-of-the-way place with a leaky roof. The entrepreneurs ordered in pizza and Son laid out his proposal to buy out Yahoo completely. Instead, Yang, Filo, and Moritz agreed to sell some of their stock to Softbank for a total of $30 million, while another $70 million came directly from Son into the business.

As Moritz puts it, "We watched our competitors getting bigger allies and realized that to grow faster we needed some big trains. We wanted to avoid getting gauzumped by the competition."

A team from Goldman Sachs also came calling at the urging of a young Goldman associate, Victor Hwang, a friend of Yang's from his undergraduate days at Stanford. Although initially dismayed by the informality of the operation, the Goldman team was impressed enough by the Web traffic numbers to do more research and eventually agreed to underwrite Yahoo's initial public stock offering.

Yahoo had its own reasons for doing a public offering. Unlike search engine companies such as Excite, Infoseek, and Lycos, Yahoo focused less on developing technology and more on building a brand name as the leading Web indexer and ultimate navigational portal for the Internet. Yahoo's early strategy was to position itself more as a media company that would build its image leveraging big-time and creative advertising campaigns, in the same way the early tycoons of television and radio broadcasting did. More than just raising big bucks, an IPO would also give Yahoo the serious public exposure it needed if it were to become a household name and the leading contender in the emerging Web services space.

"We didn't want to risk having the other guys go public while we didn't," says Jerry Yang. "Not only would they have the extra cash, but they could also use the stock as currency to acquire other companies. To have Excite and Lycos out there consolidating the market while we couldn't would've been a huge mistake." He adds, "I also think the market at the time was clearly receptive to a story like ours."

So in February 1996 Yahoo's executives, bankers, and venture capitalists got together in the company's newer and only slightly nicer offices in Sunnyvale to discuss the offering. At the meeting the Goldman Sachs team reported that the demand for the stock was already high. They hadn't even built their offering book yet, and the requests to buy flowed in. Yahoo was a pure Internet play in a frothy market, and the bankers wanted to cash in; they figured they could charge up to $25 per share, allowing Yahoo to double up on its valuation.

"This was Goldman's first big Internet deal," says Yang. "They would have felt bad leaving money on the table."

But one of Yahoo's founders, the cerebral and normally quiet David Filo, was wary of getting too greedy; he wanted instead to reward investors by giving them a reasonable deal. The more experienced managers also realized if the stock started out lower and continued to go up, this would be great publicity for Yahoo and help boost its brand recognition, especially if their competitors' stocks dropped below their initial prices. Yahoo's team took the long view. "We didn't want to be viewed as a company that went up and then went down," says Yang. In essence, Yahoo wanted to create an investor brand as well as a company brand by establishing the best stock performance record among its competitors.

Since Softbank had just paid approximately $13 per share for the private stock holding, the team thought this was a good target price for the public offering.

In what they called "the fastest IPO known to man," Yahoo filed to go public in the first week of March and was a public company a month later. During that period, Goldman Sachs got over 100 Yahoo-related phone calls a day, and the bankers claim there was in excess of 100 million shares of demand for Yahoo's 3-million-share offering.

In the first round of trading, the stock went up to $24.50 per share. Shares changed hands several times and peaked at $43 before coming down to $33 at the end of the day. The total market value came to almost $850 million.

In the months immediately following its IPO, the market for Internet stocks went into a downswing, but Yahoo stock never traded below its offering price, unlike its competitors. Its early branding strategy had succeeded.

Since the fourth quarter of 1996, Yahoo always showed a profit. And the year 2000 was no exception as Yahoo posted a profit of $291 million on $1.1 billion in sales. This made the company one of the few pure Internet players to consistently operate in the black. But Yahoo was not exempt from the effects of the deflated Internet Bubble. By the first quarter of 2001, Yahoo's stock price was down more than 90 percent from its fifty-two-week high of over $200 per share a year before. And the company was facing something of a crisis. In spite of having 185 million users, Yahoo was only expecting ad sales of $170 million in the first quarter, down from a forecast of $320 million only a few months before. Sales were off because advertising from Internet companies had fallen far faster than expected. Meanwhile with the economy as a whole slowing, established national advertisers proved reluctant to jump in and fill the ad vacuum on Yahoo.

That Yahoo would survive was not in doubt, since the company had $1.7 billion in cash, although its precipitous drop in market value made it an attractive takeover target. In March 2001, Tim Koogle announced he was stepping down as CEO and a worldwide search for a replacement began.

Yahoo and Amazon were among the Internet's first-generation elite. Yahoo had followed the old rules: It was profitable before going public and had raised plenty of money in private financing before its IPO. Its founders, David Filo and Jerry Yang, each retained a 15 percent ownership in Yahoo, while Sequoia Capital ended up with 17 percent and Softbank, 37 percent.

Meanwhile Amazon had survived by doing a junk-bond debt

financing and then two convertible bonds, rather than another public offering. From 1997 through the end of 2000, Amazon had received $2.8 billion in funding. But by early 2001 its debt was trading at fifty cents on the dollar, and with its stock price down 86 percent from its peak, Amazon now had a $130 million annual interest expense. It also seemed that more than $2 billion had been spent to attain a mere top-line annual growth rate of 17 percent. And more than half of Amazon's customers were ordering something once from Amazon, but never coming back.

In February 2001, Lehman Brothers' convertible bond analyst Ravi Suria was predicting that Amazon's working capital would turn negative by the end of the year. In other words, there would not be enough cash coming in to cover expenses. His analysis showed that Amazon ended 2000 with approximately $386 million in net working capital and almost $2 billion in debt, but he expected cash outflows to be $440 million in 2001. Not surprisingly Amazon executives took issue with Suria's calculations and conclusions, and the *New York Observer* reported that Amazon board member and Kleiner Perkins venture partner John Doerr called Lehman Brothers to strongly protest the report before it was released to the public.

We chose to open our book by telling the inside stories of the Amazon and Yahoo IPOs because we feel they represent the high drama of life inside the Internet Bubble. In this world, entrepreneurs, professional managers, venture capitalists, and investment bankers all work together to plot strategy, make decisions, and raise big bucks at a rate of speed unprecedented in the history of business. Read on as we describe what it's like to live and do business during a mania, and what companies and investors are doing now to survive and prosper in the aftermath of the Darwinian shakeout.

# Doonesbury

# *INTRODUCTION*

> We have witnessed a cruel correction—a 7.5 on the
> Richter scale. I have not witnessed such a brutal
> market beating in the 15 years I have been helping
> technology companies go public.
> —Brad Koenig, managing director and head of the
> technology-banking practice, Goldman Sachs

In June 1999, when we submitted our final manuscript for the
first edition of this book to our publishers at HarperCollins, the
concluding thesis in our epilogue was very clear:

> The bottom line to our analysis is very simple. With very few excep-
> tions, every one of the 133 public Internet companies is overvalued.
> Our advice to Internet investors is equally simple: If you hold any of
> these stocks, it's time to sell. Yes folks, if the Internet gala hasn't ended
> by the time this book hits the streets, it will probably end sometime
> soon thereafter. So it's time to get out.

Of course, no one listened to us—at least at first. By the time
our book finally hit the bookshelves on November 1, 1999, the market capitalizations of the Amazons and Yahoos continued to climb
literally by the billions, and Internet IPOs were still very much in
fashion. By March 9, 2000, another 200-plus Internet companies
had gone public, bringing the total to 378. These companies had a
collective market capitalization of an incredible $1.5 trillion. This
number was truly amazing when you figure that it was supported
by a meager $40 billion in total annual sales, most of which were
concentrated in the hands of a few companies such as Qwest, AOL,

and Amazon.com. And most incredibly, 87 percent of those 378 Internet companies had yet to even show a quarterly profit.

But we all know the rest of the story. It is clear that a major Day of Reckoning came the day before our taxes were due, when on April 14, 2000, many of these Internet companies saw their stock prices take a 50 to 70 percent whack in price. And since that day, a Darwinian shakeout of the Internet business has ensued with a vengeance, with almost daily reports of once promising public and private companies slamming their doors shut for good. Since the Internet industry walls started to shake in the spring of 2000, we have counted over 600 Internet companies that have laid off a total of over 60,000 employees through February 2001. And 130 dotcom companies have closed down altogether.

By the time we submitted the manuscript for the second edition of *The Internet Bubble* on December 22, 2000, the total market capitalization of the over 370 public Internet companies had plummeted by 75 percent. That means that over a trillion dollars of value had evaporated in just under a year. Of the 378 public Internet companies we follow, 211 had seen their stock prices crater by more than 80 percent (see Appendix C, "The Internet Wasteland"). Former high flyers such as DoubleClick, InfoSpace, Internet Capital Group, Priceline.com, PSINet, Red Hat, and VerticalNet—once considered to be core Internet holdings—were now threatening to become penny stocks. And it wasn't just the underperformers that had taken a serious whack in price. Even Internet brand names such as Amazon (down 86 percent), Yahoo (down 88 percent), and C/Net (down 84 percent) had seen their stock prices pounded, way down from their fifty-two-week highs. In fact as of March 7, 2001, Yahoo was at its original IPO price and Amazon's stock was below its orginal offering price.

The three sectors that had clearly taken the biggest hit were retail e-commerce, content companies, and telecommunications-enabling companies. As Broadview International's CEO, Paul Deninger, said, "We spent a whole year wondering how many pet stores were going to be successful on the Internet, only to find out that the answer is 'zero!' "

In our first edition, we divided the publicly held Internet companies (which then only numbered 133) into five sectors. The table below shows the average loss in each sector between the time we finished the first edition and December 15, 2000.

---

### Average Net Loss of Internet Industry Sectors (6/30/99 through 12/15/00)

| | | |
|---|---|---|
| **Commerce** | −82% | (100% of the companies lost value—32 out of 32) |
| **Content** | −68% | (100% of the companies lost value—27 out of 27) |
| **Services** | −81% | (100% of the companies lost value—18 out of 18) |
| **Software** | −26% | (74% of the companies lost value—20 out of 27) |
| **Telecom service** | −68% | (90% of the companies lost value—26 out of 29) |

---

Indeed, as the head of Goldman Sachs's technology practice, Brad Koenig observed, "We have witnessed a cruel correction—a 7.5 on the Richter scale. I have not witnessed such a brutal market beating in the 15 years I have been helping technology companies go public." Former secretary of the Treasury Robert E. Rubin told a gloomy crowd last fall at Internet World in New York City, "A share of stock is worth its future earnings, and that is true whether it is a steel company or an Internet company. Too many investors lost hold of that reality and now they are paying the price."

## Is the Party Really Over?

Does all this mean venture capitalists will become stingy again and only invest in friends, and friends of friends, at low-low prices? Will investment bankers go back to insisting that entrepreneurs prove their business models and show profits before they will take their start-ups public? Will hot IPO stock prices stop doubling and even tripling on the first day of trading? Will *Fortune* 1000 employees and

MBA students forsake their dreams of overnight riches and halt their exodus to dotcom land? Is the party *really* over?

One thing for certain is that the IPO window is closed shut for conceptual, non-income-producing deals. In the summer of 2000 we saw a dramatic illustration of this reality when Hollywood-based Pop.com, a fledgling entertainment Internet company funded by entertainment heavyweights Steven Spielberg and Ron Howard, announced it was shutting its doors for good. In mid-November 2000, we saw another example of the lack of appetite for Internet deals in the public market when Playboy.com announced that it postponed its IPO, in spite of growing its Web traffic by over 150 percent in the previous twelve months. The problem was, it just wasn't profitable yet.

Given the downturn in the IPO market, it's not surprising that a study by PricewaterhouseCoopers LLP found that Silicon Valley VC funds, which had set investment records for six straight quarters, saw their total funds dip for the first time in the third quarter of 2000. Driving this decline in venture capital fund-raising was, in part, a new cautionary attitude among top-tier VCs. A significant example of this new mentality was displayed when a seasoned team of venture partners at Crosspoint Venture Partners announced in November 2000 that they were not going to close a new $1 billion fund, even though investors had already committed to giving the firm the money. "Unless we can look our investors in the eyes and say we believe we have a great model to make all of this money, in good conscience, we can't go forward," said Crosspoint's founding partner John Mumford.

Indeed, by fall 2000, even the most active VC firms in Silicon Valley had slowed down their investment activity dramatically. While Kleiner Perkins's John Doerr was still saying that it was "a great time to be an entrepreneur" and that "the future of the Internet is still largely ahead of us," his firm's pace of investment had slowed markedly. Stewart Alsop of New Enterprise Associates (NEA), a venture partnership that closed a record-breaking $2.2 billion fund in September 2000, also admitted that in spite of NEA's newfound cash, his partners decided to take it slow. "The venture capital gold rush mentality is gone, and everybody is taking more time to do their homework on each deal," he told an audience in November at the Churchill Club, a Silicon Valley speaker's forum. Another significant factor is that many firms are saving up their cash to fund their existing portfolio companies, which, in the more heady days, they thought they could take public quickly to raise more money.

So sudden was the shift in the venture capital markets that the editors of *Red Herring* magazine predicted in the December 4, 2000, issue that one of the top ten trends in 2001 would be a major shakeout in the venture capital industry and that virtually every VC firm would see a significant downturn in its return on investment. "Drowning in money, the venture capital industry has grown too big, too fast," the editors warned. "Now comes the inevitable shakeout. In 2001, only the strongest firms will survive, and the pretenders will go out of business."

The winners will be top-tier firms like Accel Partners, Kleiner Perkins Caufield & Byers, and Benchmark Capital—firms that have track records in backing successful technology hardware and software solutions that help connect consumers and corporate customers. The losers will be the VC funds that invested only in electronic commerce and e-media companies, as well as incubators and so-called "Internet holding companies" like CMGI, Internet Capital Group, Idealab, and Divine Interventures.

"It's welcome to the National Football League," says venture capital veteran John Shoch of Alloy Ventures. "Many of these VCs who are getting carried off the field right now thought they were playing touch football," he observed last fall. Wall Street Internet analyst turned venture capitalist Lise Buyer, now of Technology Partners, agrees. "The free ride is over, and the game's getting a lot tougher," she says. "I think we'll see people drop out of the business because it's not fun anymore, or because the returns are not as rich," Buyer predicts.

The moral to the Internet Bubble story is that venture capitalists funded too many companies, and investment bankers took too many unproven start-ups public. As Broadview's Paul Deninger noted, "The idea that 'The Internet is going to change everything!' was used as a good excuse to fund thousands of companies, over two-thirds of which had absolutely no business plan."

## The Next Big Thing

A great question at this point is: If it ain't the Internet, what's the next big thing? Our answer to this very important question is the same as it was in the first edition—in spite of the manic-depressive investment climate we've lived through in the last few years, the high-tech opportunity is still the next big thing. As Intel chairman Andy Grove recently reminded us, "The high-tech industry is humongous! Over any period of time, the high-tech megasector has rewarded investors pretty well, and there's no reason to believe that won't continue."

To underscore Andy Grove's assertion, it's worth reviewing the following industry growth statistics:

- The new growth industries—defined as information technology, entertainment, media, health science, and finance—contribute over 50 percent of the gross domestic product growth and new jobs in America. (Gartner Group)

- The technology industry is now the third largest industry in the American economy, trailing only real estate and health care. Worldwide, information technology spending in 1999 was $2.1 trillion; that number is expected to swell to well over $3 trillion by the year 2002. (Gartner Group)

- Over 60 percent of America's households are connected to the Internet—by 2005, a billion people in the world are expected to be online. (International Data Corporation)

- 70 percent of U.S. companies now have an active Web site, and in 1999, $145 billion in business-to-business (B2B) transactions were handled online. (Gartner Group)

Driving this growth in the technology industries is, of course, the huge and spontaneous build-out of the digital network. And, as ZDNet's Dan Farber describes it, we are merely in the caveman period of the Internet. For Internet users, it's not hard to imagine (and appreciate) that the Internet we see today is not the Internet we will be living with in twenty-five years. The Internet today is clunky, unreliable, and far from ubiquitous. A mere 3 percent of the world's population has Internet access—180 million out of a world population of 6 billion. Even in rich nations, Internet penetration is still only 35 percent.

To fully appreciate where we are in the Internet boom, it is helpful to compare it to the development of the computer industry. The computer age was divided into several stages. First there was the mainframe, then the mini-computer, then the personal computer, then the local area network (LAN), and finally, client-server computing. While investors were going through each of these development stages in the computer industry, they were thinking about each new innovation as a separate investment era. But when you add it all up, it represents a fifty-year investment boom based upon some model for computing at each stage.

Over the last six years we have witnessed the development and wide acceptance of an entirely new computing and communications platform, based on open Internet standards and protocols. We have also seen the successful rollout of some basic enabling software such as browsers, Web servers, and other e-commerce services that sit upon this new infrastructure. What we haven't done yet is begin to really exploit this new platform, but that is quickly changing. In the second phase of the Internet boom, we will see the emergence of what investors like John Doerr of Kleiner Perkins and Roger McNamee of Integral Capital Partners refer to as "Evernet," where literally billions of devices will be on a high-speed, broadband, multiformat Web. "Everything that is interesting in the marketplace today derives from the transition to real-time computing," declares McNamee.

The most significant economic consequence of this new paradigm is that it will make it increasingly easier for companies to communicate and manage their relationships with their customers and suppliers. For example, there are new applications like Zaplet that are turning electronic mail into a powerful new collaborative software platform for employees and customers. We have also seen the rise of companies such as MarketSoft, Ventaso and eConnections, which have created new software applications that enable supply-chain management in ways that could never have been imagined in the past. "These new Internet applications are giving companies that successfully deploy them a significant productivity boost," contends Dell Computer CEO Michael Dell. "Look at Dell: We've been able to increase our return on investment capital by 250 percent!"

Advancements in communications hardware are also creating new growth opportunities. The consensus is that the future of the communications business rests upon optical networks. The leaps in bandwidth performance resulting from advancements in photonics (i.e., data carried by light waves) are even sharper than the performance increases we've seen in the semiconductor industry. One might say that Metcalfe's law ("Network value rises by the square of the number of terminals hooked to the network") is eclipsing Moore's law ("Computer power doubles every eighteen months"). The result is expressed in Gilder's law (named after industry pundit George Gilder), which states that "bandwidth grows at least three times faster than computer power." Therefore, if computer power doubles every eighteen months, communications power doubles every six months. As an example, we can note that backbone bandwidth on a single cable is now a thousand times greater than the entire average traffic on the global communications infrastructure five years ago. In other words, more information today can be sent over a single cable in a second than all the information that was sent over the entire Internet in one month in 1997.

The biggest drivers of Gilder's law are the leaders in the networking equipment space, including Cisco, Corvis, Sycamore Networks, and Extreme Networks. But while Gilder's "telecosm" is moving faster than the microcosm, innovations in the networking semiconductor sector are also creating several growth company opportunities. Hot new semiconductor companies such as Applied Micro Circuits, Broadcom, and PMC Sierra are all helping to enhance the performance of the new networks.

## The Changing Faces of the Web

Perhaps the most exciting result of the convergence of these new technologies is that it will broaden the face of the Web as we know it. We have heard both John Doerr and Bill Joy, the crafty cofounder and chief scientist of Sun Microsystems, insist that we have seen only one of six different forms of the Web that will come on stream. And as each of these new Webs rolls out, it will provide the opportunity to create hundreds of new start-ups.

The original World Wide Web was invented by the British physicist and programmer Tim Berners-Lee and his team at the CERN physics research center in Geneva. This narrow-band implementation of the Web was designed for the personal computer. Now ten years after its creation, Berners-Lee is nurturing this Web into a gigantic brain that he calls the Semantic Web. The goal of the Semantic Web is to make it easier for computers to locate and process data. The Semantic Web will automatically process instructions on the Internet that currently require human intervention. And in spite of the fact that we will experience a proliferation of devices hooked to the Internet (from digital phones to television sets with their own unique Web browsers) there is no reason to think that the current PC version of the Web will become obsolete. Our guess is that the PC-based Web will continue to be our most powerful interactive device—it will be our major control center.

The second form of the Web is what Bill Joy refers to as the broadband/entertainment version of the Web, where interactive games, music, and full-motion video are available over the Internet. This content will be leveraged by interactive TVs, media-rich PCs, MP3 players, and game platforms. This version of the Web is just beginning to emerge, with an estimated 7 million users with broadband access in the United States today. That number is expected to swell to well over 10 million by 2002. Most entertainment experts we've spoken to think that at least 10 million U.S. consumers will have to have broadband capability before the economics kick in and you can start creating profitable broadband-based entertainment. In addition to increases in bandwidth performance and wider access, the broader deployment of video servers, such as TiVo, Replay, and Geocast, will also help foster the development of this face of the Web.

Most of the new broadband service companies in this space today are hatched in the entertainment industry. The problem here—as with the first generation of business-to-consumer online companies—is that when you look at the bottom line, you quickly discern that no one in Hollywood is making money on the Web yet.

We've also seen a plethora of lawsuits surrounding online content companies, lawsuits in which the established industry players are taking on upstarts such as Napster and MP3.com over intellectual property issues. No matter how this issue sorts out, the unauthorized free distribution of content cannot continue forever. Artists and producers need to be paid for their original content in order to keep producing content. This is not a problem, however. History shows that as long as you give consumers a reasonable and easy way to pay for things, they will, because most people are honest. This was certainly the case as the PC software industry developed. Over time, software piracy, at least in America, went down as a percentage of loss in the industry. We expect this will eventually be the case, as well, in the content piracy wars.

But these issues obviously will need to be sorted out before the entertainment Web kicks in. Additionally, the old guard in Hollywood will have to surrender to the Internet, which they have largely refused to do so far.

We also believe that the AOL/Time Warner merger—the ultimate old economy company joining with a new economy company—will result in a combined operation that will pioneer many new online entertainment subscription services and accelerate the proliferation of video services and content demand over the Internet. Based upon these developments, as well as the trailblazing efforts of other big players such as Yahoo and News Corp., a whole new generation of start-ups in this area will finally find their feet.

The third Web that will come into play is the smart-object-based home network, which Bill Joy believes will be the most fascinating version of them all. This setup will allow us, for example, to completely network our home entertainment center, which will become increasingly Internet dependent. It will also allow your home security system to be networked to your office, car, and cell phone, as well as allow you to control all the other electronic devices in your home, including climate controls, watering systems, and coffeemakers. This Web would mean that how we operate our lives at home will be completely transformed.

The fourth form of the Web Joy describes is the mobile Web. This Web will be accessed by digital phones, wireless e-mail devices, and pocket computers produced by companies like Palm and Handspring. Many analysts believe that sometime by mid-2003, the number of Web-enabled handsets will swiftly surpass the number of personal computers connected to the Internet. This is easy to believe if you consider that there are already twice as many cellular phone subscribers as there are Internet users. Meanwhile Europe, which has a significantly higher cellular phone penetration and a much more homogeneous digital phone network than the United States, should benefit greatly from the mobile Web boom. With 12 million subscribers to the NTT DoCoMo I-mode Internet service, Japan can also claim to be a leader of the world in wireless Internet access.

Potential winners in the wireless space include applications infrastructure companies such as Japan-based Access Company, iDini, and OnScan, all of which target business-to-business niches. Handset makers like Nokia and Ericsson should also benefit. The rapid proliferation of mobile Internet devices, which are projected to reach a couple of billion by the year 2005, may well pave the way for a boom in mobile electronic commerce. Already, mobile commerce revenue surpassed $3 billion in 2000 and is projected by some to bloat up to $210 billion by 2005.

But as bullish as we are on the prospects of wireless communications, there are enormous technical and regulatory limitations to this particular sector. In our view, investors should beware the many hyped-up wireless application companies that may end up being as valueless as many of the "dot bombs."

The creation of the mobile Web will facilitate the fifth form of the Web—the voice Web—in which telephone functions and voice services are available over the Internet Protocol (IP) network. "Clearly, voice, data, and video are all moving into a single IP network even faster than we thought," Cisco Systems' CEO John Chambers remarked last fall. Companies such as Cisco Systems and Nortel are beginning to create routers that will allow traditional telephone switch technologies to operate over the Internet. There are also voice Web services, produced by new players such as TellMe, that are becoming very popular.

Finally, a business-to-business (B2B) version of the Web will emerge, in which machines are programmed to talk to each other and execute business transactions. B2B transactions over the Internet represent well over two-thirds of the total annual revenue of the entire Internet economy and are expected to continue to represent this percentage for the next several years. Given these numbers, one could easily make the case that from the entrepreneurial and venture capital perspectives, B2B electronic commerce represents the single largest Internet opportunity today and the single largest opportunity for the foreseeable future.

The godmother of the Internet, analyst Mary Meeker of Morgan Stanley Dean Witter, predicts that the big Internet story of 2001 may very well be the new efficiencies created by the B2B phenomenon. For example, some analysts predict that the B2B exchanges being set up in the automotive industry, which will provide a more efficient market for car parts, could reduce the cost of making a car by 14 percent.

The steam age moved production from the household to the

factory, railways allowed for the development of mass markets, and with electricity, the assembly line became possible. Internet-based B2B technologies are now offering the means for a sweeping reorganization of business, from online procurement, to decentralizing operations, to making outsourcing a much more attractive alternative. "The new opportunity is for every company to link to all their customers and suppliers, not just at the corporate level, but the individual level as well, and in real time," exudes Roger McNamee.

If you want our long-term bet, we would say that the lion's share of the B2B revenues will be generated by existing manufacturers. For example, Cisco Systems is already selling billions of dollars of its networking equipment online.

## Long Term, Things Look Good

These "six faces of the Web," as well as other new Web functions, will serve to reignite venture investment in start-ups. "I actually like the entrepreneurs that are coming into our office today'better than during the Bubble," venture capitalist Tim Draper observes. "The suits that want to get rich quick are gone, and the folks that want to change the world are back."

"The main difference between now and 1995 is that you can actually find lots of employees who have experience using Internet technologies," says C/Net founder turned venture capitalist Halsey Minor. "You also have a much more mature set of Internet solutions to work with."

But as with the first generation of the Internet, there will continue to be a lot of experimentation. In the first phase of the Internet boom we saw that e-media and e-commerce, especially business-to-consumer, were two industry sectors that couldn't find their way to profitability. Yet there were also many new, cool companies that emerged as technology solutions: enterprises such as Yahoo, eBay, Inktomi, Broadcom, Extreme Networks, and Verisign, to name just a few.

The bottom line is that we continue to believe that when future scholars reflect back on this era, they will observe that the first major phase of the Internet revolution was a classic industrial mania that resulted in excessive financial speculation, both private and public. But that will not be the end of the story. The next phase of the revolution will have a socioeconomic impact that will rival that of the electric light, the telephone, and the automobile. And the investors who exploit this phase of the Internet will profit handsomely.

## The Second Edition

When we were researching the first edition of *The Internet Bubble,* our main adviser, Roger McNamee of Integral Capital Partners, wisely counseled us to not try to play stock analysts. Our main role, he reminded us, was that of investigative reporters. We agreed, and ultimately our analysis and conclusions came from interviews we did with over 100 industry insiders. We tapped the wisdom of some of the smartest and most successful players in technology and finance, from Microsoft's Bill Gates, to entertainment investment banker Herb Allen Jr., to veteran venture capitalist Don Valentine. Virtually all those we interviewed agreed with the book's basic premise that the Internet market was ripe for a huge shakeout and that individuals could experience a 50 percent-plus meltdown in the value of their Internet stocks if they didn't sell before the Bubble burst.

As we went about our business interviewing insiders, Roger would often refer to our project as "the diary of a mania" because we were capturing the story while it was happening. For the sake of posterity and our own edification we have preserved that "diary" in this edition, with some new examples and "postmortem" on the aftermath of the Internet shakeout. We have indeed been living through a classic industrial mania surrounded by a financial bubble, just like that of the railroad boom, the launch of the automobile industry, and the original development of the biotechnology market. It has been a wonder to behold.

We have also preserved and updated our behind-the-scenes look at the financial wizards who funded the Internet craze, including the venture capitalists (led by Kleiner Perkins Caufield & Byers) who set out not only to invest in hot new Internet companies but also to create whole new industries. Also updated is our discussion of the investment bankers of high tech—how they compete for deals, spin shares, help their favorite institutional investors flip stock, and profit mightily from investor mania.

We have also maintained our discussion of our original Bubble calculation methodology, based on a formula provided by onetime industry analyst Bill Gurley, who is now a general partner with venture capital firm Benchmark Capital. Many readers and reviewers found our Bubble calculation particularly helpful and enlightening, and some used it as a tool for their own investment analysis. The details of the formula and application are contained in Appendices A and B.

We have also fully revised our discussion of the New Economy. It is our opinion that the so-called Long Boom thesis, which was so popular as the Internet Bubble was building and the NASDAQ continued to climb, has essentially been disproved. The twenty- to thirty-year unbroken accelerated growth scenario has been undermined not only by the bursting of the Bubble but also by distinct indications of a down cycle in the larger technology market, as well as hints of a slowdown and possible recession in the overall economy. Cycles are a simple reality of economic markets. In the midst of these cycles, meanwhile, there are socioeconomic issues, both inside and outside the Bubble, that we have touched on in this revised chapter.

Finally, for the benefit of individual investors, we profile some of the most popular Internet companies and analyze the winning characteristics of the industry leaders that are emerging from the ashes of the Internet shakeout. We also suggest how the outsider can learn to invest wisely, just like an insider. We conclude with an open letter to Internet stockholders that recaps the lessons of the Internet Bubble and provides some insight into how investors of all stripes can profit from the next new waves of the Internet.

# Doonesbury

WOW, POPPY! WE'RE SURE BURNING THROUGH A **TON** OF MONEY!

WELL, WE'RE TRYING TO POSITION OUR-SELVES TO GO PUBLIC, HONEY...

IN THE INTERNET BUSINESS, PROF-ITABILITY IS FOR WIMPS. IT MEANS YOUR BUSINESS PLAN WASN'T AGGRESSIVE ENOUGH. IT'S OKAY TO LOSE A LOT OF MONEY, AS LONG AS IT'S ON PURPOSE.

8-25

OH.

WILL ALL THIS BE EXPLAINED IN SCHOOL?

NO, IT'S TOO NEW.

# INTERNET MANIA

**We have never had something so disproportionally
publicized by everybody in the world as the greatest
coming of anything ever as the Internet.**
**—Donald Valentine, Sequoia Capital**

*I*n the last five years, individual investors have poured millions
into more than 2,000 Internet start-up companies with nothing
more on their minds than striking it rich. The result has been Internet mania and a financial bubble.

But manias and bubbles are nothing new. The classic historic
case of a mania, of course, is the tulip mania of seventeenth-
century Holland. The country's extremely prosperous mercantile
culture created a place, as the historian Simon Schama puts it,
"where a glut of capital washed around looking for a place to settle," and in which "thousands were eager to squander what disposable income they had in the irrational hope of instantaneous
wealth." And this wasn't just the elite, but "modest folk" such as
artisans, millers, weavers, carpenters, smiths, maidservants, and
barge keepers. People of all grades converted their property into
cash and invested in tulip bulbs.

There was about a two-year buildup of the tulip market before
it took off in the year 1636—and then came crashing down for good
in April 1637. At the peak of the mania, tulip prices doubled or
tripled by the week or even the day, and the object became to snap
up the tulip shares and then off-load them at a choice markup.

People eventually saw that this frenzy couldn't last forever. And
when the full panic hit, prices dropped by the hour, and the tulip
shares became worthless. Those who had borrowed to buy the

bulbs went bankrupt. "Substantial merchants were reduced almost to beggary, and many a representative of a noble line saw the fortunes of his house ruined beyond redemption," wrote Charles Mackay in his classic study, *Extraordinary Popular Delusions and the Madness of Crowds*.

Almost a century later, Europe indulged in two other speculative schemes. But the financiers of these bubbles were far more calculating. Both these schemes—the Mississippi Company/Banque Royale speculation based in Paris and the South Sea Bubble headquartered in London—were designed to retire extensive government debt incurred from foreign wars. The idea was to sell banknotes and/or stock to the public. The stock was supposed to be backed by the vast riches that were to be mined in the New World. The French expected to find gold in their Louisiana territory, and the English planned to explore South America for similar riches to underwrite their public offerings. Trouble was, nothing was ever found, and the stock turned out to be worthless.

When a run on the Banque Royale notes started, the suave chief financier and notorious gambler John Law hired some street beggars to pose as miners and march through the streets of Paris pretending they were off to mine gold in Louisiana. A few weeks later, shareholders recognized the beggars in the street, and the run on the notes began again. Of course, there was still no gold available for exchange. The scheme collapsed and onetime millionaires were now impoverished.

Similarly, the South Sea stock had escalated from £128 per share to £1,000 per share before it went into a tailspin, yet not before the insiders dumped their stock and made huge profits. "I can measure the motions of bodies," Isaac Newton once observed, "but I cannot measure human folly." Yet in spite of this astute observation, even he was to lose £20,000 in the speculative orgy of the South Sea Bubble. The sight of some people becoming so effortlessly rich had proven too much for most, so they had rushed in to join the mania.

John Kenneth Galbraith in his book *A Short History of Financial*

*Euphoria* claims that these speculative manias had all the predictable features: large leverage, individuals convinced of their own sense of financial acumen, investment opportunity rich in imagined prospects, and escape from sanity in the pursuit of profit.

In the latter half of the nineteenth century, America had its own version of speculative mania in the form of railroad stock speculation. Ultimately, many of the stocks sat underwater or failed completely as railroad bankruptcies piled up losses totaling $3 billion by the end of the nineteenth century. Around the same time, America also experienced the Comstock Lode silver rush. Historian Oscar Lewis describes Comstock mania:

> Its silver mines became a sort of national anodyne, a sure avenue of escape into a land where every dream came true and every illusion had the substance of reality. All over America millions believed that there, granted the opportunity and a bit of luck, one's vision of wealth and power and prestige would surely materialize. The nation never had a more satisfactory wishing well.

After a concerted rush to buy silver stocks, the boom eventually collapsed, and the average investor lost out. In the end, only the insiders prospered. Lewis concludes:

> Thousands were impoverished by the enormous stock losses. . . . So widespread was this experience, and so painful, that the public was eventually forced to conclude that Comstock speculation was a losing game to all except the few who controlled the producing mines and who, having day-by-day knowledge of their prospects, knew in advance of the public when to buy or sell. Realization that the cards were stacked against them came slowly to thousands of bemused and hopeful gamblers.

The twentieth century had speculative manias as well—the Florida real estate boom and the stock market frenzy of the 1920s, for example. In both cases, many stories circulated of fortunes made overnight, and there was constant talk of prime real estate, hot companies, and surefire stock tips.

By 1927, though, the Florida land boom was a bust; nevertheless, stock prices rose on Wall Street and people continued to buy. "Thousands speculated without the slightest knowledge of the companies upon whose fortunes they were relying," writes historian Frederick Lewis Allen. All sorts of people were in the market; it was a national mania that everyone expected to go on and on. A substantial portion of the American economy was supported by this wild rise in stock prices. Even one of the era's most esteemed economists, Irving Fisher of Yale University, got completely caught up in the speculative euphoria of the time; in the autumn of 1929, just before the crash, he said, "Stock prices have reached what looks like a permanently high plateau."

## The New Mania

Veteran technology investor Roger McNamee likes to distinguish between the industrial and technological manias that led to something lasting and mere fads such as the tulips that came to nothing. "There were a whole bunch of industries funded on the backs of gigantic manias, many of which led to great industrial revolutions," he says. "We like to speculate on things that are new and different— it's in our genes. When great new technologies come along, whether they are canals, railroads, autos, computers, or the Internet, everybody wants a piece of the action. Speculation tends to go hand in hand with entrepreneurship."

But McNamee also carefully explains that during these financial manias, which generally span a three- to five-year period at the beginning of any new industrial boom, capital is infused rather indiscriminately into the industry. On the upside, this infusion of funds stimulates a huge burst of creativity, accelerates the development of new markets, and keeps the United States on top. Eventually, though, a Darwinian process sets in where the companies with sustainable business models survive, but the vast majority of start-ups implode and go out of business.

Investors in past industrial manias such as autos, steel, and canals were all big spenders who poured tons of capital into numerous companies. In the first decade of the twentieth century, 508 automobile companies were started, including Ford Motor Company; now only a few remain. The personal computer boom was similar. For the Internet boom, even more money is available as angel and corporate investors and even day traders have joined the mix, providing billions in risk capital. "The level of money and the level of company formations has skyrocketed—it's really quite amazing," observes Bill Gates.

But as is the case during all financial manias, McNamee suspects that the average dollar invested in the Internet space will have an extraordinarily low return. "It will be a number of years before the business models become standardized sufficiently enough for the Internet industry to take off," he believes. To bolster his case, he points to the increase in the wealth of Microsoft's chairman and CEO, Bill Gates, whose stock holdings were worth only $5 billion in 1990 but got as high as $90 billion in 1999. Even at the end of 2000 his holdings were still worth $42 billion, significantly higher than a decade before. "Microsoft has been around for twenty years, but only in the last five years has its value spiked," McNamee states.

## Internet IPOs for Sale

As capital floods the market, companies not only get started faster but go public sooner. Many have only a vague idea about what their strategy is, other than that it has something to do with "grabbing some Internet real estate." Venture capitalist Ann Winblad of Hummer Winblad Partners, which has placed big bets on the Internet, puts it succinctly: "There are companies where, even if you squint, you can't figure out what their business models are." Winblad also points out that some are not companies at all but merely a business built upon a single product.

So how do so many fledgling Internet companies go public? As in other manias leading to bubbles, there is a whole financial food chain that benefits from the process—in this case the entrepreneurs, the venture capitalists, the investment bankers, and certain large institutional investors and mutual funds. Venture capitalist Don Valentine of Sequoia Capital candidly calls it a "greed system" and states bluntly, "No one in the chain is doing this for altruistic reasons."

In the Internet boom era, venture capitalists were pushed by both their investors and the entrepreneurs they invest in to shoot quickly for an IPO. "When the market is hot, there's pressure to take your portfolio companies public because every other venture capitalist is doing it," says Bob Kagle of Benchmark Capital. (Benchmark funded eBay, one of the few Internet plays other than Yahoo that went public as a profitable company.) Valentine offers a sober motive: "To us, going public is just another means of financing the roll-out of a company. Yahoo is a good example."

But quick IPOs require willing investors, and the market over the last four years has demonstrated an insatiable demand for Internet stocks. "More than 95 percent of the other venture capitalists I work with like to say, 'The ducks are quacking; it's time to feed them,'" says Jim Breyer, managing partner of Accel Partners, whose Internet home runs include UUNET and Real Networks. But as investor demand rises, the quality of the companies generally sinks. "The quality bar to go public has been lowered and lowered and lowered," says Brad Koenig, managing director and head of the technology investment practice at Goldman Sachs.

Indeed, the investment banks willingly accommodate their investors' desires for technology IPOs, which lets the banks collect their 7 percent underwriting fees and sign on new clients to manage their follow-on offerings. This overheated banking environment has led to one of the most frothy IPO eras in history. "You have investment bankers leaning out of their shoes to find things to take public," declares Sequoia's Valentine. But the bankers make no apologies about taking fledgling companies public to meet this demand. "It's our job to put food on the stoop," declares Cristina Morgan, managing director at the investment bank Chase H&Q. "If the cat eats it, we've done our job."

Investment bankers also make their money by keeping their big institutional clients happy. These investors control huge blocks of cash and use this financial power to bang on the bankers for big stakes in hot IPOs. And given the huge competition for IPO shares from the over three dozen primary institutional investors around the United States that favor technology stocks, it's almost impossible for most individual investors to secure any IPO shares on their own.

One way individual investors have been getting in on hot Internet stocks is through specialized mutual funds that buy technology stocks early in the game—including private mezzanine rounds before companies go public, as well as IPOs. Between November 1, 1998, and March 31, 2000, for example, investors poured over $72 billion into technology and small-cap growth mutual funds. About $11.4 billion of that total flowed into funds specializing in the Internet such as Amerindo Technology, Munder NetNet, WWW Internet, Monument Fund, and one simply called Internet Fund.

What whets the public appetite for these investments is the innate human tendency of wanting to get something for nothing—a bit like the lottery. That's how, in 1920, Charles Ponzi convinced investors that he could pay them 50 percent interest for the use of their money for just forty-five days. It was too good to be true. Ponzi took in $7.9 million, and the early investors were paid with funds raised from later ones before the whole scheme collapsed and the latecomers lost all of their capital.

During manias, public investors tend to forget how much time it takes for viable companies to become established and for an industry to mature. "The investment maniacs in the public market end up sacrificing their net worth for the sake of the industry as a whole, something they obviously wouldn't do if they knew better," observes McNamee. "There's a thinning of the herd, and the greedy lose their capital on behalf of the insiders."

The added danger is that life in the Bubble also encourages the maniac speculators to overspend and overleverage themselves, racking up high credit-card bills and other debt that could easily send them into a financial death spiral when the Bubble bursts. As stock prices today have escalated, so have consumer spending and debt. Debt as a percentage of personal income rose from 58 percent in 1973, to 76 percent in 1989, to 85 percent in 1997. Total credit-card debt soared from $243 billion in 1990 to $560 billion in 1997. American families carry an average of more than $7,000 in credit-card debt.

"The State of Working America," a report published by the Economic Policy Institute in Washington, D.C., reported that in 1999 the total value of all outstanding household debt reached an unprecedented high in the United States, for the first time exceeding 100 percent of the total disposable income of all households. Economist John Schmitt, one of the report's authors, says, "The financial boom we're living in is partly financed by debt and so when the debt comes due or unemployment starts to rise again, that [financial] bubble could burst and make the downturn worse than it otherwise would have been."

Meanwhile one American family in sixty-eight filed for personal bankruptcy in 1998, seven times the rate in 1980. By 1999, the number of middle-class families declaring bankruptcy exploded to 1,281,000 from 313,000 in 1980. In 1981, these people owed non-mortgage debts equal to nine months of income, compared to more than twenty-two months in 1997. "The next time the business cycle hits bottom," says Elizabeth Warren, a Harvard Law School professor and coauthor of *The Fragile Middle Class* (Yale University Press, 2000), "many people who are now solidly employed may find themselves out of work with bankruptcy as their only recourse."

Part of this consumer debt was being used to finance the purchase of stocks. Consumer leverage found its way into the stock market during the big NASDAQ run-up that hit its peak on March 10, 2000, with a record close of 5,048. During this time, margin debt (i.e., speculating on stocks with borrowed money) was rising at a faster rate than it did even in the 1920s, when the peak annual increase was 56 percent. Over the twelve months through the end of February 2000, the increase in margin borrowing was 75 percent, and most of that came after the NASDAQ market began to take off in late October 1999. The total volume of margin loans at that time was $252 billion.

Under Federal Reserve rules, investors may borrow up to 50 percent of the initial value of stock they buy through a margin account. After that, a maintenance requirement set by the stock exchanges kicks in: The investor's equity—the market value of stock minus the amount owed to the broker—may not fall below 25 percent of the stock's market value.

Because of this requirement, if you buy on margin and the value of your stock goes down too far, the brokerage firm will sell your stock to raise cash to pay off your margin loans—without asking you. If you borrowed more than the current (lower) value of the stocks, you can wind up owing your brokerage more than your stock is worth.

And of course, you have to have a cash account at the brokerage. After all, it's not like they're going to take the loss if your stock falls. They'll just sell your stock and take your cash to cover it. And if somehow your cash account comes up empty, you need to find the money to pay off the debt.

Many speculators got caught short in just this way after the April 2000 market plunge, when the prices of their stocks fell so far that they owed more than 75 percent of the value of their brokerage accounts. The brokerages sent out margin calls, forcing the investors to come up with more money or sell their shares. Many investors had to sell, and thus lost money during the major NASDAQ correction and initial deflation of the Internet Bubble in April 2000.

And the seduction of margin investing was not limited to the mom and pop investor; nor did all these bills come due immediately after the April correction. A case in point is Pete Musser, a professional investor who built his company Safeguard Scientifics over forty years. The seventy-four-year old CEO had never sold a share of his company's stock. But during the Bubble he bought blocks of Internet company stocks on margin, borrowing money from his brokerage firm to help pay for his purchases and using his Safeguard stock as collateral. But in late September 2000 when Safeguard's stock slid from a split-adjusted high of $98 to $19, the value of his holdings came so close to the total of his debt that his brokers demanded their money back. To help pay down that debt Musser had to sell most of his Safeguard stock—7.5 million of his nine million shares—at a loss. *Fortune* magazine reported that he had taken on almost $100 million in debt. Ultimately Musser ignored the extreme risk Internet stocks contained. "I got seduced by the value of my holdings," Musser told *Fortune*. "I didn't count on the market going off by 90 percent in six months. I wasn't ready for that. I got caught up in the exuberance of the moment." Not surprisingly, Musser has vowed never to buy stocks on margin again.

Meanwhile Internet mania has not been limited to investors in public companies but has been rife among employees of private companies as well. Many technical workers, managers, and rank-and-file members of start-ups worked night and day at slave wages in the hope that their stock options would some day pay off. In spite of much publicized Internet IPOs, the reality is that for every company that gets started, only about one in ten either gets necessary funding or makes it to an IPO. So if an employee works at one of the other nine out of ten companies, his or her options will prove worthless in the end. And even for those who get stock from a company IPO, unrealistic expectations tend to prevail. "Greed, fear, societal pressures, assert themselves," says Gabriel Fenton, an options expert at PaineWebber and coauthor of the book *Employee Stock Options: A Strategic Planning Guide for the 21st Century Option-aire* (Stillman Publishing). "A lot of people have based their lifestyles on expectations of a 15 to 25 percent growth rate for their options. They're over-leveraged and if things flatten out, they'll be upside-down. They're not going to have the money they had."

In fact, some employees who loaded up on their companies' stock in the midst of the Bubble were in for a particularly rude surprise when they calculated their taxes for 2000. They discovered that their tax liability for their stock was based on the price of the stock at the time that they exercised their options to buy the stock. Even if the stock price plummeted, as most Internet stocks did in 2000, the tax bill remained unchanged. Even worse, some who loaded up on company stock and assumed it would keep going up in price treated their paper gains at the time as real and even borrowed against them. They assumed the money would be there when tax time came, but in fact owed more money in taxes and in the debts they incurred than they got out of their stock options. In some cases, the money owed in taxes alone was in the millions of dollars.

## Bubble Values

In the midst of the Internet Bubble, stock valuation has been a big topic of debate. Stock security valuation is a challenge that goes back to the 1934 publication of the book *Security Analysis* by Benjamin Graham and David Dodd. Graham and Dodd tried to provide a logical way of evaluating stocks in the wake of the speculative frenzy that led to the Great Crash of 1929. In the 1920s, as in earlier decades, stock was valued subjectively, as much on the basis of rumor and "hot tips" as on anything else.

Graham and Dodd argued that share prices should follow a company's economic fundamentals, which they attempted to evaluate systematically. Their approach relied heavily on a company's historical earnings and on the balance-sheet values of tangible assets such as inventory, equipment, and the proverbial "brick-and-mortar." Today, there is far greater emphasis on a company's future earnings power and on its intangible assets such as intellectual property and brand names, a measure especially true of Internet and software companies.

The traditional method of stock valuation tries to predict the long-term cash flows of a company, discounts those amounts back to the present, and then divides by the number of shares. As this process is much easier said than done, most analysts use a "good enough" proxy for cash flow called the price-to-earnings (P/E) formula in which you come up with an earnings multiple.

A further attempt to refine the formula for Internet companies is to do the proxy valuations based on EBITDA (earnings before interest, taxes, depreciation, and amortization).

The classic P/E ratio essentially shows how many more years of current earnings it would take to cover the current value of the shares. The higher the ratio, the more investors are betting on earnings to grow in the future. Beginning in 1950 and for several decades after, the typical P/E ratio was around 14. By the first quarter of 1999, the S&P 500 Index average had a P/E ratio of about 31, and the S&P 500 Technology Index was almost 59.

P/E ratios still involve a certain amount of guesswork, and Internet companies must figure out what their income stream will look like in five years and what the real prospects for growth are.

Although the public market historically has had difficulty valuing new technologies and their growth potentials, the increase in stock prices, without question, has been wildly exaggerated for Internet companies.

"There was no economic basis for those Internet stock valuations," admits Andy Bechtolsheim, cofounder of Sun Microsystems and an active angel investor in Internet companies. Bandel Carano of Oak Investment Partners agrees: "My view is that in the long run, technology businesses are worth between 10 and 20 times earnings, that's all. And it's 10 to 20 times the next twelve months' earnings, not five years out."

At some point, these darlings of cyberspace had to grow up and be valued like real companies. Meanwhile, it's difficult to predict earnings for technology companies, partly because technology dislocations happen all the time. It's tough enough for franchises such as Microsoft and Intel to deal with this changing landscape, never mind the young technology company whose business model might be completely overthrown by unanticipated dislocations. This volatility is especially true in a new industry such as the Internet.

"When I got in the venture capital business in 1983, everybody had to own technology stocks," says Carano. "But by 1987, technology was considered an uninvestable asset class by professional money managers for exactly this reason—its unpredictability. Lots of people got burned. Right now, it's technology again, and they're willing to pay year 2005 earnings discounted back only 10 percent to justify today's stock price. Hello? It's hard enough to project Coca-Cola's next quarter growth rate, which is much easier to analyze than an Internet company's."

Bill Gates preaches the gospel of unpredictability even for Microsoft, which has grown at a steady rate of 40 percent-plus over the last twenty years. "Coca-Cola will make its money off the same soft drink formula in ten years. In those same ten years, Microsoft will have had to completely reinvent all its products and our whole company," says Gates. "That's why I have always thought Microsoft was overvalued in the market."

This notion of dislocation and unpredictability is captured in the main thesis of Clayton Christensen's best-selling analysis, *The Innovator's Dilemma* (HarperBusiness, 1997/2000). Christensen demonstrates in painstaking detail, using numerous examples from the high-technology industry, that technological change and innovation can be highly disruptive. On the positive side, this allows nimble start-ups to successfully exploit first-mover advantage in the pursuit of new markets. The downside is the unpredictability—putative leaders in an industry or market segment can become tomorrow's also-rans, even if they are currently successful in delivering upgrades to large customer bases. And this does not even take into account the many start-ups that pursue innovative markets but fail. Technology markets by their definition are ever-changing and volatile, with a high mortality rate for the pioneers and sometimes displacement of even those companies that have been historically very successful and well managed.

As an early indication of displacement and failure in the Internet market, Morgan Stanley Dean Witter's spring 2000 Technology & Internet IPO Yearbook noted that while 54 percent of Internet

IPOs were trading above their IPO price, only 35 percent of Internet IPOs were trading above their first day close as of May 2, 2000. Morgan Stanley's report concludes: "We believe most Internet companies will fail—when all is said and done, 30 percent of Internet IPOs will be trading above issue price, 70 percent below issue price." The report concluded that overall 90 percent of Internet stocks were still overvalued at the time.

Over against its predicted failure rate, Morgan Stanley's research also showed that 5 percent of Internet companies had created 68 percent of market value. Don Valentine corroborates this from a venture capitalist's perspective. "If you look at twenty or thirty years of history, a Sun Microsystems or a Cisco Systems happens only once in a while," he says. "There aren't many companies like that for the long term. We venture capitalists, by exception, create great companies."

Prior to the stock deflation of April 2000, there were different attempts to justify the valuation of the go-go stocks. These new valuation methods ignored fundamentals such as revenue growth or profit margins. One attempt used Web site traffic as an indicator of at least relative valuation of a company with competitors. "Yeah, people came up with all these metrics to try to justify the stock price. It's all bullshit," says Bruce Lupatkin, former head of research at Hambrecht & Quist and a longtime technology analyst.

A more serious alternative to P/E ratios was a method called Economic Value Added (EVA), which tried to measure the level of growth required to justify the current stock price. But when Amazon hit a price of $214 per share (presplit), the EVA formula showed that its revenue would have to grow almost 60 percent per year for ten years, reaching annual sales of $63 billion by 2009 to justify its price.

By comparison, Microsoft's growth has averaged 43 percent per year since it went public in 1986. Amazon would have to outpace Microsoft to reach the level of growth needed to make Amazon's stock price reasonable at even $214 per share. Yet Amazon stock went up to more than $350 per share, with a market value of nearly $17 billion in late 1998, after CIBC Oppenheimer analyst Henry

Blodgett, now an Internet analyst with Merrill Lynch, set his twelve-month target price for the stock at $400 per share. Not long after, Amazon stock did a three-for-one split. By the end of the first week of January 1999, the split stock price was up to over $160 per share. Presplit, that would equal $480 per share. Amazon's market value was more than that of JCPenney and Kmart combined.

That companies keep their stocks moving up by splitting their prices on a regular basis still bewilders industry players and has become an inside joke. Roger McNamee was in rare form in spring 1999 while addressing an audience of institutional investors in San Francisco: "Betting on Internet stocks, it's actually pretty easy. Here are the rules: 50 bucks a share is cheap; $150 a share is fairly valued; but at $200 a share, the stock is cheap again because that means you are about to have a four-for-one split."

"I had spent a fair amount of time trying to make an argument for the valuation of these Internet companies," says Lise Buyer, Internet analyst turned venture capitalist. "I couldn't do it. So I fell back on the Graham and Dodd comment that the buyer of such stocks was not making an investment, but a bet on a new technology or a new market. They were engaging in an odds-setting exercise rather than a valuation process."

## Say Hello to Mo

It's important to note that the go-go stocks were boosted largely by momentum investors—people who weren't afraid to buy high, with the bet they could sell even higher. Momentum investors buy the stocks simply because they're going up in price, not because of a company's underlying sales, earnings, or other business fundamentals. This kind of investing is driven by a certain herd psychology—if an IPO becomes "hot," the momentum investors stampede all over each other in anticipation of a huge price jump. They must buy the stock because others are buying it; people try to outguess the fashion in the stock market. Ultimately, they are looking for the "greater fool" who will pay more for it than they did.

In recent years retail day traders have driven momentum investing. These traders tune into business news networks like CNBC and CNN for continuous twenty-four-hour coverage to help them with their investing. They also do online research and tap into Web sites such as Silicon Investor and The Motley Fool, where they can chat with like-minded people. Naturally, they use services such as E*Trade, Charles Schwab Online, and Discover Online to trade online. At an average fee of $15 a trade, online brokerage commissions are about 70 percent lower than what they were even three years ago, making the online services even more attractive to users.

An estimated 5 to 7 million day traders were online in the first quarter of 1999; their number was projected to go up to 18 million by 2002. Their activity accounted for 25 to 33 percent of all retail trading and was increasing quickly. Overall, online day traders accounted for about 14 percent of the stock market's daily trading volume, and about two to three times that for many Internet stocks. In many cases, day traders had taken over the main trading of Internet stocks from the major institutional buyers. In November 1998, for example, the average trade size of Yahoo was 438 shares, 453 for Amazon, and 310 for eBay. In February 1999 more than three out of four trades in Amazon, Yahoo, and eBay were for 1,000 shares or fewer, far smaller than the typical blocks of thousands of shares institutions usually trade.

Day traders might buy an Internet stock at $94 in the morning and sell it at $96 in the afternoon, in what's really a form of gambling. *The Economist* has dubbed this phenomenon "cyber casino" in which "shares of firms with almost no track record are being bought by investors with no experience, at prices that appear to make no sense." The magazine adds that "the casino capitalists who spend seven or eight hours a day at their PCs trading Internet shares appear to be stark, staring mad." Some of the trading was done on margin.

This type of gambling not only drove up the valuation of certain stocks but also greatly contributed to their volatility, since momentum investors like to unload their shares quickly at the beginning of what looks like a significant decline in price. "One of the most amazing things about the Internet Bubble era is that investors had become completely desensitized to one-day price drops—almost irrespective of the magnitude," says McNamee.

Even with these wild fluctuations in stock prices, day traders not only hoped to get rich, they expected it. According to a survey by the Institute of Psychology and Markets, the average investor in 1999, online or off, expected an 18.6 percent annual rate of return on stocks. With dividend yields what they were, even with the Dow Jones over 10,000, that kind of return would have put the Dow at 45,000 in 2010 and at 210,000 a decade after that.

## Hope Floats

Another factor that drove up Internet stock prices was their generally narrow float—the limited number of company shares available to public investors. In January 1999, while 51 percent of Yahoo's shares were available for public trading, only 35 percent of the stock of Amazon, At Home, and C/Net was; eBay had a mere 9 percent available. The entire float of most of those stocks could be turned over in less than a month. Amazon's actually turned over twice a week in January 1999.

When demand is high and the supply is limited, the prices of these stocks skyrocket. Their superhigh prices result from too many buyers chasing too few shares. As one Wall Street insider put it regarding small stock floats: "If it's thin, it's a win."

One main reason for the small float is that venture capitalists and other insiders keep more of the stock from their Internet start-ups for themselves. In 1999–2000, these companies offered only 22 percent, on average, of their total capitalization to public investors, therefore allowing insiders to retain more decision-making power after their companies went public. It also positions them to sell their stock at a greater profit following the significant share appreciation typical in bubble markets.

Many insiders can sell after 180 days following the IPO—the end of the so-called lockup period. The selling of shares by Internet company insiders picked up considerably in the fourth quarter of 1998 and the first quarter of 1999. In March 1999, right as the 180-day lockup ended, executives and other insiders at eBay filed to sell $1.1 billion worth of stock. By then, eBay stock, the best-performing IPO in 1998, had appreciated more than twenty-five-fold from its IPO value in September of 1998, and its market capitalization was $23 billion. The insiders sold the secondary offering of 6.5 million shares of eBay at $170 per share in April 1999.

And in the midst of the big NASDAQ run-up that started in fall 1999, there was an explosion of stock sales by venture capital investors and their partners who were seeking to solidify their profits as quickly as permissible following the IPOs of companies they had bankrolled. Throughout most of the 1990s, sales of this so-called restricted stock averaged $1 billion to $2 billion a month, according to First Call/Thomson Financial. But beginning in November 1999, such sales averaged $12.4 billion.

## Breaking the Record

The IPO historic record breakers were the onetime darlings set up for the biggest falls. These stocks started out with an offering price at anywhere from $9 to $28 per share and skyrocketed on the first day of trading, often to over $1 billion in total market value. In recent times, this IPO group has included Earthweb, Theglobe.com, eBay, Marketwatch.com, iVillage, Priceline.com, and VA Linux. "We call these gigastocks," jokes Andy Kessler of Velocity Capital, which made a boatload of cash betting on its own gigastock, Inktomi, which provides search engine technology for Web sites.

Earthweb, for example, is an online provider of technical information and computer software for Web site designers. But Earthweb gets its revenue from advertisers and had not turned a profit by the time of its IPO on November 10, 1998. It had lost $7.8 million in 1997 and $5.3 million in the first nine months of 1998. It sold 2.1 million shares, a 27 percent stake, on its first day of trading as its stock price soared from $14 per share to a closing price of $48.69—a 247 percent gain. In December 2000, the stock price was underwater at $13 per share.

Just two days later, Theglobe.com, which helps clients design Web pages, went public in December 1998. It offered 3.1 million shares at $9 per share, and the first-day closing price was a whopping $63.50, a record 606 percent gain! Its market value was $622 million, even though the company had $11.5 million of losses in the first nine months of 1998. By the end of the year, its stock was down to just over $32 per share. And by July 1999 was around $18 per share. The free fall continued as the stock plummeted to 30 cents a share in December 2000, making it a penny stock in which investors had no more interest.

The online auctioneer eBay is even better known. On September 24, 1998, it went public at $18 per share; seven weeks later its stock was up to $174 per share and its market capitalization was a staggering $7 billion. During that period, eBay's stock turned over at a rate of more than 5 million shares per day on five separate days, a stunning record of activity, given that eBay's float was only 3.5 million shares. By the end of 1998, eBay's stock had multiplied ten times within ten weeks, amounting to an increase of more than 1,400 percent and a stock price of over $240 per share. It took Microsoft four years to achieve that kind of stock price growth. (For more on eBay, see the chapter "Leaders of the Internet Pack.")

In 1998, Internet offerings jumped an unbelievable 70 percent, on average, in their first day of trading. In 1999 the IPO frenzy increased, as almost a quarter of the offerings done in the first quarter of 1999 and a whopping 57 percent of IPOs in the second quarter were for Internet-related companies.

Marketwatch.com, a financial news Web site owned by CBS, went public on January 15, 1999, at $17 per share and closed at more than $80 per share. Its basket of public shares flipped over not once, not twice, but three times within the first twenty-four hours, driving the opening day price up nearly 475 percent. But by December 2000 the stock price was down to $4.50 per share.

Not far behind Marketwatch was Priceline.com, an online service that allows users to locate their favorite prices for airline tickets and hotel reservations. Priceline issued 10 million shares that were originally priced at $16 per share, but which opened at $81. Its closing price was $69, an increase of 331 percent. In December 2000 its price was at $2.50 per share, and the company's future was in doubt.

iVillage, an online service specifically for women, was another hot first-quarter IPO, going out at $24 per share and closing at over $80 after soaring as high as $100 on the first day of trading. The first trade of the day was valued at more than $95. It didn't seem to matter that iVillage had lost almost $44 million in 1998 and $21 million a year earlier. By December 2000 the stock price was down to $1.25 per share, and speculation was rife that the company might be bought or go out of business.

The all-time first day record breaker, however, was reserved for VA Linux Systems, a Sunnyvale, California, company that sells computer servers powered by standard Intel Pentium processors that run on Linux, the free UNIX-based operating system. These servers are designed to deliver Internet products like Web pages, e-mail, and other network services. The IPO was conducted on December 9, 1999, and the company reached a market value of almost $10 billion by the end of the day. This was astounding for a tiny company with little revenue, powerful competitors like Dell and IBM, and no expectation of earnings in the foreseeable future. In fact, the company had been bleeding money in its six years of operation, and had lost nearly $30 million in total. Nevertheless, shares of VA Linux Systems surged 733 percent, setting a record for an initial public offering. The stock was priced at $30 a share and closed at $250 a share on its first day of NASDAQ trading. In early November 2000, after the company warned of slowed sales growth, the record-breaking stock went down to $18 per share. By February 2000, it plummeted to $5 per share, well off its first day closing price. The company reported a net loss of $13.4 million and laid off one quarter of its workforce.

In the frenzied Bubble environment, insiders were all too eager to take their companies public. "The first thing we told our companies was, 'Go sell your stock. Take advantage of it,'" says Sandy Robertson, cofounder of the investment bank Robertson Stephens. "It's like the way the old Green Bay Packers coach Vince Lombardi used to tell his running backs to run for daylight. When you see the daylight, go for it." Edmund Cashman, head of the syndicate desk at investment bank Legg Mason Wood Walker, is even more blunt: "It's the Wall Street way. We're all greedy as hell."

But someone still had to buy these Internet shares in the after-market frenzy. "People were buying Internet stocks as if they were Beanie Babies," said Lise Buyer. "A Beanie Baby is worth 23 cents, but temporarily I've got to pay $20 for it. And I'll pay even $150 for it, until I'm no longer interested, and then I'll say, 'Damn! it's just a piece of felt and some beans. What was I thinking?'"

Indeed by January 31, 2000, even before the big Internet market shakeout in April 2000, Internet stocks such as barnesandnoble.com, Value America, DLJ Direct, eToys, iTurf, ZapMe!, 1-800-FLOWERS. COM, and iVillage had already made Morgan Stanley's list of the fifty worst performing technology IPOs since 1980. By June 1, 2000, Deutsche Banc Alex. Brown had identified some twenty-five unprofitable Internet commerce, portal, and content companies that lacked sufficient cash to stay in business another six quarters. The list included eToys, iVillage, Theglobe.com, Value America, as well as Looksmart, Netzero, Goto.com, and Marketwatch.com. Value America filed for bankruptcy on August 11, 2000, and shut its retail operations. The company had failed just three months after a reported $90 million bailout. Meanwhile, by December 2000 several other companies, more than 200 total, had entered the "Internet Wasteland" (see Appendix C) with stocks that were down by 90 percent or more from their fifty-two-week highs. This list included Ashford.com, At Home Corporation, barnesandnoble.com, Buy.com, CMGI, DoubleClick, Drugstore.com, Internet Capital Group, and Rhythms NetConnections. eToys filed for bankruptcy in February 2001.

## It All Started with Netscape

Perhaps the most famous Internet IPO is Netscape's, whose offering on August 9, 1995, generated a frenzy of interest. Internet analyst Mary Meeker calls that date "the start of Year One in the online era." One venture capitalist traces Internet mania back to the Netscape IPO. "What you found," he says, "is that certain traders, mostly institutions, made a lot of money from the quick rise in Netscape's stock."

Netscape's IPO started with a share price of $14 that doubled to $28 per share the day before the offering, and went from 3.5 million shares available to 5 million. The stock closed its first day of trading at $58.25. In the aftermarket, the stock went as high as $87, but by 1997 it had dropped almost as low as its offering price. It finally crept back up into the 20s and 30s in 1998.

Paul Deninger, chairman and CEO of technology-investment bank Broadview International, says, "If you bought Netscape just after the IPO and held it, you were screwed. If you bought Netscape within six months of the IPO, you were screwed. You were so far underwater you can't even imagine." Fortunately for Netscape, the company was eventually bought by AOL in late 1998 for $4 billion, a hefty premium over what their stock price was trading on the day the deal was inked. In spite of this handsome price, the sale of Netscape marked a rather unceremonious ending to Netscape's fairy-tale story as an Internet pioneer. Just two years earlier, Netscape had commanded 80 percent of the Web browser market; now it clung to barely half of it. As one pundit put it, "Netscape devolved from a browser business into a schizophrenic quilt of a part-portal, part-enterprise software, part-browser company."

In retrospect, the early publicity from Netscape's IPO may have backfired. "I think they went public a year to eighteen months too early," says Jim Breyer of Accel Partners. "If they had waited, and had not charged for their Internet browser but continued to build a presence with it, instead of tipping off Microsoft the way they did through their massive public offering, Netscape would have been fundamentally more successful long term. It was a strategic mistake."

As Michael Cusumano and David Yoffie point out in their book *Competing on Internet Time: Lessons from Netscape and Its Battle with Microsoft,* Netscape's overpriced stock also put pressure on the company's management to constantly meet Wall Street's high expectations on a quarterly basis. One result was that Netscape felt it had to keep charging for its Internet browser for the sake of the additional revenue, while Microsoft gave its browser away and grabbed more and more market share. By the end of 2000, it was Microsoft that had more than 80 percent of the browser market.

## The Strange Case of K-Tel International and Other Internet Wanna-bes

To recognize just how absurd the mania had gotten, you don't have to look any further than K-Tel International, a company best known for selling the music recordings of fading pop stars on late-night television.

Before marketing such music compilations as "70s Teen Heartthrobs," K-Tel sold contraptions like the Miracle Brush lint remover and the Veg-O-Matic vegetable slicer and dicer. It branched out into music when it began selling a compilation titled "Hooked on Classics," in which classical music was played to a disco beat. In 1984, after disco slumped and K-Tel's investments in oil, gas, and real estate went south, the company went bankrupt.

Eventually the company pulled out of bankruptcy, and until April 1998 its public stock was very thinly traded, with only a few hundred shares changing hands on most days. This all changed when K-Tel suddenly announced that it planned to open an Internet record store. Its stock jumped from about $4 per share to almost $40. According to the *New York Times,* company founder Philip Kives of Winnipeg, Canada, who owned 80 percent of K-Tel, quickly sold 2.6 million shares after the stock price spiked up.

By October 1998 the share price had slumped again to about $8.

Yet in early November, K-Tel announced it would sell music on Playboy's Web site as well as in a nonexclusive way on Microsoft's MSN online shopping channel. K-Tel's stock immediately shot up 93 percent. On some days more than 20 million shares changed hands, which was impressive, given that only 8.3 million shares were available for trading, 4 million of which still belonged to company founder Philip Kives.

Apparently, it didn't matter to stock buyers that K-Tel had lost money in three out of the previous four years, posting a loss of $3.1 million in the last quarter before the Playboy announcement. Or that the market for selling music online was already crowded, led by powerhouse Amazon and its nearest competitor CDNow. In fact, Amazon had featured billing on Microsoft's shopping channel, while K-Tel was only one of six others listed in the music and video section. And only 121,000 people had visited K-Tel's Web site in September 1998, compared with 2.2 million for CDNow during the same month.

By November 1998 K-Tel International was in danger of getting delisted from the NASDAQ stock exchange, since the company's total assets of $900,000 had fallen well below the minimum requirement of $4 million to stay listed. The company obviously did not have the tens of millions of dollars required to compete on the Internet. Not surprisingly, the threat of delisting caused K-Tel's stock to plunge from almost $40 a share to $10. By December 2000, the stock was down to a mere 37 cents per share.

But K-Tel wasn't the only ridiculous example of an Internet wanna-be. Books-a-Million, an Alabama-based company with a little-known chain of bookstores in the Southeast, suddenly announced on November 25, 1998, that it planned to sell books on the Internet. The company's stock rose from $4.38 per share the day before the announcement to $47 only three market trading sessions later. On one day, more than 8.2 million shares changed hands, driven by day traders, with the average trade for the overall session being only 437 shares. Company executives sold their shares like crazy. A report in *The Wall Street Journal* helped spur a general sell-off, and the stock dropped to $14.94 per share.

The Internet rumor mill only got worse. At the end of 1998, a motorcycle maker named Bikers Dream merely suggested it might set up a Web site to sell motorcycle parts, and suddenly its stock was the hottest in America. The stock jumped 167 percent in one day, with shares changing hands eight times as frenzied day traders swapped the stock back and forth. The next day, the stock came back to earth with a thud when traders finally realized that the company's Web site wasn't even up and running.

Around the same time, clothing wholesaler Active Apparel Group began promoting its Internet debut in news releases and on CNBC. Active's Web site was also not up and running, but this didn't keep investors from bidding up the company's stock price from $1.25 per share to as high as $25. According to the *New York Times,* several company officers and executives took advantage of the surge and sold close to $1 million of their shares. The share price plummeted thereafter, and was still below $5 per share in February 1999, even though the company's Web site was actually operational by then. Active Apparel nearly got delisted from NASDAQ and ended up listed on NASDAQ's less prestigious small-cap stock exchange.

These company stocks are just a few examples of securities that reached irrational heights in recent years simply because they had the word "Internet" or *.com* briefly associated with them. This kind of craziness led Rick Berry, director of equity research at J. P. Turner & Company in Atlanta, to quip, "The frenetic buying of Internet stocks is going to make the tulip buyers of the seventeenth century look like value players."

## Volatility and Shakeout

Internet mania has contributed heavily to stock market volatility, even though pure-play Internet stocks make up only about 15 percent of the NASDAQ and about 8 percent of the stock market overall. Speculation in these stocks was like a grand game of musical chairs in which speculators hoped, often in vain, not to be left without a place to sit when the music stopped.

In a study of stock trading patterns for 1999, for example, investment research firm Sanford C. Bernstein found that among NASDAQ stocks the average holding period was five months, down from roughly a two-year holding period a decade before. And for the fifty NASDAQ stocks with the heaviest trading, investors held their shares for just three weeks, on average. The entire share base of DoubleClick, a company that specializes in Internet advertising, turned over twenty-one times in 1999. So a lot of churning was going on as speculators ducked in and out of tech stocks hoping not to get caught holding the bag.

The volatility continued into 2000 as dramatically illustrated by the case of Emulex, a fiber-optic communications equipment company. On August 25, financial news services such as Bloomberg News, Dow Jones News Service, CBS.Marketwatch.com, and CNBC issued reports about Emulex based on what turned out to be a fake press release. The fake release reported that the company's CEO had resigned and that Emulex planned to restate its earnings for the last two years. Investors rushed to dump their Emulex shares, and the stock plunged from $103 to $45 in fifteen minutes. The drop stripped more than $2 billion from the company's market valuation before NASDAQ halted trading in the stock at about 10:30 A.M. The free fall dragged down several stocks of companies in similar businesses and even pulled down the broader NASDAQ. Once the hoax was exposed, trading on the stock was resumed.

A week after the fake posting, the FBI arrested a suspect who had apparently sent the phony press release via e-mail to Internet Wire, a Los Angeles service where the suspect had previously worked. The other financial information services had picked up the release from Internet Wire. A week before the press release, the suspect had sold 3,000 shares of Emulex short, betting that he would be able to buy the stock later at a lower price and pocket the difference as profit. Instead the stock price soared and the suspect lost $100,000. But after the fake posting and the precipitous drop of Emulex, the suspect made $240,000. Meanwhile, investors who panicked and sold their shares, or had sell orders automatically executed at preset prices, were unlikely to recover their losses.

While Emulex is an extreme example, the fact is that Internet stocks have been deflating and shaking out on a segment-by-segment basis for quite some time. It started at the end of April 1999 with Internet portal companies and online communities such as Theglobe.com. Then there were content plays and financial sites such as theStreet.com.

The most publicized shakeout, however, was in the business-to-consumer (B2C) e-commerce segment. These B2C companies, along with many of the online brokerages such as E*Trade and Ameritrade, had thrown some $2 billion at advertising in traditional media such as TV, radio, and print. The Internet gift site Send.com alone spent $20 million on advertising during the Christmas 1999 shopping season, only to log fewer than 125,000 visitors to its Web site, according to Nielsen Media Research. Some dotcoms paid $2 million for a thirty-second pop during the Super Bowl in January 2000. And this doesn't even include the additional money spent on developing the ads themselves. An *Adweek* magazine analysis revealed that e-commerce accounts generated $3 billion of the $10.3 billion in advertising billings awarded in the United States from January through October 1999.

Beyond B2C e-commerce, the next hot segments for speculation and shakeout were networking infrastructure companies and fiber-optic equipment companies, as well as wireless and mobile computing devices offering Internet connections.

In 2000, the market got a preview of mobile computing mania when Palm Inc., a spin-off IPO of 3Com, went public. The bankers initially were considering a price range of $14 to $16 per share, but given public market euphoria they were able to bump the price all the way up to an offering price of $38 for the IPO on March 2, 2000. The stock got as high as $165 per share on its first day of trading. And closed at just over $95 per share. The company raised some $874 million through its offering. Nevertheless, by March 2001 the share price was back down to $22 per share. Private companies in the "wireless space" also had no problem raising capital in 2000. A company called eFrenzy—which describes itself as "the first real-time services marketplace, customized to meet the needs of mobile users"—raised $30 million in venture capital without any problem.

Optical networking companies (which build new generation technology for routing Internet data) also were attracting a lot of attention and venture investment. In the first half of 2000, they received $1.6 billion of venture capital. Vinod Khosla, a general partner with Kleiner Perkins Caufield & Byers and a highly success-ful venture investor in networking companies, predicts that 90 percent of fiber-optics start-ups will fail. "Even though there is fun-damental value to be added in the optical networking space, you have a situation where a lot of people are investing in optical com-panies without understanding the basic trends or the technology," Khosla laments. "You will see a similar situation in the optical space as in the dotcom space." And the overfunding of optical companies could not have come at a worse time. With prices of bandwidth declining somewhere between 50 percent to 80 percent, some ser-vice providers are finding it difficult to make money.

The bubbling up of new segments accompanied by market volatility, then followed by shakeout, has been par for the course in recent years. From the beginning of 1998 through April 2000, Inter-net stocks had been through four bull markets and four bear mar-kets. The spring 2000 dotcom shakeout, in particular, wiped out almost $800 billion in Internet company stock market value. Inter-net stocks as a group, valued at $1.4 trillion at its March 2000 peak, lost almost 60 percent of its value by July 2000—erasing almost as much paper wealth as the crash of 1987. Almost half of the Inter-net companies were trading below their IPO price.

By December 2000 several once hot Internet companies were actually in danger of being delisted from NASDAQ due to insuffi-cient assets, or a stock price below $1 per share, or both. Among the companies on the brink of delisting were the Internet software seller Beyond.com, the online drugstore PlanetRx, online grocery retailer Webvan, and the sporting goods e-tailer Fogdog.

But this shakeout did not prevent the financial food chain of venture capitalists, investment bankers, and mutual fund managers from profiting handsomely. For example, between November 1998 and July 2000, Goldman Sachs, Morgan Stanley Dean Witter, and Crédit Suisse First Boston each pocketed more than $500 million in underwriting fees for Internet companies. According to Thomson Financial Securities Data, this was the most lucrative streak investment bankers have ever seen in a single sector. The financial food chain had come full circle, with the insiders reaping most of the rewards of Internet mania. As the economist Hal Varian put it, "Sure, the brokers all bought yachts, but where are the customers' yachts?"

## THE OLD, OLD THING

iTulip.com is a tongue-in-cheek Web site that tracks stock market madness. It gets its name from the infamous Dutch tulip mania of the 1630s. (In 1637, at the peak of the mania, one bulb sold for 4,200 guilders—roughly $1.5 million in modern currency). Like some other modern-day dotcoms, iTulip.com provides no real product. It does, however, offer advice, some of it written specifically for the site, and the rest available through links to articles in major publications. The advice and articles both follow and criticize Internet stock mania and signs of speculative excess in the U.S. stock markets.

iTulip.com is the brainchild of Eric Janszen, an angel investor who—with partner Jeff Osborn of Boston-based Osborn Capital—invests in Internet companies. Their investments include ArrowPoint Communications, which was acquired by Cisco Systems in 2000 in a stock swap valued at $6 billion.

So why is Janszen—an insider who's made money off of the Internet—skeptical of today's stock market? "My dad lost a ton of the family's money in the 1973 to 1975 bear market," says Janszen. And this happened despite the fact that the elder Janszen was a very bright guy; as a practicing physicist, he'd invented the Janszen electrostatic speaker at Janszen Labs, and later created more advanced stereo speaker models for KLH Audio. "My dad was sixty-six years old when the market tanked. This caused real hardship in my family," continues Janszen. "If I can dissuade one old guy with a family from putting retirement money into speculative stocks, then all this extra work on iTulip will be worth it."

# Doonesbury

# VENTURE CAPITAL COWBOYS

**There are more venture guys doing more deals with more dollars at higher prices than ever before. In the Internet boom there is just more of everything.**
—Roger McNamee, Integral Capital Partners

In the supply-and-demand chain of the Internet Bubble era, venture capitalists (VCs) are the suppliers. Since the Netscape IPO in August 1995, VCs have poured billions of dollars into hundreds of Internet start-ups.

The VC Internet frenzy is fed partly by the increasing number of investors who have jumped into the game. Beginning in the early 1990s, huge public pension funds started allocating large sums of money to venture capital investments. And who could really blame them? While the average venture capital rate of return over a thirty-year period is estimated to be an impressive 23 percent, in the last five years the best funds have brought in rates of return between 50 percent and 150 percent—ungodly numbers that seduce even the most mild-mannered institutional investor.

In addition to the professional VC firms, the number of corporate investors has grown rapidly. Technology blue-chip companies such as Intel, Microsoft, and Hewlett-Packard have joined the VC business, investing billions with a vengeance. Intel's senior vice president Les Vadasz, for example, boasted to us in May 1998, "We will invest $300 million this year in start-ups—all equity deals." Many of Intel's investments such as Inktomi, C/Net, Verisign, and Broadcom turned into huge Internet boom stocks. By the end of the second quarter of 2000, Intel's venture arm, Intel Capital, held stakes worth $7.5 billion in 450 companies.

The other significant type of venture capital investor that has emerged in the market over the last few years is the "angel" investor. The term "angel"—originally applied to wealthy individuals who financed Broadway productions—now refers to cashed-out entrepreneurs who pump their personal wealth into young companies. This used to mean shelling out $50,000 or maybe $100,000, but recently these angels have raised their financial stakes into the millions, and now compete directly with venture capitalists, often to their chagrin. "The problem with angels is that they take vacations," says Michael Moritz, the partner at Sequoia Capital who sniffed out and seed-funded Yahoo.

Whether the new and old investors get along or not, the huge inflow of venture capital to fund the commercialization of the Internet should be no surprise. Whenever any huge commercial idea has popped up in the U.S. market, from railroads to the personal computer, risk-loving American investors have historically jumped into the opportunity with both investment feet, and the Internet has been no exception. So when the most powerful people in Silicon Valley meet for breakfast at Buck's Restaurant—presided over by owner and self-proclaimed "Prime Minister" Jamis Mac-Niven—to plot their next moves in the Internet boom, they are merely continuing America's time-honored gold-rush tradition.

The great irony of the Internet boom era is that the very VC community that pumped up the Bubble by funding so many new start-ups is also the perpetrator of its deflation. By oversupplying the market with new companies, the VCs have satiated public investor appetite, and demand for overvalued Internet stocks has evaporated. It happened in the personal computer boom, when the VCs funded too many personal computer and disk-drive companies, and it's happened again with the Internet.

This chapter examines the VC industry from its early roots to the multidimensional business it has evolved into today. We cover early success stories such as Intel, Apple, and Cisco and the generational changes in the VC business from the early venture days to the Internet boom era. Most important, we present a venture business that had too much money chasing too many Internet deals. More specifically, this economic environment led to outrageous company valuations and an undisciplined investment market. It is our view that in the aftermath of the burst Internet Bubble, there will be a shakeout not only in Internet companies but in the venture capital world as well.

## Venture Capital Pioneers

Venture capital in America is nothing new. In some form—whether as angel investing from high-net-worth individuals, classic risk capital, or even junk bonds—venture capital has been instrumental in financing everything from canals, railroads, steel, and automobiles to the information-technology industry. One of the most active VCs in the Internet space, Tim Draper of Draper Fisher Jurvetson, whose own Silicon Valley VC roots go back three generations, likes to recall Queen Isabella's investment in Columbus for inspiration. "She was the original seed capitalist," Draper enthusiastically told a Harvard Business School audience in the fall of 1998.

The first generation of info-tech VCs was not much different from America's early investors. In the 1960s and the 1970s, second- or even third-career businessmen, playing largely with their own money, began investing in promising technologies and companies. "In the 1960s when I started, there were very few venture capitalists around, maybe twelve to fifteen in the San Francisco Bay Area," says Pitch Johnson of Asset Management, who made early, big bets on Amgen and Octel. This cadre of venture cowboys, which included characters such as Johnson, Bill Draper, Bill Edwards, and John Bryan, would lunch together every week at Sam's Grill on Bush Street in San Francisco and interview entrepreneurs. These meals would end by their asking the entrepreneur to step outside while they passed the hat to see how much money they would come up with.

But willing entrepreneurs in those days were hard to come by, so VCs spent a lot of time hustling around trying to find and create deals. Beginning in 1961, two of the modern pioneers of venture capital, Arthur Rock (credited with coining the phrase "venture capitalist") and the late Tommy Davis, used to ring people up from their small office on Montgomery Street in San Francisco to let possible investors know they had found a deal, usually in electronics, and ask them to chip in enough money to make the deal work. "When the phone rang in our office, we would get excited because it might be a new deal!" recalled Rock. In the Internet boom era, Davis's successor firm, Mayfield Fund, receives over 1,000 new business plans per month.

Perhaps the most important contribution the early VCs made was developing the legal and compensation structure for the business. Bill Draper and his lawyers at Cooley, Godward were the first to structure the modern venture capital partnership, where the general partners (the venture capitalists) typically charge the limited partners (the institutional investor) a 2 to 2.5 percent annual management fee on these funds as well as 25 to 30 percent of the carry, or the percentage of the profits earned on the fund. This equation has translated nicely in the Internet era, when some VC funds reach $1 billion or more in total and where the average general partner pulls down a few million in salary before he even places a successful bet.

## Silicon Valley's Early Success Stories

Before Rock teamed up with Davis, his first Silicon Valley investment came at the request of Eugene Kleiner, then one of the scientists working under William Shockley, the Nobel Prize–winning inventor of the transistor (Kleiner would later cofound the legendary VC firm Kleiner Perkins Caufield & Byers). The idea Kleiner and his partners had for silicon transistors eventually became Fairchild Semiconductor, the mother of all semiconductor companies.

In a later fund, Rock provided the seed capital for two other Shockley refugees, Bob Noyce and Gordon Moore, who also helped Kleiner start Fairchild. The company they pitched to Rock was, of course, Intel, and given their reputations (Noyce was general manager of Fairchild Semiconductor and the inventor of the integrated circuit, and Moore was also a distinguished engineer and Fairchild executive), they had little problem raising the money. In a 1994 *Red Herring* interview, Rock recalled the story behind raising seed capital in 1968 for Intel, the biggest hit of his VC career.

> Gordon Moore and Bob Noyce had become disenchanted with Fairchild [Semiconductor]. Sherman Fairchild had died, and the new management of the parent company were kind of autocratic people located on Long Island who didn't understand how things worked out here. For instance, they didn't appreciate the concept of giving employees stock options, even though the year before Intel was formed, the semiconductor division of Fairchild represented 110 percent of the company's profits. So, because of our long association, Gordon Moore and Bob Noyce contacted me to see if I could raise some money for a new venture they wanted to start that would focus on the semiconductor memory business. I told them I would, and we ended up putting together $2.5 million to start Intel. At $300,000, I think I was the largest single investor. The rest came from private individuals. We later raised another $3 million in a second round, and that was all the private venture capital that went into the company.

Amazingly, it took only $5.5 million in private capital to build Intel into America's most profitable corporation. Equally astounding, though, was the fact that the business plan it took to raise that money was only a page and a half long. "It was a document I wrote to sell the deal. But, of course, I don't think anybody turned me down," Rock said with a chuckle. "An unfortunate thing happened to the venture capital business. People started running their business plans by lawyers, who find all sorts of things left out that they think people might sue you over. Now we have huge business plans!" he moaned.

Today, seasoned VCs have tried to reverse the trend of bloated business plan summaries by using e-mail. "If it can't fit in an e-mail, it's too long to read," says Ann Winblad of Hummer Winblad Partners, who got word of some of her firm's biggest Internet success stories over the Internet itself.

The story behind the bespectacled and button-down-collared Rock's later investment in Apple in 1976, which came through his affiliation with Intel, was quite different from his Intel experience.

> Mike Markkula, who had just retired as a vice president at Intel, approached me about Apple. I was a little skeptical when I heard about Steve Jobs and Steve Wozniak. With their jeans, beards, and sandals, you might say they weren't exactly my style. But I went down to what I think was called the Homebrew Computer Show in San Jose. There were a lot of companies there, and I had never seen this before or since, but almost everybody at the show was crowded around the Apple booth trying to get a turn at their mock-up computer, which at the time was sold in a kit that you had to assemble. I literally could not get next to the booth. It was amazing! I thought it was great! I really thought there would eventually be a huge market opportunity. But, again, I was still a little uncomfortable with the two founders; it probably had to do with our age difference—both were barely twenty years old—but that's why I didn't invest more than I actually did, which was $57,000. Of course, I went on the board, and recruited Henry Singleton, who was the CEO of Teledyne, on the board. Markkula and the two Steves had recruited Mike Scott out of National Semiconductor to serve as president, so I began to feel a little better.

By the time Apple went public in December 1980, Rock's $57,000 investment was worth $14 million, and if he had held all his stock, it would have been worth $274 million in 2000 (1.9 percent of Apple's market in September 2000). Similarly, Rock's $300,000 investment in Intel had appreciated an incredible 50,000 percent since 1968 and was worth over $1.5 billion in mid-2000.

Rock, the initial chairman of Intel, remains on the company's board today, and served on the board of Apple until the computer company competed against Intel in 1994 by joint-venturing with Motorola and IBM to build the PowerPC microprocessor. "Motorola had taken out an ad in *The Wall Street Journal* stating that they were taking Intel head-on, and it was signed by Motorola, IBM, and Apple," Rock recalled in the *Red Herring* interview. "Within a week of the ad, articles started appearing in *Business Week* and other major publications stating that Apple and Intel were going to have head-to-head competition. Once I had decided I had to get off one board or the other, it was perfectly clear to me which board I would remain on. I own twice as much stock in Intel as I do in Apple, and I have been on Intel's board for twenty-five years, versus thirteen years on Apple's board."

In spite of such early successes, the total amount of new money committed to venture capital in the 1960s was only about $100 million annually, and that number increased gradually in the first half of the 1970s. What opened the way for modern venture capital was the "prudent man rule" of the mid-1970s that allowed American institutional investors to allocate hundreds of millions of dollars for illiquid investments such as venture capital funds. "Institutional investors became the fountainhead of money," says Don Valentine, legendary general partner at Sequoia Capital, also an early investor in Apple. "It allowed our funds to grow from $5 million to $50 million to $150 million."

The liberalization of investment rules in the 1970s and a decrease in tax rates on capital gains made increasing commitments to venture capital feasible and attractive. Overall, in the late 1970s and early 1980s the funds available for venture capital investment increased sharply—they shot up from $100 million in 1975 to $1.3 billion in 1981. Most of the new capital came from institutional sources, a tremendous windfall not only for Sequoia Capital but for other early venture capital firms such as Mayfield Fund from Menlo Park, the East Coast's leading VC firm Greylock Management, and the increasingly influential Kleiner Perkins Caufield & Byers.

The other big development of this time was the emergence of NASDAQ as the primary stock exchange for most of the venture-backed high-tech companies that did not qualify to raise money on the New York Stock Exchange. NASDAQ provided a ready outlet for numerous successful initial public offerings. Apple Computer, for example, was worth $1.8 billion on New Year's Eve 1980—more than Chase Manhattan Bank, Ford Motor Company, or Merrill Lynch, and twice as much as the combined market value of United Airlines, American Airlines, and Pan American. The success in the stock market of venture-capital-backed companies such as Tandem Computers and Teradyne also gave the venture industry a real boost.

## Changing of the Guard

By the mid-1980s, though, a change was in the wind. The Old Guard venture capitalists were joined by fresh-faced kids out of business school. While most of the Old Guard (and even some of the next-generation VCs who had joined them in the early '80s, such as John Doerr of Kleiner Perkins) had some industry experience, these young folks were making venture capital their first and primary career.

Members of this group included Stanford Business School graduates Geoff Yang, who joined Institutional Venture Partners; John Walecka, who was signed on by Brentwood Associates (Yang and Walecka were later to come together as members of a new partnership, Redpoint Ventures); and Harvard MBAs Jim Breyer, who landed at Accel Partners; Tim Draper, who started his own fund; Tench Coxe, who went to Sutter Hill Ventures; and Ofer Nemirovsky of Hancock Venture Partners. Another member of this generation, Bandel Carano of Oak Investment Partners, earned not an MBA but a master's in engineering at the age of twenty, and has been described by Stanford's former Engineering School dean James Gibbons as "the smartest student ever to graduate from the school of engineering." Every one of these VCs is now counted among the most successful and wealthy of their generation.

"When I graduated from Stanford in '85, there were thirteen

people from my class who came into venture capital," says Yang, who made a name in the business early by funding two high-profile networking deals, SynOptics and Wellfleet Communications, which netted his firm a 2,000 percent return when the two companies merged to become Bay Networks. "Our entry into the business also signaled the end of the venture capital generalist era and the beginning of specialization," explains Yang, who chose communications technology as his specialty. Similarly, when Ofer Nemirovsky started at Hancock Venture Partners in late '86, he remembers "floundering around" for a year before sending a memo to his partners announcing that he intended to specialize in software deals.

Most significant, the entrée of this hoard of MBAs into the VC business meant that the new investment decision makers in Silicon Valley had little or no operating experience. It didn't take long for resentment to grow between the new VCs and the Valley entrepreneurs. The ill will between the two groups culminated in the legendary cover story in the June 1990 issue of *Upside,* drafted by the king of Silicon Valley lore Michael S. Malone, called "Has Silicon Valley Gone Pussy?"

> These VCs—Rock, Valentine, Perkins, et al.—were very successful. Too successful, because their very success attracted not only half-assed competitors, but, worse, mountains of investment money. This money had to be invested, and that meant more people managing the funds. Unfortunately, the VCs were no more resistant to the siren call of respectability than their investment banking counterparts. And soon, the extra offices all over 3000 Sand Hill Road filled with venture pussies. By the mid-1980s, to visit a VC was to expect to be introduced to a parade of button-down, horn-rimmed post-adolescents in pleated flannel trousers. The older VC would intone proudly, "Randolph here just joined the firm. He's Choate/Brown/Harvard MBA" as junior shook your hand firmly and tried to conceal a supercilious smirk under a dewy upper lip.

## Lessons Learned from the 1987 Crash

Before the 1987 market collapse, venture investing reached $4.18 billion, the peak for the decade. More money was committed than could be wisely invested, with inexperienced venture partners raising new funds and rates of return suffering accordingly. "I joined the business not long before the stock market crashed in October 1987," says Accel's Jim Breyer. "At that time, there were some new technology trends people thought would become important—artificial intelligence, pen computing, and robotics were all hot areas of investment. But they were all spectacularly unsuccessful."

However, despite these tough times, Breyer and the others regard the collapse of the IPO market in '87 as an important learning experience. Gone were many of the "me-too" deals that allowed VCs to make money by following the pack. Instead, younger venture capitalists had to dig more deeply to find investment opportunities.

These young VCs also responded to this challenge by finding mentors, just as John Doerr relied on Kleiner Perkins cofounder Tom Perkins to teach him the business. Bandel Carano, who had three home run investments early in his career—Parametric Technology, Synopsys, and Wellfleet Communications—received invaluable advice from Oak Investment's lead partner Ed Glassmeyer, who took Carano to meetings and, in Carano's words, "made me successful." Tim Draper, who also earned a huge early investment return by seed-funding Parametric Technology, had to look only as far as his father and grandfather, who pioneered the business of venture capital in Silicon Valley.

And there were still great investments made in the '87–'90 time period. Cisco Systems received a venture investment of $2 million in late 1987 from Sequoia Capital. In 1988 the company's sales were less than $10 million, but by 1997 they were $6.4 billion, and by late 1997 its market capitalization was $60 billion. And if none of

Sequoia's original venture shares had been sold, they would have been worth over $6 billion by 1997.

Even though Cisco and other successful investments of this time provided some glimmer of hope, the initial public offering market dried up when the market crashed in the fall of 1987. According to financial research firm Securities Data Company, in 1987 the number of IPOs (fifty-one) and total dollars raised in these offerings ($774 million) were at historical low points and didn't begin recovering until 1991. In 1987 the average internal rate of return (IRR) on venture funds neared what one could earn in a passbook savings account at a bank: about 6 percent. The process that had created the initial boom had reversed itself. Institutional asset managers pulled back on their commitment to the venture capital industry, diverting capital to other sectors. "When institutional investors saw the dismal VC returns, they got the hell out of Dodge," explains Tim Draper, who at the time chose to raise his next fund from wealthy individuals at $250,000 a pop.

According to the National Venture Capital Association, capital commitments to venture capital firms plummeted, declining to a ten-year low of $1.27 billion in 1991. Under pressure, many of the venture firms imploded and broke up, and many venture capitalists exited the business. Most of the venture funds were ten-year limited partnerships, so one person was left standing to oversee what remained. Some of the portfolio companies were what the VCs call "the living dead"—they didn't go out of business but instead barely hung on, providing some jobs, eking out a payroll, but making very little, if any, profits.

But this shakeout was not necessarily a bad thing. "The most sane environment, if you had to pick a median for the last two decades, would actually be the 1992–1994 time period," says Jim Breyer of Accel. "We didn't have the backlash of the late '80s, but we didn't have the frothiness and the frenzy we've had in the last several years. In the 1992–1994 time period, we had very solid companies completing public offerings." He adds, "A company could not complete a successful public offering with top underwriters unless it had a history of profitability. Otherwise the underwriters didn't feel they could sell it to the right institutional buyers."

## The MBAs Go Marching On

With the advent of the Internet Bubble era and the influx of a couple of more waves of young venture capitalists, the venture culture has gone through yet another transformation and is ripe for another shakeout.

"When I joined the venture capital business in 1987, that was also the year when Harvard Business School sent 30 percent of its graduates, its highest ever, to Wall Street. Three months later, the market crashed," says Accel's Breyer. "Today, we see extraordinary numbers of Harvard Business School and Stanford Business School graduates wanting to get into the venture capital business and into Internet entrepreneurship. It's an all-time high, and you can bet it's an indication that something's up." Bill Sahlman, longtime head of Harvard Business School's entrepreneurial studies, agrees. In a speech to East Coast entrepreneurs and VCs in the fall of 1998, Sahlman mused, "I figure that at least 10 percent of Harvard's MBAs want to become venture capitalists, suggesting historically we are at the top of the market."

The biggest downside to this new supply of Generation X venture capitalists is their inclination for a catfight. "It was much more collegial when I first got into the business," says Redpoint's Yang. "Now, you've got all these new firms coming in and a bunch of young, assertive people who want to make their mark. That part has made it a little less fun. They're ownership hungry. They're competing hot and heavy because they're absorbed by a goldrush mentality."

Breyer agrees, "The technology business has become trendy and faddish to an extent that it wasn't in the early '90s. Everything has happened more quickly than anyone expected, and that has driven venture capitalists to get very aggressive."

While these young VCs think they are geniuses, it's only

because they have played the game during the Internet Bubble era, when returns have been fast and easy. And when you dissect their investment behavior, the newbie VCs often behave more like sheep, or "sheep following sheep" as someone put it—doing the same thing and making the same kind of investments as everyone else. And this "If you have a search engine company, then I better get one, too!" mentality is never more true than during technology booms and bubbles.

The personal computer bubble is a great example. After all, where are the "me-too" computer products from Atari, Commodore, Kaypro, Tandy, Osborne, ITT, Fortune Systems, or Texas Instruments? All once looked like great investments but have long since been relegated to the PC dustbin.

Paul Deninger, chairman and CEO of technology investment bank Broadview International, is even more blunt about the caliber of the new Internet VC. "There are some real doofuses investing in the private equity market," he says. "All it takes is one doofus in a deal to drive the value up. All it takes is four doofuses to invest in the fifth, sixth, and tenth disk-drive company to totally screw up the market."

## PC Booms and Busts

The ups and downs of the modern-day VC business since it was initiated in the early '60s are related to three technology booms: the personal computer, networking equipment and software, and now the Internet. Unlike the networking boom, the PC boom was characterized by a big bubble and its eventual explosion.

According to Don Valentine of Sequoia Capital, an early investor in Apple Computer, the problem with the early PC era was its undefined purpose and undefined markets: "When the PC was made, it was looking for an application. For years, people asked, 'It's nice, but what does it do?' The answer was, 'It doesn't do anything.'" He adds: "In 1978 we couldn't figure out who the customer was. Was it the education market? Was it the business market? You had a very embryonic product that didn't solve any problem. So it took a long time and there was a lot of wreckage; companies like Osborne and Commodore crashed because there was no market. In the beginning, there was no demand, no buyers." (This attitude partly led Don Valentine and Sequoia to cash out early on its investment in Apple, thereby losing millions of dollars in future investment gains. This move underscores the fact that even VC industry veterans such as Valentine often miss emerging new markets.)

"High expectations caused the air in the PC bubble," says Bill Brady, a veteran technology-investment banker now with CS First Boston. "When ten PC companies went public within a two-year period of time, people finally had to face the fact that seven of those companies weren't going to make it because they weren't viable."

An even better known example in technology finance circles of sheep following sheep is the Winchester disk-drive story documented by Bill Sahlman and Howard Stevenson of Harvard Business School in their famous case study "Capital Market Myopia."

From 1977 to 1983, venture capitalists invested an astounding $400 million in forty-three disk-drive companies. Each company had competent management and aggressive financial projections, and each player needed only 10 percent of the potentially huge market to thrive. But the market could not sustain forty-three new entrants, let alone the more than 100 domestic and foreign players active in the market at that time. The inevitable result was mayhem and a brutal mortality rate. Inflated expectations had created a scene where too many VCs funded too many in each segment of the PC industry.

There were some benefits of the PC boom. The disk-drive business, although intensely competitive, resulted in a few, very strong, globally competitive American companies like Quantum and Seagate. By overfunding the birth of the industry, the United States became the world leader in disk drives, and consumers benefit from high-quality, high-capacity disk drives at low prices. In summary, a well-funded, competitive marketplace creates strong companies, high rates of innovation, and job formation, while enhancing the global competitiveness of the domestic economy.

Meanwhile, the VCs were the biggest moneymakers in the disk-drive business. Just as in the Internet Bubble era, VCs could generally hand over the shares in newly public disk-drive companies to their limited-partner investors at reasonably high values and claim victory. However, Bill Sahlman also observes: "Typically, the public ended up holding the bag as competitive pressures resulted in major disappointments for post-initial public offering investors."

In their classic book *Venture Capital at the Crossroads*, authors William Bygrave and Jeffry Timmons document this lack of payoff for public investors:

The public lost interest in speculative IPOs because—in sharp contrast to the returns of venture capital investors—theirs were dismal. . . . Public investors did better in IPOs of profitable companies that did not rush to go public, than in those of losing companies that did. . . . They got the message: Beware of venture-backed IPOs. After 1983, many of those IPOs turned out to be terrible investments. Some IPOs such as Victor Technologies and Priam went bankrupt, and investors lost everything. Consequently, while holders of S&P 500 and Dow Jones stocks were enjoying record-breaking gains, public holders of venture-capital backed high-tech stocks were enduring losses.

## Networking: A Boom Without a Bust

In contrast to the sheeplike behavior in the midst of the PC bubble and disk-drive mania, venture investing in networking start-up companies such as Cisco Systems was much more calculated and sober. And it's no wonder that these investments came during a less frenzied time in both venture capital and the public stock market.

"In the beginning, the PC business did not solve a problem; it merely provided a glimpse of an emerging new market. But once the PC became somewhat useful, the next natural evolution was to link the computers. When Cisco came along, the environment desperately needed a solution," says Donald Valentine, an early investor in Cisco. "It was the company with the product that was a solution."

Bill Brady, part of the banking team at Morgan Stanley that took Cisco public in February 1990, agrees. "It was so clear if you read the prospectus. It was a whole new product. Network routers replaced bridges. It was logical. It had the best technology and a great market position." Yet as great as Cisco was, it was not a bubble stock. "I think it had a $13 million revenue quarter before it went public. It was profitable for four quarters," says Brady. "We priced the deal at $18 per share and it went to $22. It didn't blow out, yet everybody knows the history of its stock price since then. Cisco was about as high quality of an IPO as the public could ask for."

But the larger point according to Valentine is that Cisco was one among many networking companies that succeeded. "For microchip and PC companies, there were lots of wrecks," says Valentine. "But, unique in the networking world, there are almost no busts." He adds, "What's different is that it's the first time a whole lot of companies were financed dealing with a precise problem—in this case, how to get the networks to work at all and to work at high speed. The customers came out of the woodwork to buy, overcoming all the market development problems and risks."

## Back in the Bubble with the Internet

The recovery of venture capital returns starting in 1991, and the emergence of Internet commercialization beginning in 1994, pushed the pendulum back in the direction of overfunding. For example, in 1999, venture firms raised $46.55 billion from investors eager to join the party. Meanwhile, venture capitalists injected $48.34 billion into more than 3,600 start-ups in 1999, a 152 percent jump from 1998, and more than the combined totals of the previous three years, according to Venture Economics. One company alone, CarsDirect.com, received $280 million in its third round of financing in 1999. This trend continued in 2000, when VCs doubled their stake and put a whopping $104 billion into companies.

Without a doubt these massive capital inflows were a major cause of the Bubble. "The money has sloshed into venture capital," says Asset Management's Pitch Johnson, a VC since the early 1960s. "It hasn't flowed in—it's sloshed in and gone past the balance point." Indeed, by the beginning of 2000, some $100 billion in venture capital was sloshing around in the market.

Not surprisingly, in this capital environment venture funding levels of high-tech start-ups went up by a factor of ten or more in just five years. What used to be a $300,000 seed financing round in 1995 became a $3 million to $5 million round by 1999. The typical $1.5 million first round grew to $15 million, and the traditional $3 million second round became $30 million. And the top venture funds themselves were ten times larger than they were just a few years ago; a $1 billion fund was no longer unusual, with some twenty of them in existence by mid-2000, according to Venture Economics. And in September 2000 a veteran VC firm, New Enterprise Associates, raised an unprecedented $2 billion, the largest pure venture capital fund ever.

Although some of the firms planned to deploy their big funds over two to three years, much of this new cash was still being burned up big-time by Internet start-ups. The average monthly burn rate per start-up went up from half a million dollars a month in the mid-'90s to somewhere between $1 million and $2 million a month by 2000. As a result, instead of raising new funds every three or four years, venture partnerships were forced to raise new funds inside of twelve months. Crosspoint Ventures, for example, closed a fund of $300 million in mid-1999, and by December it had to raise another fund of $600 million to keep up with demand.

Horsley Bridge Partners, a private equity fund of funds, closed its sixth fund in July 1999 on committed capital of more than $1 billion from thirteen limited partners. "We thought that would hold us for two years," says managing director Phil Horsley. "Not so. The new year found us right back in the fund-raising mode. Our target for Fund VII, scheduled to close before mid-2000, was committed capital of $2 billion. The venture industry is running flat out."

The pace of investment left little time for due diligence. The decision cycles were compressed; start-ups were going from seed financing to IPO faster than ever. The whole process could go by in eighteen months rather than the four or five years it took as recently as the mid-1990s. "One first-tier venture firm did twenty-eight transactions in October 1999," reports one Silicon Valley insider. "Their explanation was they had discovered that it was costing them money to say no to any deal that made it to a second interview.

"A partner at another top firm," the insider continued, "said, 'We've had more deals that we've turned down generate a billion dollars of market value than we had total successful deals five years ago.' The clear implication was that they couldn't afford to say no to any deals that could get in the front door."

Indeed by November 2000, Chase Capital Partners, for example, was actually issuing press releases boasting that they had done the most venture deals—fifty-one—and put in the most money—more than $315 million—in the third quarter of 2000. New Enterprise Associates was second on the list in number of deals—thirty-nine— with a total investment of almost $280 million.

As recently as 1996, the best venture firms only did about a dozen deals in a whole year. The high-volume deals done by Chase and others raised the issue of the quality of the deals. Had proper due diligence been done on these companies, and could the venture firm find competent management to run these operations?

Meanwhile, many corporate venture investment programs and venture leasing firms had suspended due diligence altogether, and simply followed the best venture firms into investment deals.

VCs had so much capital to put to work, and were so ownership hungry, that syndicating with other firms in the first round became far less common. "Five years ago, 80 percent of our deals were syndicated—we had at least one other firm as partner," said Jim Breyer, managing partner of Accel Partners. "In 2000, 80 percent of our deals were solo." Less VC syndication meant that most start-ups had the benefit of just one VC brain rather than two or more on their boards. "The amount of help you get from your venture capital investor is not the same as it used to be," says Pitch Johnson. "And in many cases it's unsatisfactory. VCs run to too many board meetings; they haven't got time." Indeed more investments in a short time span with less syndication meant that VCs had to serve on more boards overall—fifteen to twenty per partner, in some cases.

When cash-heavy start-ups receive little guidance from their VC backers, these operations can acquire some bad habits. There was a strong temptation for start-ups to spend their way through challenges rather than learn to execute properly, listen carefully to customers, and build their businesses. "There was so much capital in the market, you could paper over a lot of problems," says Benchmark Capital's Bob Kagle. "It used to be that a company had to make significant progress before it could get a second round of funding at a good valuation. But there was far less scrutiny of companies for these second rounds. My biggest fear has always been that all this excess was going to kill the Silicon Valley goose that's laid the golden egg."

## My Brand Is Better Than Your Brand

All the venture capital flowing around and all the excess may have meant that more deals than ever were getting done by a larger number of venture groups, but it has not meant a lessening of competition among the elite firms.

Venture capital continues to be a multitier industry. In the top tier are a small group of venture firms such as the venerable Kleiner Perkins and Sequoia Capital and the hotshot firm Benchmark Capital. (See the box "Making the Grades" for more examples of firms and for criteria for making the top tier.) These firms work with an experienced group of limited partners, win the best deals, and generally wield most of the power in the VC business. In the lower tiers are the less experienced venture capitalists and entrepreneurs, funded by new entrant investors such as large public pension funds.

But even within the top tier, the branding of the venture firm has increasingly become critical to seeing the best deal flow. No matter how much money VCs throw at large pools of start-ups, every firm still wants to finance the next Yahoo or eBay. And success breeds success—if a firm can finance some real winners, then it increases the odds that it will be able to get a look at the next winning deals.

The elite VC brands also attract the best banking sponsorship for their start-ups. As a result, even seasoned entrepreneurs with access to plenty of capital have to choose a brand-name venture firm if they hope to get the IPO sponsorship of top underwriters like Goldman Sachs or Morgan Stanley.

A recognizable venture name also helps start-ups attract management talent, the best lawyers, and even office space—and it helps with raising a late round of financing. "A hard-working, well-intentioned, but obscure venture partnership doesn't have the right kind of contacts," says Jonathon Sweemer, former managing director of Nassau Capital. "It's the brand name that helps open doors."

In many ways, with this new emphasis on branding, institutional venture capital is starting to resemble investment banking. "I think we're seeing the emergence of a very different kind of financial services firm," says Phil Horsley. "It's going to be some combination of an investment banking firm, a merchant banking firm, and a traditional venture capital firm."

This trend is reinforced by the fact that a fair share of people coming into VC firms today started out as investment bankers, market analysts, or attorneys. And as with investment banking, personal net worth is becoming more important as an end in itself rather than as a lucrative by-product of building solid companies. Industry insiders readily admit that today's venture industry is far more greed-driven than ever before, and that some investments are made just to be flipped into the market or sold to the highest bidder. The quest for money is largely driven by ego and the competitive desire to keep up with (or surpass) one's VC peers. The ultimate goal is the *Forbes* 400 list. And as VCs strive for that goal, more time and energy is going into the toys that money can buy. "Some of these VCs are just pretending they're having partner meetings; they're just going through the motions," says a Silicon Valley insider. "At the same time, a certain attention to detail is going into the house in Aspen or customizing the jet."

Not every beneficiary of the huge returns is happy with this obsession with money. One very successful VC said, "I have a lot of friends in the business who said five years ago, 'If ever I could get $25 million or $50 million after tax, I'm outta here. What a rat race. I'm going to balance my life out.' Those same people have blown through that number and are saying they have to have a billion dollars. They already have more than they can spend rationally."

Even so, the most honest VCs recognize that the real heroes in all this are the entrepreneurs. They're where most of the good ideas come from. "Our industry is made up of a bunch of lemmings," admits Benchmark general partner Andy Rachleff. "When was the last time you heard an original idea from a venture capitalist?" Entrepreneurs are the true visionaries who create new industries and ultimately change the world. "If we don't watch it, we'll start believing that it's our money and our great professional management that's built Silicon Valley," declares Crosspoint Partners' John Mumford. "But it's the entrepreneur's blood, sweat, and tears and sacrifice that have built all of this, and we VCs are simply privileged to be part of it."

## Corporations Join the VC Game

Even as venture capital partnerships pit their brands against each other in the competition for deals, some large corporations such as Intel, Microsoft, and Softbank have jumped with both feet into the venture-funding game.

Intel, for example, invested a remarkable $2.5 billion in about 200 companies through 1998. In 1998 alone Intel made more than 100 investments; 80 went to new start-ups, about one-third of the deals were overseas, and 75 percent of them involved the Internet.

And by the end of the second quarter of 2000, Intel's venture arm, Intel Capital, held stakes worth $7.5 billion in 450 companies. Intel's strategy involves helping the overall market grow rather than making quick money, an approach they see as complementary to VC efforts rather than competitive. "We like to make sure the company has some other professional money, so we have other board members helping the entrepreneurs," explained longtime Intel senior vice president and board member Les Vadasz, who heads his company's strategic investment operation.

By the end of the second quarter of 2000, meanwhile, Microsoft had a portfolio of equity investments worth $17.8 billion. For this quarter, 31 percent of Microsoft's pretax profits were from its investments, providing earnings of $1.1 billion. In fiscal 2000 alone, Microsoft made 100 investments totaling $5.4 billion.

In 1994, corporate venture capital made up only 4 percent of total venture capital investments. In 2000, that number was up to 17 percent.

Meanwhile, VCs and corporate investors have also worked together. One example is Microsoft's investment in New Enterprise Associates' venture fund NEA VIII. "We are using the premise of their investment in the fund as a way to introduce them to those companies which could benefit from a relationship with Microsoft," says NEA general partner Art Marks. "We are financial optimizers. We try to make the most of our investments." Companies like Microsoft especially help the VCs by buying some of their portfolio companies outright, providing high returns for the VCs. Two dramatic buyouts Microsoft made during the Internet Bubble era were for the fledgling start-ups WebTV and Hotmail. Microsoft purchased both companies, which had little or no revenue, for over $400 million each.

An interesting side story to the Hotmail deal was that in spite of the gigantic return Hotmail's VCs made on Microsoft's acquisition, Hotmail's lead investor, Tim Draper of Draper Fisher Jurvetson, thought it was too early to sell. "When Sabeer [Bhatia, Hotmail's CEO] returned from his first meeting with Microsoft, he had dollar signs in his eyes, and I thought, Uh-oh, we've got trouble," recounts Draper. And Draper's wariness paid off; Hotmail's sales price eventually more than doubled because of his persistence that Hotmail remain independent. "I thought Hotmail could have been the next Yahoo," says Draper. Even Bill Gates admitted to us in February 1999 that Hotmail's perceived value had shot up tremendously since the acquisition in December 1997, and that Draper had the right instinct that it was too early to sell. "The guy at Microsoft who did the Hotmail deal had to slink around the office for a few months because everyone thought we had paid a pretty big price," recalled Gates in early 1999. "In today's overheated Internet market, the same guy looks like a hero, because if we had to buy Hotmail today, it would probably cost a couple of billion dollars."

In addition to big high-tech companies such as Intel and Microsoft getting into the venture-investing act, as well as 350 other corporations by the year 2000, the likes of Arthur Andersen has also gotten into the mix. Arthur Andersen's financial services runs a $500 million venture fund and its consulting arm (recently renamed Accenture) has a $1 billion fund. Even leveraged buyout (LBO) funds couldn't resist following the money into venture investing: Hicks, Muse, Tate & Furst, for example, raised $2 billion to invest in Internet and communications companies. Phil Rotner, managing director in the Office of the Treasurer at MIT, called this LBO participation "history in reverse." "A decade ago, when venture returns were low, venture firms such as TA Associates and Summit Partners decided that they could do buyouts," Rotner explained. "Now you have buyout firms deciding they can do venture investing."

## Angels Take Flight

A true indicator of a bubble environment is not only the overabundance of money in increasingly large venture capital funds and the emergence of the more aggressive corporate investor, but the growing number of investors, loosely known as "angels," putting money into high-tech start-ups.

Many of these angels are cashed-out entrepreneurs with time on their hands and money to burn. In Silicon Valley these guys are epitomized by a group calling themselves the Band of Angels. Begun in January 1995 as an investment club with 12 members, they now have more than 120 angels in the group. The size of their investments has continued to spike up, from a pooled amount of $500,000 per start-up to a blockbuster deal in summer of 1998, where forty members of the Band invested a combined $4 million into a company called SendMail.

Meanwhile another group called Angel Investors, led by Ron Conway, did seed-level investments in 230 Internet and other high-tech start-ups by fall 2000, most notably putting money into Loud-Cloud, Napster, and Google. All told Conway invested some $160 million.

Then there are the flush individual angels. For example, two of the cofounders of Sun Microsystems, Bill Joy and Andy Bechtolsheim, each put $1 million into the SendMail deal, bringing the angel funding to a total of $6 million. This compared, at the time, with an average first-round venture capital investment of $6.5 million in high-tech start-ups.

Bright Light Technologies, a company providing a technology that combats online "spam," or junk e-mail, also got some heavy angel funding from Band of Angels members as well as from Bechtolsheim, venture capitalist and Compaq board chairman Ben Rosen, and tech industry pundit Esther Dyson. These and other angels put in a combined $2.75 million, with venture capital group Accel Partners providing an additional $2.75 million, for a total of $5.5 million of start-up funding in 1998. Unlike SendMail, Bright Light at least had some professional venture capital funding.

While the recent level of angel investing expands the size of the overall venture pool available for promising new start-ups, it also impacts traditional venture economics. In the heat of competition between the angels and the professional VCs, private company valuations have skyrocketed, meaning VCs now ultimately pay more for less. Angel investors, for example, valued SendMail at an unprecedented $20 million at the time of their investment, and Bright Light raised its angel round at a $10 million valuation.

One main reason for these high valuations is that angels typically accept higher figures than do venture capitalists, in part because angels do less research on these companies and their markets and don't feel pressure to please limited-partner investors. Hans Severiens, director of the Band of Angels, admits as much: "The angels are freer to invest on their gut," he says.

"I am actually skeptical of this angel experience," cautions Andy Bechtolsheim, who not only made several hundred million as one of the Fab Four that founded Sun Microsystems, but more recently sold his eleven-month-old networking start-up, Granite Systems, to Cisco for $220 million. "I think any start-up would be best advised to get money from a true VC. For major deals I don't think angels are a predictable source of funding."

Meanwhile, Bechtolsheim defends his own angel investments as primarily in the electronic development space he understands well, and "where I know the people and they know me." His role, though, is mostly passive—he does not regularly advise most of these companies or sit on their boards. He expects most of his companies to get acquired rather than to go public. He does admit that the red-hot SendMail and Bright Light deals he invested in are exceptions to his typical strategy.

Bechtolsheim isn't the only one skeptical of overinflated angel activity, in spite of his own high-priced investments. "Today's angels scare the hell out of me; they're so emotional," says Integral Capital's Roger McNamee.

Predictably, venture capitalists don't like the expensive competition from angels for early-stage deals. "They don't deliver the value-added," says Winblad. "They might be there for a few rah-rah phone calls, but they don't wrap good business practices around the companies. They are not in the full-time profession of building businesses. I do it full-time. I have my money from institutional investors who won't give me any more unless I make money for them."

The abundant angel money that's jacking up company valuations is not always beneficial for the entrepreneur. If a start-up's valuation gets ahead of itself, it becomes difficult for the company to grow into that valuation and to get additional private financing down the road. "It has created a chaotic effect," adds Winblad. "The capital structures are not done right."

Whether venture capitalists like it or not, the growth of angel funding of technology deals is part of the Bubble. In simple economic terms, angel money has greatly lowered the barrier to entry for Joe Entrepreneur to obtain venture capital. Many more companies—particularly Internet-related companies—are funded as a result.

## Incubators or Incinerators?

Another competitor to VC firms that's emerged in the midst of Internet mania is high-profile incubators or "Eco-Nets" (Economic Networks) such as Idealab and Divine Interventures. These entities are best described as VC firms on steroids. Incubators are breeding grounds for start-ups. Not only do they serve up cash to invest and have partners who will happily sit on your board, but they also eagerly set up your accounting books and network connections, help you recruit your receptionist, give you a free office or two, and build your Web site. And these incubators, which pride themselves on having "management expertise," claimed they could churn out companies in thirty- to sixty-day cycles.

But Divine Interventures itself barely squeezed onto the public market in July 2000 after numerous failed runs at an IPO. Soon thereafter it began running into stock troubles, with its stock at less than $2 per share by the end of November 2000. Divine also suffered board departures and executive shake-ups, and tried to shift its strategy to avoid working with early-stage start-ups to concentrate on mergers, acquisitions, and roll-ups of companies.

In October Idealab canceled plans for is own $300 million IPO. By November 2000, it had spawned more than forty companies, including seven IPOs, but was definitely feeling the chill of the post-Bubble market.

According to the National Business Incubation Association, 100 new incubators were hatched in the last few months of 1999 and in the first quarter of 2000, bringing the U.S. total to a whopping 800. About half of those were of the venture capital variety. Eco-Net fever had also spread to Europe, where, insiders told us, approximately 140 incubators were formed in the United Kingdom in 1999 and early 2000. Not to be forgotten were Internet companies like Beyond.com and Cybershop that failed at their original business missions but reinvented themselves as incubators, or i-holding companies. One of the more absurd examples was Outlook Sports Technology, a golf accessory manufacturer, which changed its name to eFusion Fund with a new mission to incubate Internet companies.

A variation on the incubator model is publicly held venture capital funds such as CMGI and Internet Capital Group (ICG), which have attracted a lot of attention in the stock market and among venture capitalists and entrepreneurs. ICG was founded in 1996 and by 2000 had stakes in more than thirty-five business-to-business e-commerce companies. Before the big April 2000 shakedown, ICG was enjoying a significant markup in the stock market with a market capitalization of $34 billion, even though the absolute best-case combined future value of its holdings totaled only $28 billion. ICG had gone public in August 1999 at $6 per share and had risen to $200 by the beginning of 2000.

Founded in 1995, CMGI had a similar dynamic, with its stakes in more than fifty-five Internet companies and a market cap of $36 billion before the April correction. CMGI launched two venture funds, each worth $1 billion, in January 2000, and immediately began raising a third. "To me, ICG and CMGI are like the go-go conglomerates of the 1960s," said Paul Deninger, chairman and CEO of Broadview International Bank. He described their strategy as "Go public, get a big cap, and then do arbitrage by buying companies or percentages of companies with the big cap."

Institutional venture firms were tempted to follow the public-holding-company model, at least while the market caps were high. "Of course it was tempting," said a prescient Paul Deninger in January 2000. "If there's a quarter on Lexington Avenue, you're not going to jump into traffic to pick it up. But do you risk it for a $100 bill? A $1,000 bill? What if it's a billion dollars? The temptation to some of these VCs is going to be high even though they know that there is a risk they are going to get hit by a runaway Yellow Cab."

Indeed after the April 2000 washout, the market caps of the public VC firms and incubators had come back to earth. As the technology market cooled, incubators' share prices turned icy. By November 2000, CMGI's share price was down more than 85 percent for the year to $10 and ICG had similarly tumbled to $6. In September 2000 Dave Wetherell, the CEO of CMGI, announced a new "emphasis on growth and profitability" based on plans to streamline CMGI's lines of business and venture funds. *Red Herring* venture capital editor Larry Aragon commented that "CMGI still had a long hike to get out of the canyon."

By the end of 2000, both ICG and CMGI had begun to scale back. ICG had laid off fifty employees, or 35 percent of its staff, and was trying to decide which of its B2B companies to stop funding. CMGI's @Ventures VC arm had endured a string of portfolio company woes, including the closures of Mothernature.com, Furniture.com, and Productopia, and layoffs at OneMediaPlace and Foodbuy.com. CMGI said it planned to whittle down its unwieldy network of seventeen companies to just five or ten by the close of its fiscal year, which ends in July 2001. From its peak of $163 in January 2000, CMGI's stock price plummeted 97 percent to $4 by March 2001.

Wall Street in general had become less receptive to the kind of companies that most incubators were nurturing—early-stage businesses with big ideas but no products or profits. So the "time to market" had lengthened for many Internet companies in the incubators' portfolios. This meant that the risk of owning these companies had increased while the real value of an incubator's investments had decreased sharply. The whole incubator trend looked to be no more than a fad. In fact according to research done by the Aberdeen Group, the number of incubators in the United States had fallen to 138 in January 2001. Aberdeen forecast that the number would fall to 76 by January 2002 and to just 55 in January 2003.

"Incubators were compelling in 1998 and 1999, because the time frame for creating market value in ventures was very short," said Roger McNamee. "If recent trends persist, it will take much longer to build market value in new ventures. This suggests that some incubator funds will ultimately incinerate the capital that goes into them."

## The Internet Shakeout

The bottom-line question ultimately was whether the Internet go-go companies that the VCs funded could maintain their long-term market value. "The Internet industry dilemma to me is the same as the early PC one," remarks Sequoia Capital's Don Valentine. "You have to pace your investments in the Internet according to the value it creates for customers. The VC industry has gotten way ahead of itself in evaluating where the value exists, and the result is the funding and creation of unnecessary companies. What will we do with 2,000 companies? Do you think five years from now we will have 2,000 Internet companies? It's a repetition of the disk-drive mistake, the PC mistake. We always make that mistake when there is too much money."

Investment banker Bill Brady agrees. "You could compare the number of PC and disk-drive companies that went public to the number of Internet companies that have blown out of the public gates in the last few years. Of all those disk-drive companies, how many are still companies today? It's like 10 percent. You could argue that only 10 percent of the public Internet companies will be viable in the long run."

The usual argument is that it's different this time. Even for the

PC and disk-drive booms, venture capitalists at the time argued that the venture industry itself had improved and was therefore yielding higher-quality companies. There was more later-stage follow-up financing, more value-added assistance provided to company management, better underwriters, and just better all-around technologies than before, they said.

The truth is that venture funds raised in noneuphoric, bear markets, for example 1987–1988, have done the best and have had the least wreckage, whereas those raised during a bubble—like 1982–1983—have done the worst. "History tells you that the funds raised now will underperform," says Brad Koenig, managing director and head of the technology banking practice at Goldman Sachs. "So I think we will see some real correction here, and not only with Internet companies. There will be a shakeout in hedge funds, in the money management business, and in investment banking. And there will be a shakeout in the venture capital business."

Historically, a venture shakeout has been tied to the public market: Once the IPO window closes, venture funding also drops significantly; many venture capitalists and VC firms below the top tier simply go away over the following two years. This public market/venture capitalist pattern could be seen clearly in the years 1980–1995, with the venture capital shakeout occurring largely in the late 1980s.

Setting the stage for the shakeout are the 1,000 venture capital firms raising venture money, at least 400 of which have been launched in the Internet era, most of them with little experience outside a bull market. Basically, any new investor or venture capitalist who came into the business after 1992 has operated only in an easy-money environment. "There are a number of venture capital firms and individuals in this business who have never seen a down cycle," observes Kleiner Perkins general partner Joe Lacob.

Inevitably, VCs will have to go back to basics when the bull market ends. They'll have to be more cash conservative and willing to syndicate their deals to minimize risk; there will be no easy exits through quick IPOs or mergers. It will be a difficult adjustment, and many won't make it."

Without a hot IPO market, even the surviving venture investors will feel less sure of themselves. "Suddenly, you've got a lot to do working with your companies that don't make it out of the IPO gate," says NEA's Art Marks. "It will also get harder for your companies to raise money."

There are signs that this is already happening. "There are a lot of people baby-sitting a lot of companies wondering what the hell to do with them," declares Ann Winblad. And many of these can't even think about going public, especially when the IPO pipeline narrows or closes. She adds, "A lot of bunts in this game are concealed by acquisitions."

In essence, the venture capital world lives in its own distorted reality. One thirty-something venture capitalist who started his career at the tail end of the burst in the PC bubble worries that his peers have become so swept up in Internet mania that they have forgotten their economic lessons. "This is a repeat of a cycle," he states vigorously. "The only difference is that the financial markets are more extreme, and it's even easier to make money than it was in '83. If anything, it's gone to our heads even more."

Another concern is that many VCs appear to have taken advantage of the public investor drunk on Internet stocks. "The venture capitalists who have made the most money right now in this part of the cycle are the most promotional venture capitalists, the ones who hype the most and play into creating high multiples for their companies," the same VC complains. "It doesn't mean there aren't a lot of good entrepreneurs or venture capitalists, but when it becomes easier to make money by promoting stock than by building underlying businesses, people will shift their attention to promoting their companies."

It is true that those venture capitalists who were early to the Internet have cashed in big. Luck and timing have typically played a large role. There's also a sense that old strategies and time-tested investing methods got in the way of exploiting the Internet revolution. For example, many venture firms had enjoyed quite a bit of stability by focusing on specific markets, such as chip deals, computer deals, or software. These venture capitalists knew their markets and specialties, knew what to look for in a deal, and generally stuck to their tried-and-true referral networks for business plans.

In contrast to the old segmented investment strategies, the Internet represents a blending of numerous technology segments. VCs who were semiconductor, communications, media, content, and software specialists now need to work together as a team, focusing on this huge technology revolution—which, in turn, is segmenting into various markets. Those VCs who jumped on this opportunity reaped the rewards. "Three years ago, I was pretty nervous about the public Internet market," says Benchmark's Kagle. "I could have crawled under my desk and sat there, but I would have missed one of the greatest opportunities of all time."

## The Venture Capital Shakeout

Fortunate timing aside, the venture capital industry in recent years has been overbloated and undisciplined. They may have chalked up some big scores, but by oversupplying the market with young, unproven companies, they set up the whole Internet market for a Darwinian shakeout. As if to signal the reality of such a shakeout, the top-tier firm, Crosspoint Venture Partners, decided in late 2000 to pull the plug on its own $1 billion fund. This raised eyebrows because Crosspoint had been one of the most successful VC firms in recent years, backing such mega-hits as Ariba, Brocade Communications, and Juniper Networks. One of Crosspoint's funds, raised in 1996, has turned $100 million into $4 billion. The money for the new fund had already been committed by its investment partners, but the thirty-year veteran firm decided it could not be invested wisely at the time. "I frankly think it's smart," said Jesse Reyes, vice president of venture data firm Venture Economics. "Crosspoint could be the first venture guys to say that the emperor wears no clothes."

Not long after the Crosspoint announcement, Hummer Winblad Venture Partners had to write off more than $44 million in one fund because of worthless investments in Net retailers Gazoontite, HomeGrocer.com, and Pets.com. Though that was just three companies out of thirty-seven in the fund, the write-offs represented more money than the firm had lost in total since its founding. In the fourth quarter of 2000, COMPAQ's venture arm was forced to write down $1.8 billion.

"When the Bubble burst, all hell broke loose," angel investor Ron Conway told *Business Week*. Twenty of the companies Conway backed and an estimated $10 million in seed capital were wiped out. He was planning to shut down his Angel Investors group once the last two funds ran their course.

And Angel Investors will not be alone. From 1996 through 2000, the number of venture firms more than doubled to 1,010, the number of companies financed surged 150 percent to 5,380, and the amount of money invested soared nearly tenfold to $103 billion, according to Venture Economics. Meanwhile the average one-year return to venture funds had sunk from a high of 164 percent in 1999 to 37.6 percent in 2000. And in the fourth quarter of 2000, VC returns were negative 6.3 percent. In the wake of the burst Internet Bubble, the venture capital bubble was poised for a major deflation with a shakeout of venture firms to follow.

## MAKING THE GRADES

What makes a venture capital partnership great? The Massachusetts Institute of Technology auditions numerous venture partnerships every year to determine which ones to invest with. The university is already investing with some of the best in the business, but is constantly evaluating venture performance based on very sophisticated criteria. "The hardest part about deciding who you go with in recent years is that everybody was coming in with absolute numbers that looked terrific," says Phil Rotner, managing director in the Office of the Treasurer at MIT. "And, of course, the usual question about these numbers was, are they sustainable and repeatable?" While some investors would say that it's better to be lucky than good, limited partners like MIT are very interested in fund-over-fund performance that goes beyond the occasional home run investment or a single fund that performs well.

How are those returns measured? Limited partners use three criteria: internal rate of return (IRR), multiples, and if-held value. They also consider less quantifiable factors.

IRR is based on a complex formula that shows the rate of return received by the investor taking into consideration all of the cash flows and remaining residuals. Phil Horsley, managing director of fund of funds at Horsley Bridge, points out that measurement by IRR has to be carefully qualified. "Keep in mind," says Horsley, "that IRRs on funds less than three years old are not meaningful. In fact, we pay attention to IRR only if a fund is at least five years old."

Because short-term IRRs are not meaningful and yet the venture cycle is faster than ever today, most limited partners tend to prefer multiples (cash on cash) as the best measure in the current environment, that is, how much money a venture fund returns to a limited partner compared with how much the limited partner put in. Crosspoint Venture Partners, for example, had a fund in the late-1990s with an astounding multiple of 50X. But even a 20X return for a venture fund is outstanding compared with the 3X that was considered quite respectable just a few years ago.

Beyond IRRs and multiples, limiteds also like to look at the if-held value of the companies that VCs invest in. The if-held value measures what the venture partnership's original investment in a company would be today if their limiteds had never sold their stock distributions. This metric highlights the ability of a venture partnership to help create great stand-alone companies—the true long-term industry leaders. Kleiner Perkins Caufield & Byers likes to point to the if-held value of such companies as Sun Microsystems, America Online, and Verisign. Sequoia Capital takes special pride in the if-held value of Cisco Systems and Yahoo.

A strong if-held value indicates that the VCs help their companies recruit great management, develop and refine strategy, and forge advantageous partnerships. "When I invest in a venture firm, I want to buy into an unfair deal flow," says Jonathon Sweemer, former managing director of Nassau Capital. (Nassau managed Princeton University's private equity and real estate investments.) "I want to have unfair leverage. I want strategic relationships for our portfolio companies that are superior. I want a venture partner, such as Jim Breyer at Accel Partners, who can reach virtually anybody at a Microsoft, an Intel, an Oracle, or a Cisco, and see how that relationship might work to the benefit of our investments."

Ultimately, if-held value means more than simply distributing the IPO stock to limited partners and declaring victory. Any stock distributions made need to be of high quality, with no hidden land mines, and the stock should continue to increase in value after the limited partners receive it.

Alongside the metrics, most careful limited partners also look at what MIT's Rotner calls "soft points." Chief among these is partner chemistry—how well the VC team blends and works together, and ultimately stays together. This applies both to firms that have one or two highly visible rainmakers and firms that seem to have parity across the partnership. Partner chemistry, for example, has become a hall-mark of Benchmark Partners.

Closely allied to partner chemistry is managing intergenerational transfer—the ability to pass the baton from one generation to the next without breaking stride. One long-established venture firm that has modeled this process very well is Greylock Management.

According to limited partners we interviewed, in addition to the firms mentioned above, other venture firms that have demonstrated an impressive combination of the right qualities are Battery Ventures, Communications Ventures, Foundation Capital, Matrix Partners, Menlo Ventures, North Bridge Venture Partners, Redpoint Ventures, and Sigma Partners. And though some venerable firms, such as Charles River Ventures, Mayfield Fund, and Mohr Davidow Ventures, may have missed the first wave of the Internet, they have been able to successfully reinvent themselves and post the kind of returns that show that they are truly top tier. For all of the above firms, the right combination of winning qualities contributes to a venture firm's franchise factor. It's the networking effect all over again—success breeds success.

# Doonesbury

POPSTER, HOW COULD WE BE SPENDING THIS MUCH?

WELL, A LOT OF IT'S PAYROLL. WE HAVE TWO GUYS WORKING IN THE GARAGE AND 20 MORE FROM THEIR HOMES.

8-27

BUT DON'T WORRY, HONEY— I'M MEETING WITH UNCLE BERNIE TODAY, AND I'M SURE HE'LL EVENTUALLY COME THROUGH WITH ANOTHER ROUND OF FINANCING!

BUT WHAT IF WE RUN OUT OF MONEY BEFORE THEN?

ACTUALLY, WE ALREADY HAVE. EVERYONE'S WORKING FOR STOCK OPTIONS. DO YOU KNOW WHAT STOCK OPTIONS ARE?

SURE! THEY'RE LIKE LOTTERY TICKETS. RIGHT?

SHHH!

## KLEINER PERKINS CAUFIELD & BYERS:
# LEADING THE VENTURE CAPITAL HERD

> We consider it our responsibility that our companies never run out of money. We help them hire the right people, and we help them identify the risks and put those risks behind them. If anything, we have been accused of being too involved.
>    —Tom Perkins, cofounder, Kleiner Perkins Caufield & Byers

Of all the venture capital firms involved in the Internet boom, none has had the impact of the Menlo Park, California–based venture powerhouse Kleiner Perkins Caufield & Byers (KP). Beginning with its 1994 investment in Jim Clark and his start-up Netscape, KP focused on investing and creating companies in the Internet space with a vengeance. Very early in the game, the partners at KP divided up the Internet market into what they considered emerging new sectors, and began making their bets in each category. In the portal game, KP bet on Excite / At Home; in e-commerce, they put their market muscle behind Amazon.com; and in the networking and communications space, they helped start companies such as Juniper Networks, Cerent, and Concentric Network. All in all, KP has funded some of the most richly valued Internet companies over the last five years, covering virtually every segment in the emerging Internet market.

But even KP has seen its share of woes. In the first edition of *The Internet Bubble,* we showed a chart of the public Internet companies KP had funded up through June 30, 1999. We noted that the combined market capitalization of all of KP's public Internet companies represented 40 percent of the total market cap of all the public

Internet companies, thereby demonstrating KP's power in the marketplace. But this scenario was not to last. At the end of this chapter is a revised table that includes all the public Internet companies KP has funded, and how their stocks performed over a fifty-two-week period ending December 15, 2000. As readers can see from examining this updated table, while KP companies still dominate many new Internet sectors, many are still unprofitable, and all have taken a market-cap whack in the wake of the deflated Bubble.

## Dividing and Conquering

This chapter tells the story of how KP came to be the biggest promoter of the Internet Stock Bubble. We first focus on the founding investment principles of the partnership as seen through the eyes of legendary KP founder Tom Perkins and current lead partner John Doerr. Second, we examine the evolution and power of the KP network of companies and executive talent. Then we describe how the partners first identified the Internet opportunity and then invested in companies such as Netscape, At Home, and Amazon. Finally, we show how KP leveraged its advantages to cash in big (and early) in the first phase of the Internet boom.

Since the firm's inception in 1972, the $1 billion KP has invested in over 400 start-ups has turned into more than 250 public companies, including Compaq, Sun Microsystems, America Online (AOL), Netscape, Amazon, At Home, Verisign, and Juniper Networks. The companies are now worth over $724 billion, generating over $100 billion in annual revenues and employing over 252,000 people.

While KP's annual return-on-investment numbers are not public, insiders say their combined funds since 1972 have generated an annual compounded rate of over 50 percent, with some of their recent, Internet-focused funds returning well into the three digits— far outpacing the historical venture capital industry average of 23 percent, and putting the firm in the top 5 percent of all venture firms. KP partner John Doerr unabashedly refers to this type of venture capital success as "the largest legal creation of wealth in the history of the planet." And these totals don't even consider KP's active list of over ninety private companies, which also represents billions of dollars in potential market value and strategic influence in the technology industry.

KP has leveraged its reputation well, raising a series of increasingly larger funds to manage, the last being Fund X, a $1 billion fund. Most of the money for this latest fund comes from institutions, including the endowment arms of Harvard, Stanford, and MIT, and nonprofits such as the Ford Foundation. KP's general partners command a 30 percent take of capital gains earned on their funds, and 3 percent annual management fees (based on the total dollar amount of each fund raised), demonstrably higher than the more typical 20 percent/2 percent fee the average venture firm commands. Senior partners John Doerr, Vinod Khosla, and Brook Byers are said to take the biggest slices of the pie, leaving the rest to be divided up by the other partners. In fall 1999, both Doerr and Khosla made the *Forbes* 400 list of the world's wealthiest individuals. Each of the venture capitalists was estimated to have paper wealth of $1 billion.

By putting these kinds of numbers on the scoreboard and exerting control and influence over its high-powered band of companies, KP has earned a godlike status inside the industry. KP's Doerr refers privately to this perception of power as the "Kleiner Mystique," and he and his partners leverage this aura to win the hottest start-ups, recruit the best CEOs, and take their portfolio companies to the public market faster than any other venture firm in the business.

Doerr's partner Will Hearst III credits the innate competitive drive within each partner for KP's success. "We think about what the other firms are doing and why we might have missed an important deal. We analyze where we went wrong, and figure out if we can get back into a market and win," explains Hearst.

Part of this aggressive nature is revealed in how KP partners work with their network of companies to influence the direction of the Internet industry and gain collective advantages. The partners affectionately refer to their portfolio of companies as the KP *keiretsu,* a metaphor Doerr came up with in the 1980s. *Keiretsu* refers to the modern Japanese system of extensive cross-ownership within a family of companies. While KP's *keiretsu* is not as formal, the sense of mutual obligation among companies is still there.

The most aggressive action within the KP *keiretsu* is targeted at destabilizing Microsoft, the software behemoth KP must keep off balance in order to create new start-up opportunities in the Internet space. Some industry insiders speculate that this battle between Microsoft and KP companies is personal, as well. "The Gates/Doerr competition goes back at least a decade, when Lotus [a KP software company investment led by Doerr] got its butt handed to it by Microsoft in the spreadsheet wars," observed a technology industry veteran friendly with both Gates and Doerr. "The battle continued when Microsoft took on Sun in the corporate computing market with Windows NT, and lives on today over the Internet," added our source, who preferred not to be named.

This high-stakes competition never rests. Just within the last couple of years, KP orchestrated two huge anti-Microsoft deals, combining two pairs of KP portfolio companies—AOL with Netscape and At Home with Excite. KP's goal was clearly to consolidate forces in the Internet portal space and keep Microsoft's MSN online service a distant competitor.

KP partner Vinod Khosla showed another example of the *keiretsu* tactic in action when he divided up the emerging Internet networking sector. Khosla's investments in this new tribe of companies—including Concentric Network, Juniper Networks, and Cerent—have brought in billions of dollars in venture capital returns. Today, Khosla is pursuing a similar strategy in the Internet software application sector with investments in companies like Asera, Centrata, Zaplet, and Zambeel.

## The KP Way

The KP partnership was distinct in the venture capital business from its very inception in 1972. The founding partners, Eugene Kleiner and Tom Perkins, were well-known high-tech entrepreneurs, and both took joy in actively assisting the entrepreneurs they funded. Eugene Kleiner was a veteran of Bell Laboratories and Shockley Semiconductor Laboratory, Silicon Valley's first transistor company (founded by William Shockley, the controversial Nobel Prize–winning coinventor of the transistor). Kleiner, along with Gordon Moore and Robert Noyce (who later cofounded Intel), became one of the famous Shockley defectors who formed Fairchild Semiconductor, the mother of all semiconductor companies.

By age forty, Tom Perkins had established his legacy by working under his mentor and Silicon Valley godfather, David Packard, and subsequently driving Hewlett-Packard into the computer business, making it the company's number one producer of revenues by the time he left. Along the way, he took $10,000 of his personal savings and built a start-up company around a low-cost, easy-to-use laser he invented. His initial investment eventually turned into $2 million when he sold it to Spectra-Physics. "I guess I was already a de facto venture capitalist before I even raised my first fund," Perkins told *Red Herring* in a 1994 interview.

Their reputations as hands-on strategic thinkers separated Kleiner and Perkins from the number-crunching money managers on Wall Street. "Kleiner and I characterized ourselves as technologists and entrepreneurs who could help start companies. We were the first industry guys to go into venture capital," Perkins recollected.

Kleiner and Perkins then picked partners who thought and acted like they did. Frank Caufield, Brook Byers, Kevin Compton, John Doerr, Will Hearst III, Tom Jermoluk, Vinod Khosla, Floyd Kvamme, Joe Lacob, Bernie Lacroute, Jim Lally, Ray Lane, Douglas Mackenzie, Ted Schlein, and Russ Siegelman are all hands-on guys with strong technical backgrounds and competitive, impatient personalities who are often more ambitious than the entrepreneurs running the companies they invest in.

"Once we sign the check, we're on the team," Perkins emphasized. "We consider it our responsibility that our companies never run out of money. We help them hire the right people, and we help them identify the risks and put those risks behind them. If any-thing, we have been accused of being too involved," he admitted.

This hands-on approach has allowed KP to build billion-dollar companies from scratch and create huge new industries. Even their first $8 million fund in 1972 (one of the largest venture capital funds raised in those days) was distinguished by two gigantic hits, Tandem Computer and the first biotechnology company, Genentech. Both companies were founded by KP partners Jimmy Treybig and Robert Swanson, respectively, in spare rooms at the firm's first offices on Sand Hill Road in Menlo Park. "Both Tandem and Genentech were high-risk deals," explained Perkins. "If we have any kind of investment formula, it's that we try to isolate whatever the biggest risk is in a given deal and structure our initial investment so the money is used to eliminate that risk.

"In the case of Genentech, clearly the biggest risk was whether or not God was going to let us create a new form of life," Perkins remembered with a laugh. "And with Tandem, we had to prove we could develop software that could work in a multiprocessing environment. The market opportunities were clear and exciting, but there were big scientific and technical risks in both deals."

John Doerr, who earned his KP stripes sponsoring the firm's investments in Compaq, Lotus, Sun Microsystems, Netscape, At Home, and Amazon, among many other successes, concurs with his mentor that the secret to venture capital success is to get the risks out of the way early. And KP prefers some risks over others. "There are basically four risks we have to confront in each deal. There is technical risk: Can we split the atom? There is people risk: Will the key players on the team stay together? There is financial risk: Can we keep the company well financed? And there is market risk: Can we get the dogs to eat the dog food?" Doerr explains. "The most dangerous of these risks is market risk. Removing market risk is expensive," believes Doerr. "We're risk takers, but we'll take a technology risk over a market risk any day of the week." KP partners find market risk deadly because it often doesn't become obvious until after a company has blown through millions of dollars.

But while KP doesn't want its start-ups spending its precious dollars educating consumers, they have built their track record upon anticipating huge markets—such as compatible PCs and the Internet—and boldly launching companies right when these new industries are ready to explode. "We look for markets that are going to change by at least an order of magnitude, the technologies that can make it possible, and great teams," says Doerr. Genentech gave birth to the modern biotechnology industry; Sun Microsystems led the move from mainframes to client-server computing; Compaq put PCs in corporate America; Lotus introduced consumers to spreadsheets; Intuit put personal finance on the PC; and in the Internet era they are betting on online services AOL (combined with Netscape's Netcenter), Excite/At Home, e-commerce portal Amazon, and a whole slew of other fledgling public and private companies in the e-commerce, media, and technology backbone space.

The willingness of KP to swing for the fences clearly separates the firm from the venture capital pack. Doerr explained this approach to us in a 1995 *Red Herring* interview:

> The venture capital industry is very fragmented. There are 400 venture firms, right? So how can any one firm develop significant market share? Only by focusing on initiatives, which means several KP partners working together to help build companies and opportunities in specific areas, such as wireless communications, interactive media, and Internet/online services. If KP really hustles, we hope to see perhaps half of the really good projects in an area. But we can't do everything. Our goal is quality, not quantity. You also have to develop competence and expertise in an industry to earn the right to advise entrepreneurs.

Even KP's competitors in the venture business concur that focusing its investments on huge potential market initiatives is one of the firm's primary strengths. Geoff Yang of the top-tier venture capital firm Redpoint Ventures told us that this practice is what he admires most about KP. "I think when they create an industry initiative, they tend to refocus the whole partnership in one form or another toward those initiatives," says Yang.

Yang's previous firm, Institutional Venture Partners (IVP), started focusing on the Internet in early 1994 when it provided the start-up capital for Architext (which eventually became Excite), along with Vinod Khosla at KP. But Yang admits that IVP made this investment as a stand-alone deal, not as part of a firmwide focus on the Internet. KP, on the other hand, had mobilized its entire firm toward making investments in the Internet space by this point, and Excite became one of over a dozen blockbuster Internet deals KP invested in before other venture capital firms even woke up to the online world.

In spite of KP's home run record, even its partners admit that some of their hits could have sailed farther out of the park. KP partner Vinod Khosla, who first came knocking on the partnership's door in 1982 as the founding CEO of Sun Microsystems, recounted recently how the computer workstation and server company he cofounded could have been worth five times as much as it is today. "I look at Cisco and can't imagine I was that stupid! Everybody at Sun, including John Doerr and [Sun's cofounder and current CEO] Scott McNealy, missed Cisco as an opportunity," Khosla lamented while hitting his forehead with the palm of his hand. "Sun was out there from the very beginning saying that 'the network's the computer,' but we completely missed the networking system opportunity. And the first network router was just a piece of software—an application built on Sun's CPUs [central processing units, the brains of a computer]."

True to the KP style, Khosla may have missed the Cisco opportunity, but it didn't mean he was giving up on the networking and communications space. Later in this chapter, we'll tell the story of how Khosla plotted a strategy of investing in the networking space that turned him into one of the most successful venture capitalists in the world.

But like other venture firms, KP has many deals that never get off the ground. In its most dramatic failure, KP tried to jump-start the pen-computing revolution by backing GO Computer, whose handheld computer operating system was to convert the 25 million PC-illiterate and keyboard-averse professionals into joining the digital age. What was supposed to be an $8 billion industry turned out to be dead on arrival as manufacturers turned out bulky, overpriced, and malfunctioning handheld computers that then-Apple CEO John Sculley referred to as personal digital assistants, or PDAs. By September 1994, *Red Herring* featured a caricature of John Doerr posing in a faux rendition of Edvard Munch's painting "The Scream" under the headline "PDA Angst."

Ironically, in a largely underreported move that demonstrates KP's intense shrewdness as an investor, the firm did not lose money on its $3 million investment in GO. When it became apparent that the market was not going to emerge, and GO continued to burn money in research and development, the company was pushed into a merger with another KP company called EO, a maker of PDA hardware. AT&T, EO's biggest investor, agreed to ante up an additional $40 million in the combined company. But also as part of that deal, KP sold half of its EO stock to AT&T. After all the money had changed hands, the $7 million KP netted on this sale was as much as KP had invested in both GO and EO combined. Unfortunately, soon after the merger was inked, AT&T closed down EO for good and had to write off its entire investment in the company.

In his book *Startup*, which tells the GO story, cofounder Jerry Kaplan concludes: "In looking back over the entire GO-EO experience, it is tempting to blame the failure on management errors, aggressive actions by competitors, and indifference on the part of large corporate partners. While all these played important roles, the project might have withstood them if we had succeeded in building a useful product at a reasonable price that met a clear market need."

Doerr admits that the most important element for the success of the start-up is hitting the market right, a skill he says requires equal parts "good judgment, sweat, and luck." The other KP investment principles include personally using the technology, talking frequently with customers, and being passionate about products. "Most Silicon Valley start-ups get their technology to work but never squarely hit the marketing strike zone," Doerr told *Red Herring*. After pondering this final challenge, he added, "There's a tremendous marketing and management deficit in Silicon Valley."

## Glorified Headhunters

The last reality—the severe management shortage of professional talent in the Internet era—is why John Doerr will whisper privately that he and his partners are often no more than "glorified headhunters." But this headhunting skill is one of their primary competitive advantages. The best example of this applied skill is the Netscape Communications start-up story. "I think Jim Clark [Netscape's founder] will give us credit for helping assemble a first-rate team in under ninety days. Two vice presidents of engineering, vice presidents of sales and marketing, and world-class CEO Jim Barksdale," recalls Doerr. Barksdale was an amazing catch for Netscape, having previously been president of both McCaw Cellular and Federal Express. It's the ability to recruit this kind of executive talent that makes or breaks Silicon Valley companies. John Doerr is famous for going to extreme measures to convince the best talent to join a KP company, including flying his private Citation jet to pick up potential recruits and close the deal.

When we asked KP partner Will Hearst what was special about John Doerr, his answer was all about recruiting:

> What makes John a great investor is his ability to recruit experienced management and come up with a complete team. Two rare commodities are engineering talent and management talent. John knows that people like Bill Joy [Sun Microsystems cofounder and the inventor of the Berkeley UNIX operating system] are like .350 hitters in baseball. The eye-to-hand coordination of a batting champion like Tony Gwynn is just not the same as the average person's. I think John feels that the vision organ of Bill Joy or an Andy Bechtolsheim [another Sun cofounder, who sold his second start-up, Granite Systems, to Cisco Systems in 1997 for $220 million after only eleven

months in business] is just much higher than the average engineer. John makes a habit of staying close to these technology wizards and uses them as sources of deals, references, and due diligence.

In this way, the KP partners' role more closely resembles that of the Hollywood moguls of the 1930s and 1940s, whose power rose from their ability to sign up talent. Indeed, much of KP's influence comes from the hundreds of skillful managers the firm has placed in pivotal jobs over the past two decades. And a well-regarded manager in KP's talent pool, such as former GO Computer executive Bill Campbell, who was tapped to become CEO of Intuit, and Mike Homer, who ended up as executive vice president of Netscape, will always be presented with new executive positions and board seats on other KP portfolio companies.

In another impressive move, John Doerr aggressively recruited KPMG Peat Marwick's vice chairman, Roger Siboni, to take the helm of enterprise software start-up E.piphany. In addition to the interesting challenge, Siboni was enticed by Doerr's promise of stock options from other KP companies in exchange for board participation. True to Doerr's word, Siboni was sitting on the boards of Macromedia, Pivotal, and Active Software shortly after he was recruited. And if E.piphany didn't work out, Siboni was also assured that he could join KP's "CEO-in-residence" program, a tradition started with Bill Campbell. "Even though I had achieved a high position within KPMG at a young age and was making a considerable salary, this was an opportunity I eventually could not pass up," recounts Siboni. As testimony to Doerr's persistence, it took him six months to talk Siboni into the job.

The most powerful members of the KP inner executive circle are also encouraged to join the *"zaibatsu,"* a personal counterpart of the *keiretsu,* where a select group of former and current KP entrepreneurs and industry insiders can invest in KP companies alongside the regular funds. The *zaibatsu's* investments can be on a much grander scale than similar opportunities offered by top KP venture capital competitors such as Sequoia Capital or Institutional

Venture Partners. While typical investments in their side-by-side funds average around $50,000, individual investments in the KP funds are more in the range of $75,000 to $300,000, and sometimes in the millions, per fund. Numerous members were given the opportunity to participate in KPCB Fund X, the $1 billion fund raised in 2000. In turn, members are expected to provide KP with the benefits of their own contacts and industry knowledge as well as with investment leads.

According to paperwork one *zaibatsu* member gave us, *zaibatsu* investors include KP portfolio company founders such as Netscape cofounder Marc Andreessen, Intuit's Scott Cook, and Sun's Scott McNealy, as well as influential outsiders such as industry pundit Esther Dyson, former Sony USA president Mickey Schulhof, and Intel chairman Andy Grove. Ultimately, the *zaibatsu* gives KP a network of influential friends and contacts who are loyal to the firm even beyond the normal functioning of the *keiretsu.* "You never want to bang on a KP company in public, because you might not get invited to invest in the next *zaibatsu* fund," said one investor who pleaded to go nameless.

To keep the key players in the *keiretsu* well nurtured and in regular contact with each other, KP also brings them together every year at its annual CEO summit in Aspen, Colorado. Executives of KP's hottest companies lodge at the genteel Aspen Meadows, home of the prestigious Aspen Institute. Here the CEOs can enjoy white-water rafting or rock climbing under the brilliant spring sun before settling down to roundtable discussions about the future of electronic commerce or strategies for increasing Internet bandwidth. More important, there are numerous quieter and smaller discussions among the CEOs about how their companies might work together. "It's an amazing experience to be around that many quality players who yield so much industry influence," gushes Siboni. Doerr invited Amazon's Jeff Bezos to the firm's 1996 summit as a successful tactic to help close KP's exclusive $8 million investment in the company.

An interesting side note is that in spite of their tremendous success as investors, some of the KP partners harbor desires to run their own companies. "We all experience entrepreneur-envy from time to time," says KP partner Kevin Compton, who originally joined the firm as an "entrepreneur-in-residence" but eventually signed on as a partner. John Doerr at one point jumped into Sun Microsystems full-time to help them through a rough spot, and he also briefly considered taking the CEO job at Netscape. And when Will Hearst finally gave up the post as acting CEO of At Home, he admits it was very emotional for him to step down.

Part of this hidden entrepreneurial ambition is certainly driven by the financial upside. "You can make more money faster as an entrepreneur," Tom Perkins says. "I tell that to a lot of people who want to get into the venture capital business." Of course, this is moot, since KP partners become independently wealthy after only a few years on the job. But even for a partner like Will Hearst III, whose inherited wealth alone makes him a *Forbes* 400 member and one of the richest KP partners, racking up a big scorecard on his technology investments allows him to earn his keep. "In the old days, the venture guys talked about making millions of dollars; now they talk in terms of $5 million blocks," muses Marc Diocioccio of Lehman Brothers.

## The KP *Keiretsu*

Industry pundit Stewart Alsop claims that John Doerr is to the venture business what Bill Gates is to the software industry. Doerr gains his stature through influencing, and often commanding, the KP *keiretsu* of over 200 information-technology companies the firm has invested in and assisted over the last twenty-five years. Doerr admits that KP gets almost all its investment leads from entrepreneurs working within the *keiretsu,* and rarely has funded a deal that has arrived over the transom.

On KP's Web site (www.kpcb.com) the firm proudly boasts: "One of the most important elements within KP's concept of value-added investing is access to a network of shared information and knowledge referred to as the *keiretsu*. The partners at KP are proud to have facilitated more than 100 alliances among the *keiretsu* network of companies."

Roger McNamee, founder and manager of the highly successful technology fund Integral Capital Partners, who also sits in the same offices as the KP partners, sums up the leverage of the *keiretsu* best: "I think the value of the *keiretsu* is really simple. There are network effects you need to leverage in order to succeed in Silicon Valley today. The *keiretsu* provides a low-drive, high-efficiency system for getting those effects."

While the wiry and hyperactive Doerr likes to play down KP's influence over these companies, particularly after they go public, each KP partner proactively encourages its companies to work together. They constantly introduce their family of entrepreneurs to each other and actively suggest licensing or marketing agreements, research collaborations, joint ventures, and (as with AOL's purchase of Netscape and At Home's purchase of Excite) even mergers and acquisitions. Sometimes this activity includes investing in each other. AOL has made multimillion-dollar investments in two other KP companies, including a coinvestment, along with Netscape, in the fledgling public travel e-commerce company Preview Media. But there is an art to peddling this kind of influence, even for KP partners. "In our business, you can't just go up to a CEO and tell him or his subordinates to go do something," says KP partner Will Hearst. "You have to lead leaders; you can't lead their companies."

Khosla describes how KP's goals almost came into conflict with the desires of the entrepreneurs in one of its portfolio companies. In 1995, six months after KP had invested in Excite, Microsoft made an offer to buy the company for $70 million, which at the time seemed like a staggering amount to a group of young entrepreneurs. At this point, Excite had only a dozen employees, six of whom were under twenty-three years of age. While Khosla vehemently opposed the deal, he ultimately left the decision in the hands of the entrepreneurs. Because KP is so hands-on, Khosla explains, the ethic is for the partners to support the CEO. "The only time we work against the CEO is when we lose confidence in his abilities and think he should be fired. In all other instances, we follow the CEO's lead," Khosla explains.

Ultimately, Excite followed Khosla's advice and refused to sell to Microsoft. The company went public in 1997 and eventually merged with another KP company, At Home, in January 1999 for a whopping $6.7 billion.

## Walking the Slippery Slope

KP's critics charge that the firm sometimes pushes its portfolio companies too hard to work together or against some other portfolio company's competitor. "The *keiretsu* can be a mixed blessing, because a fine line exists between what's right for the company in isolation and what's right for the portfolio of companies," says Jerry Kaplan, founder of GO Computer and more recently founder and CEO of another KP-backed company, OnSale, which later merged with Egghead.com. And as impressive as KP's *keiretsu* is, there is a certain danger that comes with grandiose ambitions to create whole new industries. Two cases exemplify the tricky nature of KP's *keiretsu* policy. Both stories include Excite.

In 1998, Excite paid Netscape $70 million to become the primary provider of Web search services featured on Netscape's Net-Center home page, an arrangement that guaranteed Excite millions of new page views a day. Insiders close to the situation contend that Excite's competitor Infoseek originally had a lock on this deal, but John Doerr, who sits on Netscape's board, and Vinod Khosla, who sits on Excite's board, went to work behind the scenes to cut Infoseek out.

The story goes that John Doerr attended the wedding of Mike Homer (Netscape's then–executive vice president) just as the deal with Infoseek was about to come down. Doerr, knowing that Homer's best man and then-CEO of Intuit, Bill Campbell, had influence over him, asked Campbell for help. Doerr, who also sits on the board of Intuit, was overheard at the wedding saying, "If we want Excite to get this deal, throw Campbell on it."

Meanwhile, Khosla went to work for Excite but told us that "the role KP played was only to put the companies together and suggest structures that were win/win for both parties." With Homer persuaded and Excite ready to play, there was only one obstacle left to overcome—Excite had only $9 million left in its coffers and therefore couldn't commit to the $70 million payment (to be paid in $10 million quarterly installments) to Netscape to close the deal. And Netscape needed a guarantee of payment in order to record the revenues to keep Wall Street happy. This is when Doerr stepped in again and said, "Well, Intuit will loan it to you." So Excite's management went back to Campbell and asked Intuit to loan them the entire amount.

(For the record, despite Netscape founder Jim Clark's and Mike Homer's confirmation of Doerr's participation in this deal in a *Fortune* article, Doerr denied any involvement. "I wouldn't do that," he told us at the annual National Venture Capital Association meeting in San Francisco in the fall of 1998. Khosla, while acknowledging his involvement, also contends that Doerr only became aware of the deal after it was a fait accompli.)

Intuit ultimately did a $500 million debt conversion in order to have the cash to lend Excite for its Netscape deal. According to an Intuit prospectus supplement dated May 21, 1998, Intuit provided a short-term, low-interest, unsecured loan of $50 million to Excite on April 30, 1998, "and may provide additional financing to Excite in the future." The prospectus also mentioned that Intuit held 2.9 million shares of Excite common stock, representing 13 percent of Excite's outstanding common stock at the time. It's also interesting to note that Excite would later complete a secondary public offering for $75 million, just enough to pay off its loan to Intuit.

Shortly after these transactions were completed, a founder of one of Excite's primary competitors marveled at the three-way deal. "The KP guys just did a nice little round-trip where they got the public to finance Netscape, with Excite and Intuit being sort of a passing vehicle. And Netscape got to book the money as revenues, which I thought was really clever," he said.

"If I were Netscape, I would have been friggin' thrilled," said Cristina Morgan, a managing director at Chase H&Q, commending the deal. "In order to compete today, CEOs need to be as clever as possible. If that means using their backer's other relationships to get things done, then so be it. If it works, they are all geniuses. But if the money that so-and-so gave to so-and-so to invest in so-and-so goes down a rat hole, then you aren't a genius," Morgan cautioned. "Usually when that happens, you never hear about it."

Others we talked to in the industry were more skeptical. "I am very fond of getting critical mass leverage, but as a venture capitalist, I would avoid moving onto any slippery slopes that would endanger my companies," says venture capitalist Ann Winblad of Hummer Winblad. "If these kinds of deals don't work out, they could potentially drag your company into shareholder lawsuits."

In the end, the Excite/Netscape/Intuit deal helped catapult Excite ahead of Infoseek into the number two position in the Web portal business (behind Yahoo), and Netscape built credibility for its NetCenter portal for Web customers and boosted its revenues by $10 million a quarter for seven successive quarters. For Intuit's part, its finance and small business online service, Quicken.com, got a much-needed boost by being prominently displayed on Excite's Web site. "I don't know how much of this was public knowledge, but before this deal was done, Quicken.com wasn't getting any traffic at all, and was losing to Yahoo in the finance [Web site] category," explained Khosla.

The other KP *keiretsu* deal that raised eyebrows among industry insiders was At Home's purchase of Excite. At Home and Excite were start-ups created and funded in the finest KP tradition. At Home was actually conceived and named by John Doerr, and its original CEO was Will Hearst. After KP provided its initial financing, it gathered more funding for the company from a group of cable companies led by John Malone's Tele-Communications, Inc. (TCI), and later helped recruit many of the company's top management, including Tom Jermoluk, the CEO who eventually took over the company reins from Hearst.

At Home is deploying a communications infrastructure that allows cable companies to provide Internet access through cable. Excite was founded in 1994 by six Stanford students in their rented house in Cupertino. While the company raised its initial seed money from International Data Group, a technology trade publication company founded and run by billionaire Pat McGovern, Excite didn't really take off until KP's Vinod Khosla came in and held the young team's hand through endless strategy sessions and helped to bring in experienced managers. Since those early days, Excite has evolved from a simple search engine company to one of the Internet's most visited Web sites.

In January 1999, At Home announced that it was acquiring Excite. The deal put a $6.7 billion value on Excite, a whopping 57 percent premium over its closing stock price on the same day. The irony of this purchase price was twofold. First, given Excite's second position in the search engine company race, and the fact that it lost $37.6 million on a relatively meager $155.4 million in revenues in 1998, the company was grossly overvalued. But the premium price that At Home paid for Excite meant that KP saw a big return on what might otherwise have been a poor investment.

Second, even though At Home's stock was valued at over $10 billion at the time it purchased Excite, its numbers were just as bad as Excite's, having generated only a token $48 million in revenues in 1998, against $144.2 million in losses. The combined cumulative losses over the life of both companies was an incredible $350 million. "This is a funny-money deal of grandiose proportions," an experienced technology fund manager told us.

This is also a deal many people believe was made to keep At Home alive. "At Home needed content to move beyond being merely a distribution company with heavy dependence on the cable companies," says Frank Quattrone, a leading technology banker at CS First Boston. "The merger with Excite was clearly a deal designed to save At Home," concurs Paul Deninger, chairman and CEO of technology investment bank Broadview International.

From Excite's perspective, then-CEO George Bell got nervous about his company's future when AOL bought Netscape. Bell told *U.S. News & World Report* the week the deal was announced, "I came home to my wife and said, 'I have to rethink everything I know about Excite.' " His big question was: How was Excite going to compete in the brutal Web portal competition in the shadow of the giants AOL/Netscape, Yahoo, Infoseek/Disney, NBC/Snap, and Microsoft?

Conventional wisdom in Silicon Valley has always been that, as in all media battles, only the top three portals will ultimately survive. From this standpoint, Bell's paranoia made sense, but the real question insiders were asking was: why At Home? Excite wasn't picking up any significant new users with At Home, which had signed up only 2.3 million subscribers by the beginning of 2001. By comparison, according to Media Metrix, Excite had 34 million users visit its site in November 2000, and about 100 million people have used Excite's "My Excite" feature, which allows users to create their own individualized home page to include updates on their favorite stocks, sports teams, and news.

According to what the two companies' CEOs told the *New York Times* on the day the deal was announced, Excite was uniquely positioned to solve At Home's problems. "We can take what we know about [Excite's customers] and intuit their income levels and imputed demographic profile and whether they are likely to sign up for broadband services," said Bell, adding, "That's a powerful method of cross-promotion." At Home's then-CEO, Tom Jermoluk, also noted another benefit to the deal. "The hidden gem of the whole deal is how we'll implement their targeting and database technology to deliver advertising to the individual user," he said.

Excite's defenders also say that the real winner of the portal competition will be the company that can offer fast broadband services to home and office, thus allowing customers to easily download videos and music over the Internet, engage in videoconferencing, and speed up the normally clunky Web site surfing experience. High-speed Internet lines also open the way to more efficient and reliable online shopping, banking, trading, and advertising.

Arguably, Excite should have remained agnostic on which pipe it was choosing. In addition to At Home's cable solution, new two-way satellites and DSL technology are both developing rapidly, and the portals that end up winning, we think, will offer their services across all platforms. By helping At Home focus on solving its customer acquisition problems, Excite may lose the bigger battle for customers and eyeballs.

The bottom line is that KP believes if its companies are to remain top players in the Internet battles against Microsoft, Yahoo, and the others, these are the types of inside deals they need to broker. Or so the reasoning goes. "With the industry moving at Internet speed, you need to create business partnerships to accelerate the success of your company," observes Phil Horsley of Horsley Bridge Partners, a longtime investor in KP funds. "The fact that KP can leverage the sister companies in its venture investment portfolio, where you have partners sitting on both boards, can be a real advantage."

Certainly KP and its 200-company-strong *keiretsu* is a force in the technology industry that has successfully challenged Microsoft's dominance. In February 1999, while lunching with Bill Gates at the World Economic Forum in Davos, Switzerland, we asked him about KP's strategy to prevent Microsoft from lording over the Internet in the same way it did over the PC. All Gates would say was, "I hear things, and people tell me things, but I really can't say anything for certain." KP partner Russ Siegelman, who spent seven years working for Microsoft, supported his former boss's view of KP in a *New Yorker* piece in 1997: "Bill's view of venture capitalists is they're out to make money and they will do that any way they can."

## The Internet Opportunity: Bigger Than the PC

At KP there are benefits to working within the *keiretsu* other than keeping your established companies in play. Kibitzing among portfolio company founders and CEOs has provided the impetus for some of KP's most exciting new opportunities. Doerr was originally turned on to the Internet by his good buddy, Sun's tech wizard Bill Joy, who told Doerr he should jump into the Internet opportunity with both feet. This advice gave Doerr the confidence to invest in Netscape, the Web browser developer whose early success, in essence, gave birth to the Internet industry. Doerr says that KP's interest in the Internet was also confirmed by working with the KP portfolio company Intuit. When KP first invested, Intuit was a one-product company with $35 million in annual revenues. Five years later, it has over $400 million in revenues and a significant share in three software businesses: personal finance, tax preparation, and small business. "In three years the Intuit team turned a one-legged stool into a sturdy, deep-rooted stump," Doerr says. "Regis McKenna articulated the key strategy at one of our off-sites: 'The smartest entrepreneurs aren't providing either a product or service, but both.' [Intuit founder] Scott Cook and his team deeply understand that Intuit is not just a software company, but also a service provider building enduring relationships."

And Doerr's philosophy has proven right. Whether you talk about AOL, Yahoo, Amazon, or any of the great online companies created so far, the strategy to become both a product and a service has given them domination.

"In the early 1980s, the PC was driven by spreadsheets and word processing, and lowering costs in businesses. Now the killer applications leverage the top line—helping us inform, sell, educate, entertain, inspire, even govern. I believe the Net can have as much impact as the telephone, radio, or possibly television—it will certainly be bigger than the PC," Doerr explained prophetically to *Red Herring* in 1995. "Silicon Valley is no longer about silicon; it's about networking," he said. "In the 1980s, PC and hardware and software grew into a $100 billion industry—the Internet could be three times bigger."

This new awareness inspired Doerr to sign up one of his all-time best recruits, Will Hearst, who left his family's famous media business to join KP as a partner in early 1995. "Five years ago people would have wondered: Why add a media guy to a technology venture group? Will's a first-rate technology investor. And it's also clear that there are major opportunities in new media," explained Doerr at the time. Hearst's first major assignment was to help launch At Home.

## Netscape Takes Sail

Since waking up to the Internet opportunity, KP has funded more Internet deals than any other venture capital fund, pumping more than $500 million into over 114 Net-related start-ups.

Its first major play in the Internet space was a company founded by Jim Clark, the former Stanford computer science professor who had previously founded Silicon Graphics (SGI). In January 1994, Clark resigned from his post as chairman of SGI, the multibillion-dollar visual computing company, to start an interactive software company for the Internet, then called Mosaic Communications. "The Internet is more exciting than 3-D graphics," Clark told *Red Herring* shortly after he founded the company and before taking money from KP.

At the time, Clark had bankrolled the company out of his own pocket, stating that "venture capital is good for the raw entrepreneur," which he obviously no longer considered himself to be. When pushed further about his wariness in dealing with venture capitalists, Clark recounted the story of his first start-up. "When I started Silicon Graphics, I sold 40 percent of the company for $800,000 in our first round of financing. By the time SGI went through a couple of public offerings, I ended up owning only 1 percent of the company. In retrospect, that kind of hurts. So when I started Netscape, I decided it would be a better idea to fund the company myself, since by then I had some of my own money," he said.

Clark's new start-up team included Marc Andreessen, the twenty-two-year-old whiz kid, and his development team from the University of Illinois, which created one of the first popular Internet browsers, Mosaic.

"I've learned everything I know about the Internet over the last three months. I'm convinced that the Internet is the information superhighway, and that Marc Andreessen's vision is right on," Clark proclaimed to *Red Herring* at the time.

Netscape's initial plan was to make the best Internet browser and then market and sell it over the Web. If Netscape quickly gained market share and built a large installed base of customers, the company could build a strong brand and defend its position in the browser market. This task was not difficult because distribution of software over the Internet proved to be incredibly inexpensive. In the first huge sign of the commercial potential of the Internet, Netscape sold over 10 million browsers in just nine months. "There is no other distribution system in existence that would have allowed that," Clark bragged at the time. He then accurately predicted, "We see this potential for low-cost distribution of any kind of intellectual property—whether it be software, or pictures, or movies, or CDs, or anything that can be represented as bits—as one of the most revolutionary aspects of the Internet."

Eventually, Clark decided he could use the assistance of a seasoned venture capital team to build Netscape. Before presenting his deal to KP, Clark "halfheartedly" shopped Netscape, out of a sense of professional obligation, to the two venture capital firms that were original investors in SGI: New Enterprise Associates and Mayfield Fund. This time he wasn't going to give up 40 percent for only $800,000. Instead, Clark told the venture capitalists they would have to invest at an $18 million valuation if they wanted to get in on the deal into which he had already pumped $3 million of his own money. Mayfield never called him back, and NEA was interested only if they could get in at a $12 million valuation.

At this point, Clark revisited his dream with John Doerr. "John Doerr, God bless him, had the courage to pay what at the time looked like a very high price," recalls Doerr's friend and competitor Norm Fogelsong of Institutional Venture Partners. And in many ways, KP's willingness to pay a higher price to win the Netscape deal was vintage KP. In spite of its position of tremendous strength in the market, KP still has the reputation of not cutting the toughest, tightest deal with the entrepreneurs they work with. "We try to make sure the entrepreneurs make a lot of money, too," states KP's Tom Perkins. "We like to tell the entrepreneurs that the only time we're on the opposite side of the table is when we're cutting the pie in the first round."

"When Jim called about Netscape, he really didn't need our money," recounts Doerr. "He wanted help building the team and polishing the company's strategic plan. I guess we forced him to take the money. In fact, after we agreed to invest, I think it took four or five months before he even cashed the check."

Clark concurs that KP's greatest help, other than being early believers in the Internet, was their incredible recruiting skills. "These are the ways that top-flight firms such as Kleiner Perkins can really help out young enterprises. So I don't mind if they own a part of Netscape, because they've earned it," says Clark.

And the admiration is mutual. "The high human drama here is that Jim Clark and I have always wanted to work together," recalls Doerr. "I first met him as a professor at Stanford. But Jim started SGI after we had committed to Sun Microsystems, so we competed for several years. Jim Clark has an exquisite sense of taste for the confluence of different markets and technology. He also moves with an extraordinary sense of urgency."

By the time Doerr brought Jim Clark and Marc Andreessen in to formally present their deal to the KP partners at one of their sacred Monday-morning general partner meetings in June 1994, Doerr and several of his partners had already worked with the two entrepreneurs to pound out their growth plan. Sitting in the expansive, glass-encased KP boardroom around a table that some partners jokingly refer to as the world's largest surfboard, Clark and Andreessen made their case about why their browser could become the new platform for the Internet era the way that Windows had become the platform for the PC era. Within thirty minutes the KP partners voted to invest.

Netscape would eventually use the $5 million KP invested and the proceeds of an August 1995 IPO to build one of the fastest-growing companies ever founded. But in spite of Netscape's early dominance of the Web, due to the ubiquity of its browser, Doerr and his partners were always realistic about the company's long-term success. Doerr told *Red Herring* just before the company's IPO, "The company generates 80 percent of today's Web traffic. But Internet software is going to be extremely varied, vertical, and competitive." This observation was eventually proven right, however ironically for Doerr, when Netscape was ultimately forced to sell to AOL after losing significant browser market share to Microsoft and losing the traffic battle to up-start portals like Yahoo and Excite.

## Gaining First-Mover Advantage

A big part of KP's strategy to win big in the Internet game is helping its companies gain first-mover advantage, which generally means raising big bucks through any means as fast as possible. Part of this tactic is leveraging what insiders refer to as the "Kleiner Mystique," a form of investor-relations pixie dust that KP has sprinkled on some of the most richly valued Internet companies in the public market. One longtime technology investor well acquainted with the mystique says, "It's not by accident that Kleiner Perkins deals get much higher valuations than those of other firms. It's based on knowing how to optimize company pitches and the way they present data to Wall Street. KP is good at making their companies the center of attention." Sam Colella of Institutional Venture Partners observes, "If you are an institutional buyer playing in the public market and you look at a Kleiner Perkins company, you say, 'Oh, my God. KP is behind this deal. This could be a whole new industry. Geez, those guys have done it so many times. Yeah, I had better buy this.' "

In particular, the advantage of having John Doerr on a company's team is that it helps create the impression that the company is bigger than life and thereby worthy of an equally fanciful market valuation. "The Internet is underhyped," was a classic Doerr remark when he was out peddling his Internet start-ups. Sun Microsystems CEO Scott McNealy refers to such promotional energy as "the Doerr sphere of evangelism—the art of selling some futuristic technology as the next big thing."

"He has used personal self-promotion to his advantage better than any venture capitalist on the planet—bar none—by an order of magnitude!" says Broadview's Paul Deninger. "Doerr has created a product category around the venture capital business, and he has successfully branded himself and Kleiner Perkins as the most powerful venture capitalists in that category," explains Deninger. "So is there any difference between what Bill Gates does and what Doerr does? One sells product, the other sells valuation."

The investment bankers we talked to—who regularly fall all over each other to take KP portfolio companies public—concur with Deninger. "KP is given the benefit of the doubt," believes Mark Diocioccio of Lehman Brothers. "They have a cachet and a marquee name that comes from having made people money. They can do more aggressive things because people see them as having a lot of credibility," he says. Brad Koenig, managing director and head of the technology banking practice at Goldman Sachs, who has taken several KP companies public, adds: "KP has established a dominant position. John Doerr has the image, the brand, the perception that he and the firm can add significant value both through their business acumen and especially through their *keiretsu* network of companies. It's all larger than life!"

Netscape and Amazon are two classic examples of KP companies that benefited from the Kleiner Mystique and moved quickly into the financial markets to gain market advantage. In the summer of 1995, when Netscape was a year and a half old, Doerr worked behind the scenes to convince the company's management that it was the right time to go public. Doerr thought Netscape should raise money while the market was hot on the Internet, and, more important, an IPO would give Netscape's browser business a huge boost. And it worked. "The IPO was one of the best marketing tactics we could have done," says Netscape founder Jim Clark. Indeed, the advertising value alone was worth market points and strength in the company's early days.

Amazon's founder and CEO Jeff Bezos recalls that before the company's initial public offering, he and Doerr agreed that "the Internet landgrab" was in full swing, and that if the company didn't build a war chest to capture and retain customers faster than its competitors, it would lose out big-time. So just as in the Netscape case, Doerr convinced Bezos and the investment bankers that it was time for Amazon "to put the puck on the ice," that is, to heighten its image and raise some cash by taking the company public, in spite of its losses and the fact that most of the management team had been together only four months.

Doerr also regularly argued that in the Internet era, going public early helped create a liquid currency in the form of stock that companies can use for acquisitions. To make his case, Doerr would quote what has become known in Silicon Valley as Bill Joy's law: Assume innovation will occur outside your corporation. Following this philosophy, all KP companies engage in acquisition activity and major corporate alliances. "You can't predict what some of the opportunities might be and how much cash they might require," says Amazon's Bezos.

While KP has consciously cultivated a certain mystique to critically leverage its deals, it's clearly a paradoxical strategy that involves simultaneously keeping the firm and its companies in the spotlight, yet maintaining enough distance to create a certain mystery and awe. Doerr defended himself in an August 1997 *New Yorker* piece, saying, "People criticize me for being too grandiose, and it's probably true. But why not think big? Maybe you get a big belly flop. Or maybe you get the next Netscape."

But some skeptics in the industry are more cautious about the long-term success of companies that undergo such early hype. "I think you can go back and look at some of KP's biggest promotes— such as Dynabook, GO Computing, and 3DO—all those companies were presented as bigger than life very early," observed venture capitalist Bob Kagle of Benchmark. "I don't know how many truly bigger-than-life early companies have gone on to be great businesses yet. I think it's a short list." Kagle also pointed out that a close look at KP's portfolio shows that many of KP's bigger successes were companies they invested in at later stages, after the companies had some momentum. "In some cases, like Sun Microsystems and Intuit, the companies were already demonstrating their success. So the benefits of this early game of hype get kind of fuzzy," says Kagle.

Also fuzzy is whether the early hype and ultimate overvaluation of the Internet Bubble stocks degrade the integrity of the technology financial markets. As one seasoned venture capitalist noted fiercely when we brought up the subject:

> KP can argue lots of things: "Oh, look at our companies. We've raised a lot of money so we can hire a lot of people and we employ X number of people. Isn't that great. Look at all the wealth we create." They never seem to consider the damage that could occur if the whole thing crashes. They never wonder if they could be pushing the stock price up astronomically way ahead of its time. You have to remember that companies end up having to grant stock options to new employees at those crazy prices. And even if the company does just fine, the stock still ultimately goes down to a normal valuation. Those employees end up being impossible to retain. It's just the wrong way to do business.

As the table at the end of this chapter illustrates, even KP companies have not been immune to the implosion of the Internet Bubble. By December 15, 2000, the average KP company was almost 77 percent off its fifty-two-week high. The problems discussed above have all come true. As a result of the meltdown in the Internet stock market, day traders have gone bankrupt, employees have seen the value of their stock options evaporate, and the public market has shut its door to Internet IPOs. But this is not the last word in the Internet boom.

## Rising from the Ashes

One of the great stories to emerge since the first publication of this book is the network infrastructure revolution for the Web. Arguably the leading mover and shaker behind this new wave is KP partner Vinod Khosla. A February 13, 2001, cover story in *Red Herring* by Om Malik tells the entrepreneurial tale of Khosla, an Indian immigrant who as a youth dreamed of coming to Silicon Valley and starting his own technology company.

In 1982, a twenty-seven-year-old Khosla came up with an idea for a new workstation based upon open systems like UNIX. To start Sun Microsystems, Khosla recruited what turned out to be a dream team of cofounders: Bill Joy, Andy Bechtolsheim, and Khosla's Stanford Business School roommate Scott McNealy. By the time Khosla turned over the CEO job, Sun had reached over $100 million in sales and was on its way to becoming a dominant, multibillion-dollar computer industry Goliath.

Eventually, Khosla found his way to working full-time for the KP partnership. After investing in some high-profile flops like Dynabook, GO Computer, and 3DO, as well as some marginally interesting success stories like PictureTel, Khosla got a clearer sense of where the technology industry was headed.

An early believer in the Internet, Khosla became convinced that Web traffic would explode and that there would be a huge requirement for bandwidth. He saw the need for big fat pipes to carry the massive data that would easily overwhelm the telephone companies' aging networks. Since 1995, in a very calculated manner, Khosla has brought his big idea to life. He has consistently been about twenty-four months ahead of the market, and has invested in some of the hottest companies in the Internet infrastructure space. (See table: "The Kleiner Perkins Portfolio of Public Internet Companies.")

"He delivered $12 billion back to the partnership in just the last eighteen months," KP partner Floyd Kvamme noted with admiration in fall 2000. Khosla's investments in Juniper Networks and Cerent are two of the most profitable venture investments in history. KP's $3 million investment in Juniper Networks, for example, was worth more than $8 billion by fall 2000; and his $8 million investment in Cerent turned into over $2 billion in Cisco Systems stock when the start-up was sold to the networking giant in August 1999. Three months later, Redback Networks acquired Cerent's glimmer-twin, Siara Systems, in which Khosla had also invested, for $4.3 billion.

"It wasn't luck—he went ahead and thought his whole strategy through and came out ahead of the networking industry curve," says Roger McNamee of Integral Capital Partners. "By being in the networking industry so early, I think at some level Vinod [Khosla] tipped the scales in his favor."

## Funding the Next Internet Generation

As long as Vinod Khosla, John Doerr, and the other top partners at KP remain engaged, KP will be in the business of tipping the industry scales in its favor. And while KP's investment activity, like that of other VC funds, has definitely slowed since the Internet Bubble burst, KP is still on the lookout for big, new opportunities in the Internet space. As we mentioned in the introduction to this book, KP is a big believer in the so-called Evernet—a high-speed, broadband, multiform Web supporting billions of devices—which will continue to radicalize the way we communicate, buy and sell products and services, and teach and inform ourselves. John Doerr believes that this proliferation of new devices will breathe fresh air into e-commerce.

"The next generation of software will be all about building more efficient companies," Khosla observes. His forays into this area include Asera, Centrata, Zaplet, and Zambeel. "In order to become more efficient, corporations need to communicate in real time and will need a new information architecture," says Khosla.

Whatever the next generation of the Internet becomes known for—whether it's the introduction of broadband to a mass global audience, new communications infrastructure, or cool new Internet applications and services—the one sure bet is that a smattering of KP funded companies will be competing aggressively in each new sector.

## The Kleiner Perkins Portfolio of Public Internet Companies

| Company Name | Ticker Symbol | Share price (6/30/99) | 52-week high (since 12/15/99) | Share price (12/15/00) | Percentage change (since 6/30/99) | Percentage change (since 52-week high) |
|---|---|---|---|---|---|---|
| At Home Corporation | ATHM | 53.9375 | 52.25 | 5.7188 | −89.397358 | −89.054928 |
| Amazon.com, Inc. | AMZN | 62.5625 | 102 | 22.875 | −63.436563 | −77.573529 |
| America Online Inc. | AOL | 55 | 92.62 | 48.96 | −10.981818 | −47.138847 |
| Intraware, Inc. | ITRA | 24 | 99 | 1.7812 | −92.578333 | −98.200808 |
| iVillage Inc. | IVIL | 50.25 | 27.3125 | 0.875 | −98.258706 | −96.796339 |
| Marimba, Inc. | MRBA | 52.6875 | 68.875 | 5.0625 | −90.391459 | −92.649728 |
| NextCard, Inc. | NXCD | 33.9375 | 36.875 | 6 | −82.320442 | −83.728814 |
| Rhythms NetConnections | RTHM | 58.375 | 50 | 1.0625 | −98.179872 | −97.875 |
| SportsLine. com, Inc. | SPLN | 35.875 | 83.25 | 6.25 | −82.578397 | −92.492492 |
| Verisign, Inc. | VRSN | 43.125 | 258.5 | 93.5625 | 116.956522 | −63.805609 |
| Extreme Networks, Inc. | EXTR | 29.0312 | 190.875 | 72.25 | 148.870181 | −62.148003 |
| Cosine Communications | COSN | | 71 | 14.5 | N/A | −79.577465 |
| Corio, Inc. | CRIO | | 21.75 | 3.0938 | N/A | −85.775632 |
| Redback Networks Inc. | RBAK | 31.3906 | 397 | 83 | 164.410365 | −79.093199 |
| ONI Systems Corp. | ONIS | | 142 | 65 | N/A | −54.225352 |
| Qwest Communications Int. | Q | 33.0625 | 66 | 38.9375 | 17.7693762 | −41.003788 |
| Juniper Networks, Inc. | JNPR | 24.8333 | 384.375 | 128.875 | 418.960428 | −66.471545 |
| Corvis Corporation | CORV | | 114.75 | 32.6875 | N/A | −71.514161 |

# Doonesbury

# THE I-BANKERS EMBRACE THE INTERNET

**We sell stocks at whatever price the market will bear on whatever day—that's our job.**
  **—Michael McCaffery, former CEO, BancBoston Robertson Stephens**

*T*he grand facilitators of the Internet Bubble are the investment bankers. These pin-striped peddlers of IPO shares come from large New York–based investment houses such as Morgan Stanley Dean Witter and Goldman Sachs. As the underwriters of the IPO, these banks guarantee companies they take public that their sales team will sell an agreed-upon amount of stock at an agreed price. If the investment bank fails to unload all the shares to deep-pocketed institutional investors such as Fidelity and Vanguard, they have to buy all outstanding shares themselves. For this guarantee, which rarely gets called upon, the participating banks are paid a hefty 7 percent commission on the total capital raised in the public offerings they manage. After taking a company public, bankers usually continue to work with their customers by managing follow-on equity and debt financings. So, hustling for the IPO business sits at the heart of the investment bankers' livelihood.

And the IPO business has indeed been very lucrative in recent years. From mid-1998 to December 2000, IPOs raised a total of $165.8 billion, according to a tally by Thomson Financial Securities Data—triggering underwriting fees for Wall Street firms totaling $8.7 billion. Out of the 1,103 IPOs done during that period, 363 gained 50 percent or more in price on their first day of trading, and 199 more than doubled in price.

• • •

This chapter examines the beginnings of the modern technology investment-banking industry, with a special focus on some of the early Silicon Valley pioneers in the industry as well as on the bigger New York–based banks that later joined the tech-banking game. We look at how the Internet Bubble helped foster an environment where two of the pioneers of technology banking sold the investment banks they created for top dollar to huge commercial banks, then turned around and started two new competing firms. We also examine the emergence of electronic investment banking and how it promises to rattle the industry. Finally, we look at some of the potential conflicts of interest in technology banking that are accentuated by Internet mania. Due to huge investor demand for Internet IPO shares and a highly competitive banking market, bankers have often taken companies public prematurely and helped the banks' favorite customers spin shares and flip stock for huge gains. While investment bankers will never reap the same level of reward as the successful entrepreneur or venture capitalist, they are critical players in funneling the huge level of investment dollars into new companies associated with the Internet.

## Technology-Banking Pioneers

In 1965, long before the world knew the name Silicon Valley, Sandy Robertson, a partner with the New York–based investment bank Smith Barney, was dispatched to San Francisco to scare up some business and look for prospects. South of the city, Robertson discovered a growing new technology industry that included Fairchild Semiconductor, the first major semiconductor company, whose founders and early employees would later spin out and start most of the next dozen chip companies, including Intel and National Semiconductor. Unfortunately, Robertson quickly found out that Smith Barney wasn't interested in these companies. "By 1969 I was pretty frustrated," says Robertson. "We did a private placement for Spectra-

Physics, a laser company which was one of Tom Perkins's [who later cofounded the venture firm Kleiner Perkins] first venture investments, but the bank refused to take the company public." Robertson had problems trying to get people in New York to understand what kind of products these companies produced. "I'd go back to New York for our partners' meeting and the guys there would say, 'Hey, Buck Rogers, how's our ray-gun company doing out there on the West Coast?'" Robertson recalls. After getting shot down on the Spectra deal, he had to walk across Montgomery Street in San Francisco and hand it to another East Coast transplant, Bill Hambrecht.

Just a year earlier, in 1968, Hambrecht had joined with an early venture capitalist out of Bank of America, George Quist, to form Hambrecht & Quist, a firm that combined venture capital with investment-banking services for small but rapidly growing companies in Silicon Valley. Over the years, H&Q grew into a major investment bank by underwriting deals that included Apple, Genentech, and many of the hottest IPOs during the Internet boom.

Meanwhile, Robertson left Smith Barney and eventually joined with Paul Stephens to raise $1 million to form Robertson Stephens investment bank, whose mission was to target hot new technology companies. Eugene Kleiner, later of Kleiner Perkins fame, invested in the firm as a limited partner. As for his old employer, Robertson reports: "Almost ten years to the day after we started our firm, the president of Smith Barney came to my office and said, 'Gee, we're interested in technology; how can we work together?' I thought to myself, You're ten years behind—you could have owned the place."

Despite the formation and reasonable success of specialized banks, eventually known as technology boutiques—such as the original Robertson Stephens and Hambrecht & Quist—financing Silicon Valley start-ups was not a huge business in the 1970s.

By the late 1970s, however, the big New York investment banks—the so-called bulge-bracket firms—decided to set up technology practices in San Francisco. While financing high-tech companies was still a small market—the average IPO deal size in those days was a paltry $10 million to $15 million in range, with very little merger-and-acquisition activity—even the larger investment banks began to recognize that something dynamic was happening out west. The now-defunct L. F. Rothschild was the first big bank to enter the market, and Morgan Stanley and its longtime archrival, Goldman Sachs, were all actively pitching their services to technology companies by 1980.

Opening the door to these bulge brackets were some of the best venture capital firms, such as Kleiner Perkins Caufield & Byers and the Mayfield Fund, who wanted the additional prestige and clout these New York banks could provide for their portfolio companies. "When I joined Morgan Stanley in 1977," says Frank Quattrone, now managing director and head of the technology group at CS First Boston, "the firm was basically an execution house for its existing blue-chip clients such as General Electric and General Motors. We expanded beyond that when the Kleiners and Mayfields began courting Morgan Stanley and Goldman."

Another factor was a rule change in the banking business that enabled bond issuers to switch banks more easily. This shift set off a mad scramble for clients among the investment banks, and some companies such as Exxon actually started to insource some of their investment-banking work. As a result, profit margins at the banks began to shrink, and they needed to find new markets for their services. High technology was a natural choice—it was growing fast, but it was underbanked.

A watershed deal was the public offering of Apple Computer in 1980, lead-managed by Morgan Stanley and joined by tech boutique Hambrecht & Quist as another underwriter. "Steve Jobs, who felt he had a very large company in the making, wanted a large investment bank to be the banker," says Quattrone.

Ben Rosen, Morgan Stanley's electronics analyst at the time and an early user of Apple's computers, was instrumental in forging the connection between the bank and Apple. Rosen later gained notoriety as a cofounder of Compaq Computer and a founding partner of the venture capitalist firm Sevin Rosen.

Apple was actually the first IPO Morgan Stanley had done in

almost twenty-five years, and more opportunities followed. In 1982 Kleiner Perkins asked Morgan Stanley to help arrange a private placement for its largest venture fund to date, $100 million, and a strong link between the two firms was forever forged.

Meanwhile, Goldman Sachs got its biggest break in the technology market when it took Microsoft public in 1986, thus legitimizing the bank's technology practice. Alex. Brown & Sons also had a good year in 1986, which included taking Sun Microsystems public.

Yet while the bulge brackets could offer a whole range of services, the boutique banks, living or dying by their technology deals, had the strongest technology research at the time, enabling them to participate in many technology IPOs even if they didn't lead them. This competition catalyzed Morgan Stanley and Goldman Sachs to build their own strong technology research teams and opened the way to additional business with technology companies that went beyond leading initial public offerings.

Despite its promise, the technology market remained cyclical and sometimes volatile. In 1983 the personal computer bubble hit its peak, but when it burst in 1984, some very lean years followed for tech bankers, and it got even worse after the stock market crash of 1987.

The bulge-bracket banks had enough resources to survive, but some of the boutiques struggled. Busy chasing one high-tech initial public offering after another, they came up short when the IPO market dried up. And while some good companies such as Cisco and Microsoft did go public after the PC bubble burst, the crash of '87 nearly finished off some of the boutique banks.

"I joined Hambrecht & Quist in 1982," says managing director Cristina Morgan. "I believed technology was a driving force in our economy. I looked smart in the eight-month bull market of 1983. But, frankly, I looked stupid from 1984 to 1990. You might as well have not been in the technology business—being at Hambrecht & Quist in the eighties was a joke."

Technology banking veteran Stu Francis, managing director and head of the technology practice at Lehman Brothers, provides a similar spin on his two decades in the business:

When I started in the business after finishing at Stanford in 1977 and went to a dinner party and told people I was an investment banker, they said, "What's that?" In the mid- to late eighties when I went to a dinner party and said I was an investment banker, they said, "I just read about how much money you make." In the nineties when you tell people you're an investment banker they say, "Why aren't you retired?" I think that sort of sums it up. Investment bankers used to be behind the scenes working with their clients. Now certain firms and individuals have become much more visible. It's just a bigger-time industry.

## Goldman Sachs vs. Morgan Stanley

When Morgan Stanley's top Internet analyst, Mary Meeker, was asked by *The New Yorker* in April 1999 if she had any regrets, she mentioned that Morgan Stanley had missed the opportunity to underwrite IPOs for Yahoo, eBay, and Amazon. She admitted that losing the Yahoo business was a "brain dead" mistake because she thought, at the time, that Yahoo wasn't ready to go public. Goldman Sachs was happy, of course, to sweep up the Yahoo business with no big bank competition. The Goldman banking team also outfinessed Morgan Stanley with its pitch to eBay's management to take the online auction company public. "We walked out of our meeting with eBay right then and knew that it didn't click," Meeker moaned to the *New York Times*. This loss hurt Morgan Stanley, because eBay ended up as the top-performing IPO of 1998.

And with Amazon, Meeker contended to *The New Yorker* that she wanted to do the deal but was overruled by the senior management at Morgan Stanley because the bank had a long-standing relationship with Barnes & Noble, Amazon's main rival. Frank Quattrone and Bill Brady, while still at DMG, ended up snatching the Amazon business, a deal that helped establish DMG.

But Meeker didn't rise to Internet industry stardom by resting on her laurels. Still convinced that eBay would be the online auction category leader, she kept her relationship with eBay's management a top priority in her hugely hectic schedule. Meeker, for example, spent hours reviewing strategy with eBay's CEO, Meg Whitman, even helping her review and critique her IPO roadshow presentation.

In the end, all Meeker's hustling paid off. When eBay initiated its $1 billion secondary offering in March 1998, Whitman insisted that her underwriters at Goldman share the offering with Morgan Stanley. Much to Goldman's chagrin, they agreed. "Morgan Stanley earned it," Whitman told the *New York Times.*

Meeker's persistence with Amazon also paid off. In spite of being stifled by her bosses (a decision that upset Meeker so much, she almost quit) she stayed in contact with Amazon's executive team and remained a big supporter. Amazon rewarded Meeker for her public endorsements by signing up Morgan Stanley to sell $500 million worth of their junk bonds.

In many ways, Meeker's experiences in dueling with Goldman and her former partner at Morgan Stanley, Frank Quattrone, epitomizes the longtime, often brutal rivalry among the big banks that fight in the technology space. All three firms focus like lasers on winning only the best Internet deals because in the long run, they know the banks with the best-performing IPO portfolio will reign supreme.

While Meeker's work helped keep Morgan Stanley in the running, Goldman Sachs was not about to roll over and give in. By mid-2000 Goldman was by far the most prolific underwriter of Internet companies since the Internet boom began in 1996. Goldman was the lead on fifty-one dotcom deals. Any institution buying one share of each of Goldman's fifty-one offerings, at the premarket offering price, would have seen its cumulative investment rise by just under 90 percent. Goldman's best offering by a mile was Yahoo, which went public at the split-adjusted price of $1.08 per share in April 1996 and was selling for $119 in July 2000. Goldman's other big winners included eBay and search-engine technology provider Inktomi.

The next most prolific underwriter was Morgan Stanley, which by 2000 had brought twenty-four dotcom deals to market as lead underwriter since the boom began. Institutions buying these deals had seen their investment grow by nearly 134 percent during the period, a higher return than Goldman's.

When you compare the figures of these two investment-banking kingpins with those of the other large banks, you begin to see why entrepreneurs tend to put either Goldman or Morgan Stanley on their dream underwriter list. In fact, by mid-2000 institutions had actually lost 21 percent of their money on Merrill Lynch's eleven dotcom deals, and individuals lost 51 percent. Merrill's worst deal was Pets.com, which went public with a premarket offering price of $11, sold at $13.50 on its first trade in the aftermarket, and by July 2000 was selling for $2.25, and went out of business later that year.

Investors fared no better with Donaldson, Lufkin & Jenrette. DLJ was lead underwriter in fifteen dotcom deals during the boom. By 2000, the firm's institutional clients had lost 20 percent of their investment, and aftermarket investors had lost nearly 60 percent. DLJ's biggest success was Wink Communications, which was up nearly 90 percent to institutions. But aftermarket investors in Wink were losers. Retail investors paid $31 on the first trade in the aftermarket, and the stock was selling for $28 in July 2000. DLJ's biggest dud was E-Stamp Corp., which was priced at $17 on the offer, sold for $30 on the first trade in the aftermarket, and had plummeted to $1.75 by July 2000.

Meanwhile to compete with Morgan Stanley and Goldman in the midst of the Internet boom, the Frank Quattrone–led CS First Boston instituted some new policies that made its underwriting business more lucrative than ever. First to go was the requirement that client companies show a profit. By early 1999, the bank also abandoned its policy that a company have annualized revenue of at least $10 million before going public.

Basically an inverse relationship could be observed: As the line graph measuring the fees to IPO underwriters in the U.S. market continued to work its way up from late 1995 on, the line showing the percentage of companies going public that were turning a profit before IPO went steadily down. According to Sanford C. Bernstein

& Associates, the percentage of profitable companies going public went from over 60 percent in mid-1995 to below 20 percent in September 1999 and down to 5 percent in December 1999.

As if to corroborate CS First Boston's new strategy, Jay Ritter, a finance professor at the University of Florida, showed in 1999 that companies with less than $10 million in annual sales on average actually saw their shares shoot up almost 76 percent in the first day of trading. By contrast, companies with more than $200 million in sales on average rose a mere 38 percent. Less of a track record was actually treated as more of a virtue in the public market at that time.

## Selling Out at the Top of the Market

Meanwhile the boutique banks may have been full of bravado in the early days of the boom, but in the end it was tough for them to compete with the full-service banking capabilities of the Morgan Stanleys and Goldmans. "Indeed," quips one bulge-bracket banker, "the boutiques would not have existed in the first place if the venture capitalists hadn't needed them in the early days of Silicon Valley to take their portfolio companies public."

The bigger banks were in a stronger position, able to leverage their global brands and debt-raising muscle to win most of the big deals. In fact, with only a few exceptions, Morgan Stanley, Goldman, and the Quattrone-led CS First Boston generally cherry-pick the best tech deals.

This competitive reality led to the sale of four of the industry's top tech banks—Alex. Brown & Sons, Robertson Stephens, Montgomery Securities, and Hambrecht & Quist—to large commercial banks. Other than competitive pressure, part of what inspired the sale of these tech banks was the deregulation of banking. In November 1996 a change in Section 20 of the federal banking laws allowed large commercial banks to own and operate investment-banking practices once again, knocking down a barrier set up by the Glass-Steagall Act, passed in the aftermath of the stock market crash of 1929 to curb the power of the money trusts that had controlled Wall Street.

More important, however, was the boutiques banks' growing sense that they were at the top of a very frothy market, and if they should ever cash out, the time was now. Alex. Brown was the first to go when it was bought by Bankers Trust in 1997 for $2.3 billion. "That got things going," says a former boutique insider. "This looked like a pretty good time to cash in. The high was high enough, so we sold out." When Bankers Trust was in turn swallowed by a larger fish, Deutsche Bank, which digested BT at the cost of $9 billion in spring 1999, the investment-banking arm was given the new name of Deutsche Banc Alex. Brown.

Robertson Stephens was next to go on the block after Alex. Brown when it sold out to Bank of America in June of 1997 for an eventual total price of $470 million. Later that year, NationsBanc bought Robertson's archrival, Montgomery Securities, for a whopping $1.3 billion. When NationsBanc then bought Bank of America, it decided to unload Robertson Stephens to avoid overlap with its earlier Montgomery Securities acquisition, so NationsBanc sold Robertson Stephens to BancBoston in September 1998 for $800 million, a huge premium over the price paid by Bank of America. BancBoston, initially valuing Robertson at $400 million, paid double to beat out five other high-caliber suitors that wanted the investment bank. "They said they'd pay full price if we gave them an exclusive look at it," a Robertson executive told us. "So they paid the absolute top."

To avoid immediate competition from an old pro, BancBoston paid Sandy Robertson a special compensation to stay out of the investment-banking business for at least a year after the acquisition. BancBoston also negotiated a penalty clause with Bank of America that would require them to pay BancBoston $400 million if they did not make good in keeping Sandy Robertson out of the business.

On the flip side, NationsBanc did not have a binding noncompete agreement with Thom Weisel, who founded Montgomery Securities in 1971. So when he left the bank in a huff in the fall of 1998, he set up a competitor to his old firm called Thomas Weisel

Partners and attracted a number of his old partners and associates from Montgomery Securities—about ninety people in all. "Our agreement to join NationsBanc was based on Mongtomery's remaining independent and staying in charge of all capital-market activities," recalls Weisel. "But they wanted to fold us into the bank, which was a violation of the merger agreement and my employment contract." He adds, "If I had a chance to do it all over, I wouldn't do the merger. Montgomery would be doing just fine on its own. But I'm on to the next chapter." But given his wealth, why is he bothering? "This is what I am," says Weisel. "I don't know what else to do. I don't intend to retire." For those who know Weisel, this was not a surprising move. "Thom is the most competitive human being on the planet," says a longtime associate.

Montgomery Securities still fared well after Weisel's departure. By January 1999, mostly on the strength of its brokerage business, revenue at Montgomery was up 80 percent above the previous year, recovering nicely from the stock market meltdown in the latter part of 1998. However, Montgomery still struggled to build up its investment-banking business, especially in the areas of technology and health care, in the wake of all the defections from those departments.

After the acquisition of Montgomery Securities, only one of the original boutique banks was left—Hambrecht & Quist. But the lone holdout would not last long. In September 1999, Chase Manhattan Bank gobbled up Hambrecht & Quist for $1.35 billion, resulting in a merged entity called Chase H&Q. In turn this entity would merge with JP Morgan in late 2000.

## Net Bankers

While Thom Weisel pursues a more traditional route back into tech banking, the other two veteran financiers prominent in Silicon Valley lore, Bill Hambrecht and Sandy Robertson, are going electronic. Hambrecht, who cofounded H&Q back in 1968, has formed his own electronic investment bank, W. R. Hambrecht & Company.

Located in a former warehouse in the city's design district, Hambrecht's new online investment bank sells new stocks over the Internet in a so-called Dutch auction, with investors setting the price. Robertson, who cofounded Robertson, Stephens & Company, backed a competing online investment operation, acquired by Wit Capital in May 2000. Wit-E*Offering could open up the stock sales process even further, with new stocks available on a first-come, first-served basis.

"The New York Stock Exchange is obsolete," says Robertson. "It's not only twentieth-century technology; it's nineteenth-century technology, in the twenty-first century. Because to have an order come down and have someone go out to make an open outcry in front of a specialist and see if you can match the orders is bizarre when you've got a computer that can match all that stuff up." He continues: "It's not like buying a suit where you have to look at the color of the fabric and feel it. You're trading a commodity; 100 shares of General Motors is 100 shares of General Motors. You don't care who sold it to you."

Looking at the numbers, we think Hambrecht and Robertson are riding on top of yet another big wave in their already distinguished careers. By mid-1999, fifty-two IPOs had already parceled part of their IPO shares for sale over the Internet. "We are in the baby-step stage," says Bill Doyle, research director of online financial services at the consultancy Forrester Research, which projects that by 2003, as much as 12 percent of IPO shares will be sold online to individual investors. Forrester also projects that 20.4 million people will have Internet brokerage accounts. "First you had the discount brokers; now you have the emergence of the discount investment banker," observes a gleeful Michael Moritz of the venture firm Sequoia Capital. Moritz is giggling because he and his partners, particularly Don Valentine, have been very vocal about what they believe have been overinflated investment-banking fees.

This time around, however, Hambrecht and Robertson aren't the only pioneers in town. Established firms like the Charles Schwab Corporation and DLJ Direct, the public online affiliate of

Donaldson, Lufkin & Jenrette, already distribute shares online and help underwrite stock offerings. There's also Wit Capital of New York, formed in 1996, which had already distributed stock in over forty deals by mid-1999 and raised almost $80 million in its own IPO in May of 1999, a year before its acquisition by Robertson's E*Offering.

While online investment banking promises to be incredibly lucrative, it will also be fiercely competitive. When the dust clears, this new industry will shape up much like the other service industries being dislocated by the Internet, with a combination of old and new dogs driving the business.

## The Squeeze Is On

The emergence of electronic investment banking undoubtedly will put a serious squeeze on the fees associated with managing IPOs. This is good news for entrepreneurs as well as for all investors.

Typically, IPOs are arranged by a lead-manager investment bank (sometimes called a bookrunner), which gauges institutional investor demand, acts as the lead underwriter, and arranges a syndicate of other banks to share the underwriting risk. Bankers also sit up late at night in smoke-filled boardrooms with company executives and lawyers to set the final IPO share price. For these services, the bankers typically charge companies 7 percent of the money raised from the IPO, in part to pay for marketing costs.

Not surprisingly, most VCs and entrepreneurs consider these fees rather exorbitant. "I think the banks are disproportionately compensated for what they do," declares Sequoia Capital's Don Valentine. "I'd like them a lot better if they charged no more than 5 percent."

Conceivably, Dutch auction systems, brought online by firms like W. R. Hambrecht & Company, could put the most pressure on traditional investment-banking fees. The auction approach has actually been in place for years and is used extensively for the resale of U.S. government securities. The issuer is the Treasury Department, and the underwriters are bankers designated by the Federal Reserve Bank of New York. Under this kind of system, potential investors set the terms of the IPO in an auction rather than by the traditional direct offer/preset price system of trading. Under Hambrecht's system, called OpenIPO, investors place bids over the Internet for the number of shares they want at prices they are willing to pay. When the subscription period ends, the managing underwriter tabulates the bids and reoffers the stock to the bidders at the highest price they can charge and still sell all the stock.

Since Hambrecht's new e-investment bank leverages the Internet as a new, low-cost research-and-stock-share distribution channel, the firm offers a lower overall banking fee of 4 percent instead of the traditional 7 percent for managing the IPO.

W. R. Hambrecht & Company claims its system also counteracts many of the abuses traditional banks engage in for IPOs. The biggest conflict always centers on who gets the hot IPO shares first. Online auction proponents claim that their approach allows small-scale investors to compete with even big institutional investors who typically get allocated the most IPO shares because they yield the greatest financial clout with their bankers. A flyer Hambrecht uses to market itself reads: "One for me. None for you . . . Most investment bankers lead a very hard life. After they take care of each other, they have to take care of their friends. And after they do that, they have to take care of the people they'd like to have as friends. You can imagine that after all this hard work, there aren't many IPO shares to go around."

On December 9, 1999, we went to observe W. R. Hambrecht's third OpenIPO in action, in this case for Andover.net, a Web-based Linux content company that was ultimately acquired by VA Linux on June 7, 2000, for a little over $250 million in stock. As demand for Andover.net was skyrocketing in the pre-IPO bidding process, W. R. Hambrecht was trying to determine the most accurate opening price. The stock opened at $18 a share and ultimately more than quadrupled, closing at $77. After the dismal performance of

Salon.com's IPO back in July 1999, W. R. Hambrecht needed a success to prove that the Dutch auction model did indeed work. Bill Hambrecht was happy with the results. "More than half the stock went to retail investors," he said.

Nevertheless, CS First Boston's Frank Quattrone is skeptical of this system as a whole: "I just don't think high-quality companies will risk going with that kind of pricing formula, especially with such little research support undergirding it." He adds, "Think about it. If your business takes small companies public and trades their stocks and not much else, that's the low end of the business. That's what these electronic offering services are going after—you bring down the fees to where you can barely make a living."

Bill Doyle of Forrester Research does not believe fees alone will persuade companies to choose online investment banks as underwriters. "Given a choice between Goldman Sachs and E*Offering, what will a young company choose? Goldman—even if E*Offering offers to do it for half," says Doyle. "When Goldman leads a road show, people pay attention," he adds.

There's also a sense that these electronic offering services, because they might become bottom feeders, will get more companies out there that don't deserve to go public.

Despite these negatives, e-banking has potential, as has been shown by all the activity in this sector. In May 2000, Wit Capital Group announced it would buy privately held rival E*Offering for $328 million in stock. Meanwhile, E*Trade Group, the third-largest online brokerage firm at that time and owner of a 28 percent stake in E*Offering, bought the retail brokerage business of Wit Sound-View, Wit Capital's online investment-banking subsidiary, for $20.5 million. "E*Offering needed more research and Wit Capital needed distribution," said Sandy Robertson.

Of all 1999 Web-based offerings, Wit underwrote 69 percent, E*Offering underwrote 18 percent, and Schwab underwrote just 10 percent, according to Thomson Financial Securities Data. Taken together, online offerings constituted 9.9 percent of the total IPO market. Not a bad slice of the pie for such a new industry.

• • •

Our guess is that all the major investment-banking firms will eventually succumb to competitive pricing pressure from e-bankers and be forced to build extensive Internet sales-and-distribution systems of their own or acquire one of the new upstarts. They will also have to compete with online bankers who propose to further lower the cost of IPOs by using the Internet to conduct "road shows." (Traditionally, just before going public, a company's management and its underwriters travel around the country and meet with groups of analysts, fund managers, and other potential institutional investors to answer any questions about the company's financial information and short- and long-term outlook.)

Big banks such as Merrill Lynch have already rattled their traditional retail broker networks by going online, and Goldman bought a 22 percent stake in the online investment bank Wit Capital for an estimated $20 million. "The bigger firms are slow to react," says Walter Cruttenden, CEO of E*Offering. "This massive distribution will win," he predicts, because it has "the most people, the quickest service, and the lowest cost." Wit-E*Offering itself faces some stiff new competition from some major retail competitors that have come together to form Epoch Partners, headed by CEO Scott Ryles. The joint venture's powerhouse investors include Charles Schwab, Ameritrade, TD Waterhouse, and three venture capital firms, including Kleiner Perkins Caufield & Byers and Benchmark Capital.

## A System in Conflict

In spite of being the gateway to IPO funds, the investment-banking industry remains controversial in its practices. "The whole investment-banking system is in conflict," complains Sequoia's Don Valentine, and many in the banking business would agree with him. Herbert Allen Jr., the billionaire president and CEO of the New York–based investment bank Allen & Co., is one of them. Although Allen & Co. has brokered some major corporate mergers in recent years, including entertainment megadeals such as the Disney–Capital Cities/ABC merger, unlike traditional investment banks, it often doesn't charge a set fee for its work. And while Hambrecht is critical of the conflict of interests in the IPO game, Allen is equally critical of conflicts in the merger business.

"I don't know how you can set a fee before you know what value you have added to the transaction," says Allen. "Most of what Wall Street does in mergers and acquisitions is non-value-added." Sometimes the bank just gives an opinion on what is pretty much a done deal. "That's not value-added, that's legal protection," says Allen. He further contends that it's unusual for a bank to come up with an original idea beneficial to both parties in a merger. "That kind of activity is in short supply," says Allen.

Allen admits that the bank did not necessarily bring much to the table in the Disney–Capital Cities/ABC merger. The three main players—Michael Eisner, Warren Buffet, and Tom Murphy—had already worked things out before they called Allen & Co. "Whatever they wanted to pay us for the deal was fine with me. It was a privilege just to be involved," admits Allen.

Allen & Co. tries to promote discussion and dealmaking among these huge entities by hosting an annual retreat at Allen's Sun Valley, Idaho, ranch. About forty major business institutions are represented, and executives like Bill Gates, Steve Case, Gerry Levin, Andy Grove, Rupert Murdoch, and Barry Diller come with their families. This retreat obviously differs from the typical scramble of technology bankers for IPOs, merger deals, and follow-on financings.

Yet even closer to Silicon Valley, investment banks such as Broadview International that specialize in technology-company mergers criticize their peer institutions. "We consider most investment banks to be securities firms because they sell securities as their primary business," says Paul Deninger, chairman and CEO of Broadview. "They do corporate finance work for companies, but companies are not their primary client—the institutional investor is their primary client. And they treat the IPO market as something meant to work primarily for the institutional investor." He adds,

"These securities firms view companies as products, not companies. When they do an IPO or walk out on the trading floor, they call it 'product,' not 'the company.' "

"Our companies and our people are treated as meat," agrees Sequoia's Don Valentine. "The banks care only about getting the transaction done and collecting their commissions. They want the shares from our company to Fidelity on Wednesday or whenever; they don't give a crap about the company."

Further evidence of the meat trading is the lack of follow-up attention for some of these companies. Investment banks bother with certain thin-margin IPOs primarily because somewhere among these companies, a few could mature into tomorrow's Intel, Microsoft, or Cisco. And as a company grows, lucrative follow-on services could make up for the IPO's paltry margins. But if a bank doesn't judge the company to have this kind of potential, its research analysts usually ignore it. And without this coverage, the Fidelitys of the world will not buy it, so the stock languishes. "It's a ball-buster job to get anyone to pay attention to some of our quality companies," declares Valentine.

## Stock Analysts in Denial

While gaining the ongoing coverage of top investment banking analysts is important to all public companies, in the midst of a volatile stock market, these analysts are often the last to give investors clues that there might be something wrong. Perennial optimists, analysts don't like to bear bad news. Consequently, they tend to be in denial if companies report weaker-than-expected earnings or if some global economic indicator portends a shrinking market for a company's products. Things will always get better next month, the analyst likes to say. There are exceptions, of course, but the lone skeptic might be regarded as a doomsayer, if not a traitor.

Besides a bias toward the positive, stock analysts at investment banks rarely come out negative because the companies they cover are often customers of their banks. More and more, analysts have become involved in the sales process. It's typical for analysts to visit prospective clients alongside corporate finance officers, who court stock offerings and merger-and-acquisition business while using positive coverage by these analysts as their best lure.

A study by Zack's Investment Research showed that among 8,000 recommendations made by analysts on stocks in the Standard & Poor's 500-stock index in 2000, only twenty-nine were sell recommendations. A study by Thomson Financial/IBES of analyst reports issued in December 2000 corroborated Zack's. Only 2 percent of all analyst recommendations that Thomson tracked were classified as "sell" or "underperform." In contrast, more than 31 percent were "strong buys," and almost 40 percent were "buys."

In 2000, Roni Michaely of Cornell University and Kent Womack of Dartmouth College published a study of high-tech stocks. They found that stocks recommended by the banks that had underwritten them would spike, and then plummet in the following months. Those stocks recommended by nonunderwriters, however, would rise over the long haul. After six months, stocks recommended by underwriters rose a median 15 percent, compared with a 20 percent gain by nonunderwriter recommendations. After two years, the underwriter-recommended stocks were down 52 percent, while those recommended by nonunderwriters were up 23 percent. "There is a bias in brokers' recommendations when they have an underwriting affiliation with a company," says Michaely. "But the public doesn't recognize it."

Chuck Hill, a former securities analyst and current research director for First Call/Thomson Securities, sees this bias as a product of fear among analysts. Analysts don't want to offend the firm's investment-banking departments or the companies they cover by saying anything negative. "There's some reluctance to put a sell on a stock," he says. "It's tougher now to be independent."

In fact, sometimes it's against bank policy to be independent. Michaely and Womack surveyed thirteen investment bankers, asking them to explain the discrepancies in their study. The bankers chalked it up to conflicts of interest. The researchers also surveyed thirteen money managers, who agreed that the differences were caused by conflicts of interest. In a speech around the same time, SEC Chairman Arthur Levitt produced an internal memo circulated at a Wall Street investment bank. "We do not make negative or controversial comments about our clients as a matter of sound business practice," the memo read.

"It's a situation people have started looking at lately. Analysts are afraid to have sell recommendations or even hold recommendations because if they downgrade a stock, the bankers could lose their relationship with the company," admits Frank Quattrone. "Some companies consider the analyst's ratings in terms of giving out the more lucrative banking business. It sets up, clearly, a potential for a conflict that must be managed properly."

Critics charge not only that analysts do less original work and more readily present data that follows the company line, but also that few take the trouble to go out and talk to suppliers, customers, and competitors to get an accurate view of what's going on.

Bruce Lupatkin, former head of research at Hambrecht & Quist and a longtime technology analyst, agrees that the role of securities analysts at banks has changed and that they're more involved in the sales process. "It's not a green-eyeshade back-office crank-the-numbers thing," he says. "The analysts have become rock stars."

But with this role have come new pressures. "One is that the companies cut you off if you say anything negative. Your information sources dry up," Lupatkin says. "Also a bit surprising, the institutional community is unhappy with the change of recommendation. They shoot the messenger. They think, 'You just knocked my stock down two points. I didn't need you to do that.' " The bottom line ultimately determines what happens. "In the end, we give the clients what they pay for," says Lupatkin.

The problem, then, is that the world of Wall Street research is clearly built to favor the banks and their clients at the expense of the retail investor. Whereas for decades research analysts had little to do with retail investors, instead working with the firm's sales team or talking only to the big-money managers—essentially acting more like a consultant to the institutional business—many analysts have now sought the limelight with regular appearances on CNN and CNBC.

Herb Allen Jr., whose investment bank Allen & Co. does not employ securities analysts, criticizes this trend. "I have a problem with the way security analysts on Wall Street are used today," he says. "They are usually fairly weak historians and very poor prognosticators. And if you're using the analyst to bring in business for the investment bank, how trustworthy is his opinion going to be on the other side when he sells some poor jerk the stock? The system doesn't make sense to me."

This reality makes Herb Allen and other critics conclude that because the analysts from the banks have grown too cozy with the companies they cover, they act more like cheerleaders or even front guys rather than true analysts.

Even so, an amazing irony emerged in the midst of the high-tech stock mania and market volatility of 2000. If an analyst did have the temerity to criticize a stock, it was sometimes the retail investor who got the most upset. For example, when Salomon Smith Barney analyst Jonathan Joseph announced on CNN's *Moneyline* program that he had lowered his rating on semiconductor companies, he received a death threat from an irate individual investor. And Dan Niles, an analyst at Lehman Brothers, has also received death threats after downgrading hot tech stocks. Niles can recall one instance when an investor sent him an angry e-mail after he downgraded Dell Computer. The investor claimed that the resulting drop in the stock had wiped out his children's college fund. The e-mailer even went so far as to threaten Niles with bodily harm if the investor ever made it to the analyst's hometown, San Francisco, Niles said.

### Stock Spinning and IPO Kickbacks

Another investment-banking practice called into question during the Internet IPO go-go days is what has become known as stock spinning. On November 12, 1997, *The Wall Street Journal* published a front-page article by reporter Michael Siconolfi titled "The Spin Desk: Underwriters Set Aside IPO Stock for Officials of Potential Customers." This article and others following it set off a storm of controversy in the investment-banking community, sparked an SEC investigation, and caused civil suits to be filed against some of the banks.

In his articles Siconolfi accused certain investment banks—Robertson Stephens, Hambrecht & Quist, and Montgomery Securities in particular—of operating "spin desks" designed to allocate chunks of hot new stocks to the personal brokerage accounts of corporate executives, venture capitalists, and other decision makers sitting on the boards of companies whose business the banks wanted. The timely allocation of these stocks made it possible for these individuals to "spin" or "flip" the shares on the first day of the initial public offering for quick profits.

The *Journal* quoted one former recipient of such spin shares, David Cary, CFO of i2 Technologies, as saying, "It's as common as water, and you can have all you want."

While most shares must go to big institutional investors such as the mutual funds, a small number were said to be set aside in a "retail pot" for certain individuals. Robertson Stephens was reported to have routinely allocated about 10,000 shares of each IPO deal to the personal brokerage accounts of executives, venture capitalists, and other special customers.

Morgan Stanley was alleged to have allocated 1,000-share blocks of the Netscape IPO to some executives, including the CFO of the then privately held Arbor Software. Arbor later chose Morgan Stanley to manage its IPO.

Cristina Morgan, a managing director at Hambrecht & Quist, defended the practice in the *Journal,* likening it to free golf outings or fancy dinners for prospective clients. "What we're talking about is trying to solicit business," she argued. "We throw lavish parties with caviar. Is that not trying to influence them?" Likewise, allocating stock "is not illegal," she said. "It's not immoral. It's a business decision. If you sell doughnuts, you do everything you can to enhance the image of your doughnut shop to customers. You're just doing your job. That's what we're all doing."

When we later asked Morgan about the spinning controversy, she called it "a tempest in a teapot" and added, "The investigators found that the stock went to retail customers of Hambrecht & Quist who had every right to the stock. Those brokerage clients happened to be, in some cases, corporate finance clients of the firm entitled to allocations in rough relationship to their investing activities with the firm." Furthermore, the allocations "were so small as not to amount to a hill of beans." As for the *Journal* articles, she declared, "This was Mike Siconolfi's bid for a Pulitzer."

Asked about spinning, Brad Koenig, managing director and head of the technology-banking practice at Goldman Sachs, says, "I would say it's widely practiced in our community. Goldman Sachs did not engage in it, but I think some firms used it aggressively."

Stu Francis, a managing director at Lehman Brothers, says, "Well, Lehman never did it. It began informally because venture capitalists and others wanted to buy the stocks. Then, as the industry got bigger and bigger and the IPO market got bigger and bigger, it became more of a standard practice. People slipped into spinning when it wasn't a problem, but it became a problem as the market got bigger."

The onetime boutique investment banks such as Hambrecht & Quist and Robertson Stephens were believed to have engaged in the practice more than the New York–based investment banks because the boutiques' share of technology underwriting had been increasingly eaten into by the larger bulge-bracket banks.

A colleague of Francis at Lehman Brothers also ascribed the practice to "a somewhat looser culture and compliant environment in Silicon Valley's financial community than what you'll find in New York."

An executive from one boutique stated, "It got out of hand. We saw some of the competition buying deals by giving an awful lot of IPO stock to the venture capitalists. It was getting a little flagrant, and it shouldn't have happened. The venture capitalists should be in the same category as the investment managers, who aren't allowed to buy these stocks."

Nevertheless by early 2001, Chris Nolan, an investigative columnist for the *New York Post*, uncovered the fact that CS First Boston was still operating a spin desk for a small group of CEOs and other well-connected Silicon Valley movers and shakers, many of whom were prospects to bring in more business for the bank. The bank had set up trading accounts which were used to buy and sell IPO stocks on behalf of the insiders. The bank was basically making hundreds of thousands, if not millions, of dollars for clients by churning IPO stock for them. These accounts were discretionary—their holders didn't have control over specific trades—so the buying and selling took place without the account holders knowing about the specific activity.

On an even more serious note, around the same time the Securities and Exchange Commission was investigating the possibility of kickbacks to banks, CS First Boston in particular, for letting certain speculators buy their way into hot IPOs. In essence, the purchaser of a hot IPO, who would not otherwise have access, would be giving back a substantial chunk of the quick profits to the underwriter in the form of a larger-than-usual commission. Specifically, the SEC was looking into whether such commission payments were made by small hedge funds and wealthy individuals to underwriters. In fact, during the height of the IPO boom, a number of hedge funds were created specifically to play the IPO calendar. Undisclosed kickbacks to underwriters, if willful, were potentially the basis for criminal charges.

In March 2001 in the midst of the SEC investigation, a class-action lawsuit on behalf of IPO investors was filed against seven investment banks accusing the banks of colluding in violation of antitrust laws in their treatment of IPOs. The lawsuit stated that in exchange for access to IPO stock, the investment banks demanded large brokerage commissions and commitments to artificially support the prices of shares after the offerings. Those commissions would typically be equal to a third of the gains made by the customer from the shares they received in the initial offering, the suit said. The suit also mentioned "tie-in purchases" requiring investors in IPOs to buy additional shares in the companies after the companies went public. The suit further charged that these purchases were made at "specified escalating price levels which were designed to push up and inflate the price of the class security to increasingly higher levels," a process known as "laddering a stock."

Some of the IPOs that were mentioned in the suit included Marimba, Ariba, United Parcel Service, and VA Linux, but dozens of other stocks were said to be involved. The suit claimed that the banks communicated with one another about their stock-laddering strategies. The investment banks named as defendants in the suit were: CS First Boston; Goldman, Sachs; Lehman Brothers; Merrill Lynch; Morgan Stanley; BancBoston Robertson Stephens; and Salomon Smith Barney.

## Flipping and Other Mutual Fund Schemes

It's not unusual in a bubble for an IPO stock price to triple or even quadruple in the early aftermarket and then decline thereafter. This pattern creates an ideal environment for another insider practice known as flipping: buying the stock once or more on the first day of trading and unloading it on the same day for a quick profit.

And it's no secret that investment-banking firms allow big institutional investors to flip, looking the other way while these investors dump hot new stocks at their whim, often within hours or even minutes of the stock's first trade. Meanwhile, the firm's stockbrokers get a commission of up to 4 percent of the value of an IPO trade, double the commission for most other stock transactions. And because the firms want to keep big institutional investors happy (since they are the source of huge trading fees), the brokers are not penalized for selling them the bulk of IPO shares, even though these investors also do most of the flipping. Mutual funds and pension funds have enough clout to avoid flipping strictures.

Since the primary client of the investment bank is the institu-

tional investor, the IPO market is treated as something meant primarily for institutions. These investors view individual companies
as a small and highly mobile part of their portfolios. They are not
committed to these companies; if they don't like them, they'll sell
them as soon as they can.

Flipping is critical to individual investors because a high propor-
tion of IPOs perform poorly over the long haul, so "while institutions dump IPOs, retail is stuck holding the bag," says Lori Dennis,
a former Merrill Lynch broker quoted in *The Wall Street Journal.*

A "flip report" prepared by investment bank Bear Stearns in
1998 showed that fifteen of thirty-three institutional buyers of Bear
Stearns–led IPOs quickly sold many or all their shares. "It's a major
problem," says Bear Stearns chairman Alan "Ace" Greenberg.
"They want it, then the minute they get it, they sell it."

Sandy Robertson, cofounder of the investment bank Robertson
Stephens, explains it this way:

> If you have a hot deal, when one of the big institutional investors asks
> you for some stock, you have to give it to them even though you think
> they're going to flip it, because they're giving you so many commis-
> sions all the time. Of the 100 institutional investors who buy the stock,
> maybe 15 want to own it over the long term. You can't say to a big
> mutual fund, "Oh, we know you're not going to hold it, so you're not
> getting any." They'll swear on a stack of Bibles that they're going to
> hold on to the stock. So you have to give it to them. That's why the
> trading volume is so high in the first couple of days after an offering,
> because there are four trades on one block of stock. You can't get
> around the flipping.

Some see a darker side to the public stock manipulations by certain large mutual funds. One venture capitalist even sees a kind of
Ponzi scheme in the way the largest mutual funds buy and sell IPO
stock in overheated aftermarkets. He believes these manipulations
are a product of the whole interdependent food chain of investment bankers and analysts, mutual fund managers, venture capital-

ists, and entrepreneurs operating in the midst of a momentum-investing environment in search of the greater fool.

"If I want to buy a highly promoted IPO," he says, "I look for a CEO and a group of venture capitalists who are very promotional and spend all their time weaving a story for the press. As a mutual fund, I then buy up the float in the hot aftermarket."

The float is that amount of stock still available for public trading after an IPO. For Internet companies, notoriously little stock has been available, making those stocks ripe for manipulation. Demand is high, but supply is limited. In the case of Yahoo in mid-1998, on average, only 8.9 million of its 93 million shares were traded—because of the demand, the price took off. And at the time, only about a third of Amazon's 49 million shares outstanding were available for trading; the entire float could be turned over in a month.

"The guys who own a lot of these small-float Internet stocks might have $100 million or $200 million worth of position in a company," says the skeptical venture capitalist, "and they can put in $10 million of buy orders to have the stock go up even in a market that's going down 200 points." He adds, "In a market that's heading up, they can keep pushing that stock up further. It becomes very controllable with these little tech stocks. So the mutual funds have promoted a handful of companies. That's why you have this two-tier market—the heavily promoted stocks and the rest, which are underwater. It's the essence of the game."

If it's tough to prove a larger conspiracy or Ponzi scheme, research does support the fact that the dotcom boom was indeed "a colossal sucker's bet for retail investors in the public aftermarket," as financial columnist Chris Byron put it. For the 170 Internet IPOs brought to market from 1996 through mid-2000 by the top eight equity underwriters, these dotcom stocks in aggregate were selling for roughly 68 percent more than the institutional investors paid in the premarket. Yet these same IPOs were simultaneously down by 23 percent from what retail investors paid on the first trade in the public aftermarket.

For example, any institution buying one share of each of Gold-

man Sachs' fifty-one dotcom IPOs at the premarket offering price
would have seen their cumulative investment rise by almost 90
percent by mid-2000. However, anyone buying these same shares
at the opening price in the aftermarket would have been sitting on
a loss of about 15 percent. Similarly, institutions that bought into
Morgan Stanley's twenty-four dotcom deals enjoyed an increase of
134 percent, while individual retail investors lost nearly 17 percent.

On a more controversial level, *The Wall Street Journal* reported
in a front-page article on July 24, 2000, that Chase H&Q pocketed
a 7,000 percent gain in eighteen months on the sale of InfoSpace
stock, a company the bank had taken public in late 1998. The controversy arose out of the fact that in December 1999 one of the
bank's analysts had published a report praising InfoSpace as a
"must-own holding" and then continued to reiterate "buy" recommendations in the weeks that followed. But while the analyst was
telling investors to load up, Chase H&Q itself was bailing out. It
sold all of the InfoSpace stock owned by the bank's venture capital
arm, plus a stake owned by an H&Q employee fund, for about $72
per share, a total of roughly $42 million. By the time of the *Journal*
article, InfoSpace was trading at $48 per share. By March 2001 it
was listed among the "Internet Wasteland" stocks, trading at less
than $4 per share, down 97 percent from its fifty-two-week high
(see Appendix C). This example illustrates again how the stock
market can be like Las Vegas, where the house holds all the cards.

In the early 1990s, venture capitalist John Doerr described the
personal computer revolution as "the greatest legal creation of
wealth in the history of the planet." Perhaps the mania phase of the
Internet boom will go down as the greatest legal *transfer* of wealth
in history.

## Investment Banking in Transition

Despite the preceding, the horizon is not entirely dark for the individual investor. New technology is helping change the rules of the
game. And whether or not the Don Valentines and Herb Allens

of the world can successfully persuade the investment bankers to cut their fees and tighten their practices, the Internet will certainly turn the industry upside down over time. Overall, we expect the Internet will level the playing field between large and small investment banks and between retail and institutional investors. And this change in the competitive landscape will undoubtedly lead to lower investment-banking fees and a more level playing field for the individual investor. E*Trades's CEO, Christos Cotsakos, calls this shift "the democratization of investment banking." Eventually, the cozy relationship between the traditional investment banks and their favorite institutional investors will be shaken, and the IPO share-hungry retail stock buyer should benefit.

# Doonesbury

# THE GREAT
# BIOTECHNOLOGY BUBBLE

> **With Amgen and Genentech, the biotech market
> broke open and a real wave whipped up.**
> —Sam Colella, general partner, Institutional Venture
> Partners

*I*n the labs of University of California at San Francisco (UCSF) in the 1970s, brilliant scientists were at work. Sequestered in dark rooms, in their white jackets with their petri dishes, these researchers were working to get inside the chemistry of DNA, trying to unlock the genetic code and then recombine different genes to form new protein molecules. Bob Swanson, a venture capitalist with Kleiner Perkins Caufield & Byers, and Herbert Boyer, a pioneer in DNA research and a professor of biochemistry at UCSF, recognized the tremendous commercial potential of these efforts. In 1976 they founded Genentech and built on these feats of genetic engineering to synthesize clinical products and build a $10.5 billion enterprise.

The efforts of Genentech raised the hopes of investors that ingenious and driven scientists could develop drugs to defeat cancer, reverse the effects of aging, and genetically engineer a brave new world in which lives could be improved and entrepreneurs and investors could get rich in the process. When the biotechnology light bulb clicked on, investors rushed toward the opportunity. Almost every major venture capital firm scrambled to imitate the Kleiner Perkins model and raised funds targeted to health care. The boutique technology-investment banks like Hambrecht & Quist and Robertson Stephens followed suit by building research and corporate-finance teams that understood genetic engineering, pharmaceuticals, and medical instruments.

This flurry of financial support led to the creation of thousands of biotechnology start-ups, hundreds of which went public. But as with all overfunded booms, the biotech industry has experienced its own Darwinian process.

This chapter looks at the great biotechnology bubble of the late '80s and early '90s, the forerunner of today's Internet Bubble. It's the story of how public investors were willing to bet the rent on the concept stocks of biotechnology companies that had no profits, no revenues, and long years of research ahead of them. We'll look briefly at how the biotechnology industry got started and how a few successful companies raised hopes for the whole industry. In the process, we tell the story of a distinguished institution, Boston University, that bet a big piece of its endowment on a supposed cure for cancer and paid the price.

Most important, while the business models and products of biotechnology are very different than those of Internet companies, the biotech bubble did set a financial precedent that carried over not only to consumer-technology companies such as 3DO, whose story we also tell here, but also to today's Internet industry.

## The Biotechnology Bubble

Kleiner Perkins partner Bob Swanson was so fascinated by the idea of genetic engineering that he quit the VC partnership in 1975 to pursue his dream. While Eugene Kleiner and Tom Perkins provided Swanson with a desk and a phone, they were initially skeptical about how quickly this science could be turned into commercial products. Still in his twenties, Swanson called scientists trying to find someone who would respond to his commercial challenge. At first there was no encouraging news, until he finally contacted Herbert Boyer, a young biochemist at the University of California in San Francisco, who together with Dr. Stanley Cohen of Stanford had done the first gene-splicing experiments two years before.

Swanson and Boyer eventually convinced Kleiner and Perkins to invest $100,000 in exchange for 25 percent of the new company.

The money helped finance a series of tests with encouraging results, and Genentech (short for "genetic engineering technology") was born. The company raised another $850,000, including $100,000 more from Kleiner Perkins. Genentech's main business goal was to commercialize recombinant DNA, in which genetic sequences from diverse origins are joined together (recombined) to form new molecules. Specifically, the company synthesized genes to produce human insulin in 1978 and a human growth hormone in 1979. To keep the research-and-development engines humming, Genentech went public in 1980 at a price of $35 per share and raised $35 million overall in the offering. At the IPO price, Kleiner Perkins' total return on its Genentech investment was an incredible 164 to 1.

In 1982, assisted by the manufacturing capabilities and financial resources of drug giant Eli Lilly, Genentech brought its human insulin drug, called Humulin, to market. Yet by 1985 Genentech earnings were only $6.5 million. What was supposed to be a blockbuster new drug, Activase, turned out to have very weak sales. In that same year, however, Genentech's new human growth hormone drug, called Protopin, received final FDA approval and started to sell. The company has sold more than $1 billion worth of Protopin since its introduction in 1985. In 1998, Genentech's revenues were $1.15 billion, and by the first quarter of 1999, Genentech's profits rose 43 percent to more than $58 million on the strength of sales for two new drugs: Herceptin for treating breast cancer and Rituxin for non-Hodgkin's lymphoma.

In the spring of 1999, Swiss pharmaceutical behemoth Roche fully acquired Genentech at a stock price of $82.50 per share. But it was Genentech's early track record and successful IPO that had inspired the venture community to place great hope in the biotech industry.

Amgen (short for "applied molecular genetics"), like Genentech, was also founded by a venture capitalist, Bill Bowes of U.S. Venture Partners. By early 1981, Bowes had rallied enough venture capital support—almost $19 million—to get Amgen rolling. Also like Genentech, Amgen quickly developed drugs it could bring to market. It went public in 1986 at a price of $18 per share in an offering that raised $43 million. After additional rounds of private and public financing, Amgen finally hit the jackpot when it went from zero revenues to $1 billion in one year on the strength of two drugs: Epogen, for red blood cell production to treat anemia, and Neupogen, for white blood cell production to stimulate the immune system. In 1998 Amgen's market capitalization was $40 billion and its revenues were $2.7 billion, primarily from the sales of Epogen and Neupogen.

A third biotech company that raised the stakes was Chiron. In its research and development, the company pursued a diverse group of drugs and medical devices, including the technology to produce the hepatitis B vaccine. Chiron limped along financially for almost five years before doing an IPO in 1983 that netted the company $20 million. In 1998, Chiron had revenues of almost $780 million and a market capitalization of more than $3.4 billion.

Throughout the 1980s, biotech mania continued to build. In those days, biotechnology had much of the cachet that e-commerce does now. In 1986, biotechnology IPOs hit a peak when there were almost $1.7 billion worth of public offerings. Looking for a quick and substantial profit, the typical venture capital attitude prevailed—$1 million in, how much out? Those were heady days for biotech.

While the market for a certain drug or medical device is more measurable than that of an information-technology product, it's also riskier to develop. Most biotech products typically require five to ten years and approximately $300 million to develop. Biotech companies must follow a tortuous course of costly research and development, manufacturing, clinical trials, federal approval, and marketing before they can see any revenues, never mind profits, from their products. There's always a high burn rate of cash.

Given how long most biotech companies took to develop a product, their IPOs were financing events rather than profitable investments for the public investor. At the IPO, people bought into concepts only, not into something tangible. "Genentech, Amgen, Chiron—those companies delivered real products and real earnings," says Asset Management's Pitch Johnson, whose firm was a big investor in Amgen early on. "Those stocks got the public thinking magical cures and wonderful drugs were just sitting out there in the future. That led to a bubble in which companies could go public on high hopes." A *Wall Street Journal* article in 1991 noted: "Inspired by the 340 percent rise in Amgen's stock in the past year, investors have rushed into biotechnology stocks in search of the next rising star in the young industry."

The biotech bubble hit a new high with the IPO of Regeneron, a company founded in 1988 with seed money from Merrill Lynch and various venture capitalists. In 1991 it went public at $22 per share, offering more than 4.5 million shares. Half of those shares were turned over—flipped—on the first day of the offering. A year after the stock offering, the price was down to $7.75 per share, and it fell to $4 per share in 1994.

In 1991 there were more than $1.6 billion worth of biotechnology public offerings and an additional $3.7 billion worth of follow-on offerings. Between the end of 1989 and January 1992, the Hambrecht & Quist biotechnology index rose fourfold. By early 1992, though, many biotech IPOs were oversubscribed; public investors still wanted the next Amgen. Instead, the first wave of the biotech market hit the beach, as one darling biotech company after another failed to bring its drug to market. The top-tier companies lost 30 percent of their value, and the second and third tiers lost 60 percent and 80 percent, respectively. IVP's Colella declares, "If, as a venture investor, you didn't get off the first wave fast enough, if you held your stocks, you didn't do well at all." Public investors suffered even more. The Fidelity Select Biotechnology Fund, for example, rose 99 percent in 1991 only to fall 24 percent in the first four months of 1992. Many investors had bought into the fund just in time to go over the cliff.

There were even whispers of fraud, when particular financiers deliberately developed certain biotech deals in which they attracted some big names, raised money at high prices, and sold them to the public just before the bubble burst. Quick IPOs for quick bucks eventually left the public paying the price. And even though biotech stocks peaked in the early weeks of 1992, there were still ninety-one initial public offerings that year, up from seventy-two in 1991. Investors still refused to run away from biotech and continued to look for opportunities to be involved in the sector. In fact, the biotech sector rallied 25 percent between June and November of 1992, but by November 1994 the average biotech stock had lost two-thirds of its peak value.

## Hope Springs Eternal

A good example in recent years of how investing in a concept company can go awry is the case of Seragin Inc., documented in the 1998 *New York Times* article "Loving a Stock, Not Wisely but Too Well." Founded in 1979 by Boston-area medical researchers, Seragin developed a drug eventually known as Interleukin-2 that looked as if it could be a "magic bullet" in the fight against cancer.

After hearing a presentation by Dr. John Murphy, the discoverer and lead developer of Interleukin-2, John Silber, the president of Boston University, grew excited about the prospect of investing in a cure for cancer that could reap tremendous financial returns for his school. The opportunity was irresistible. So Silber urged the university's trustees to invest $25 million of the school's total endowment of $175 million in Seragin in 1987. In 1992, during the peak of the biotech bubble, Seragin went public at $12 per share. Silber persuaded numerous associates, friends, and family members to buy stock in the company. He also invested $1.7 million of his own money, almost half his net worth, and persuaded the university to buy a larger stake in the company as well.

Seragin raised $52 million in public stock sales in 1992 and 1993, but its cash needs were voracious. By 1996 the company still did not have FDA approval for Interleukin-2, and the company lost $26.3 million that year, making Seragin's cumulative losses $200 million at the time. The stock had reached a high of $15 per share in January 1993, but ended 1996 at just over $1 per share. In September

1996 Boston University invested an additional $5 million through a private stock placement, bringing its total stake to $84 million.

By August of 1998, Seragin was out of money, on the brink of bankruptcy, and delisted from NASDAQ. The company was then acquired by Ligand Pharmaceuticals for $30 million, and Ligand said it would pay an additional $37 million to Seragin shareholders if Interleukin-2 ever received FDA approval. The university's Seragin stock now became Ligand stock. The school's total stake of $84 million was now only worth $8.4 million. Silber's personal stake had dropped in value from $1.7 million to just $43,000. What had looked like certain gold was now a cautionary tale about the cost of betting heavily on a concept stock.

## Public Venture Capital Precedent

Despite their risks and diminishing returns, biotech companies became a milestone in technology financing. Donald Valentine of Sequoia Capital says, "Biotech financing became institutionalized. We had an ability to start companies and raise countless amounts of money with little or no prospect of revenue for half a dozen years." Valentine concludes, "I think we financed too many biotech companies. The public was excited about all these things highly publicized by the investment bankers: This was a cure for cancer, that was a cure for heart attacks. We thought we had all the bases covered."

But in the early 1990s, most biotech solutions turned out to be just ho-hum products. There were no big barn burners. The biotech research engines by and large did not produce phenomenal drugs. The bubble popped, and as in the PC era, there was lots of company wreckage.

Much of the wreckage was of "me-too" companies, like the forty-three disk-drive companies formed in the 1980s, or all the automobile companies founded back in the 1920s and 1930s. Almost 1,500 biotech companies originated out of such prestigious university laboratories as Stanford, Harvard, Johns Hopkins, and

UC San Francisco. Yet they were financed to pursue the same areas of research and product goals. Where one or two gene-therapy companies might have been enough, for example, a half dozen were founded.

Before the biotech boom, most of the scientific research carried out at universities was funded by the government, and many discoveries were the by-product of basic research. But somewhere along the way the public decided to invest in companies pursuing cures for cancer and other potentially lucrative breakthroughs.

Each biotech company required at least $100 million to get it from nothing to something. One thousand companies were started with venture capital money, and thereafter, hundreds of them were largely financed by public venture capital. "One thousand times $100 million doesn't work," says Sequoia's Valentine.

In 1996, biotech IPOs spiked up again, to almost $1.2 billion worth of public offerings. But biotech stocks coming from those offerings and others from the 1980s aren't doing well today. The companies did exactly what they said they would do: All their scientists were locked away in their laboratories doing research. But the public had to learn the hard way that drug failure is the rule and not the exception: Fewer than one drug in ten successfully completes clinical trials. So investors got impatient waiting for positive results and drifted away because of lack of growth in the stock prices. Venture capitalists also started to bolt. Kleiner Perkins, for example, has invested in only two new biotech ventures since 1995.

In a 1998 study of their investments in these companies, Horsley Bridge Partners of San Francisco, a fund of funds that invests in venture capital partnerships and manages the stocks of portfolio companies after they go public, discovered that biotech and healthcare stocks might appreciate for a year in the public market, but those stocks languish after that. Since the biotech bubble burst in the early 1990s, the public market has not been generous to the health-care sector.

By 1998 there were almost 350 publicly traded biotech companies and about 1,000 private ones. Investors had put an estimated $90 billion into the public companies. Yet biotech stocks had risen in only seven of sixteen years. An investor who put $100 into every biotech IPO would have earned a return of only 1 percent a year.

The NASDAQ Biotechnology Index went up in late 1998, but it represented only about a 5 percent gain for the entire year and stayed well below the NASDAQ composite index, which had appreciated by almost 46 percent for the year. Only the stocks of the top ten biotech companies, which already had products, profits, and market capitalizations over $1 billion, had risen sharply. While the share prices of companies such as Genentech, Amgen, and Chiron soared, midsize and smaller companies actually stagnated or lost ground. In fact, as many as fifty of the lesser-performing public companies were expected to run out of cash within a year.

And unfortunately for the companies below the top tier, the long-predicted wave of mergers supposed to kick in following the biotech bubble had largely failed to materialize. The Darwinian shakeout continued.

So while Genentech and Amgen raised the expectations for the whole industry, they also set a precedent for public stock offerings for companies that had no profits, and sometimes no revenues. An entrepreneur could start a company with some vague, far-out idea that nobody ever questioned and take that concept public. People willingly paid for physical and financial events they thought might happen in the future. It was truly public venture capital.

## Bubble Redux

In the second half of 1999 and through 2000, biotech companies were again in vogue, in part prompted by the prospect of unraveling the human genetic code and the mapping of human proteins as a means for more rational and efficient drug design. By the end of 2000, the NASDAQ Biotechnology Index was up more than 22 percent, even while NASDAQ stocks as a whole were way down. In

2000, biotechnology companies raised a record $36.8 billion in new financing. Companies such as Abgenix, Medarex, and Millennium Pharmaceuticals had each raised more than $400 million in single transactions in 2000. Celera Genomics issued stock worth nearly $1 billion in a secondary stock offering in March 2000, more than the total raised in secondary offerings by all biotechnology companies combined in 1998 (even as, in March 2000, the NASDAQ Biotechnology Index was up a good 80 percent from the beginning of the year). In 2000, there were 54 biotech IPOs up from 14 in 1999.

The pharmaceutical companies, meanwhile, had come to rely on the biotech companies to help fill their pipelines with new drugs or to provide the latest technological tools. Many big drug companies were spending 20 to 30 percent of their research and development budgets on outside collaborations. Nevertheless, the entire market capitalization of public biotechnology companies—about $400 billion—was only as much as Pfizer and Merck combined. And according to Recombinant Capital, a financial consulting firm in San Francisco, 61 of 247 public companies it surveyed in the first quarter of 2000 had less than a year's worth of cash. Overall there were about 350 public biotech companies, 10 to 15 of which could expect to be profitable in 2001. And by the end of the first quarter of 2001, the top 100 biotech stocks were down 33 percent as a group.

In their book *Venture Capital at the Crossroads,* William Bygrave and Jeffry Timmons report that of the venture-backed high-tech IPOs done in the 1980s, 77 percent of the hardware companies and 100 percent of the software companies were profitable when they went public. This contrasts to only 20 percent of the biotech companies being profitable at the time of their IPOs. Clearly the original biotech bubble began a new trend in investing. The public was now willing to invest in mere concepts, instead of real companies. And it would not be long before the public venture capital phenomenon would spread beyond biotechnology.

## What If They Don't Come?

A prime example of this phenomenon is 3DO Corporation. Founded by the dynamic, handsome, and charismatic entrepreneur Trip Hawkins, 3DO, like Genentech, got its initial funding from Kleiner Perkins Caufield & Byers.

Hawkins majored in game design at Harvard University and after graduation served as a marketing manager at Apple Computer under Steve Jobs. In 1982 he founded Electronic Arts, a wildly successful computer games company that put out such hits as John Madden Football. Electronic Arts was also a Kleiner Perkins investment.

In 1991, Hawkins left Electronic Arts to found 3DO. The company's goal from the start was to develop a next-generation video-game system that would seriously challenge the Japanese video-game giants Nintendo, Sega, and Sony. Clearly this would be an expensive and daunting challenge, but Hawkins and Kleiner Perkins felt 3DO was up to the task.

By 1993, though, 3DO was running seriously short of cash; its burn rate was tremendous. Historically, a company like 3DO would have gone back to its venture capitalists or its other investors (in this case AT&T, Matsushita, MCA, and Time Warner) for the necessary funds to go on. Instead, 3DO decided to sell stock to the public.

The problem was that 3DO did not yet have a marketable product. And 3DO was developing technology it would license, not sell directly as its own product. The video-game multiplayer that would run 3DO's technology had to be way overpriced to support the company. It was all a big gamble.

At the time of its IPO on May 3, 1993, 3DO had zero revenues, a cumulative loss of $30 million, and no projected profitability for at least two years. In the first quarter of 1993, 3DO blew through an estimated $16 million, yet the IPO was valued at $293 million.

This was a new precedent for a consumer-technology company. It was essentially a concept stock—no completed product or revenues—in which the company asked the public to supply risky venture capital. After reviewing 3DO's published stock prospectus, *Red Herring*, in an open letter to Trip Hawkins, asked: "Given the complexity of 3DO's technology development program and business model, how do you expect public investors to adequately evaluate the risk/reward factors involved in such an investment? Isn't this the job for professional venture capitalists?"

Jim Breyer, managing partner of venture capital firm Accel Partners, says, "3DO should not have gone public because there was not a strong conviction about the business model. Unfortunately, 3DO's business was in the hands of a lot of other big strategic partners." This level of business dependency was very hard for nonspecialists to assess at the time.

Publicly, 3DO said its motivation for the concept IPO was to create higher visibility for the company, to keep its software-development partners motivated, and to build anticipation for its video-game player. But the venture capitalists also wanted to create early liquidity, diversify risk, and earn a 12 times markup on an investment they had made just two and a half years before. The old formula had been overturned; no longer was an information-technology company expected to have at least a few quarters of profit before going public.

In June 1994, 3DO did another public stock offering, this one netting $37 million. By 1996 the company had given up on the game-player business, and to stay alive proceeded to license what technology it had left, including a $100 million deal with Matsushita. In a May 1996 interview with *Red Herring*, Hawkins admitted that 3DO's original strategy was the wrong one, describing it as a "Field of Dreams" approach. "Build it and they will come. But what if they don't come?" he asked.

By December 2000, 3DO's stock was down to less than $2 per share, well below its IPO price of $15 per share.

## The Concept Deal

A big problem with the biotech boom was that too many of the companies that went public had to return to the public-market trough at the same time for additional money, thus overwhelming the public investor. The problem with 3DO and General Magic, another technology-concept deal that went public in the mid-1990s, is that a lot of time passed and their stocks languished while they tried to figure out new concepts to sell.

In the Internet boom, the majority of companies with a *.com* associated with their names were by definition concept stocks. These companies are peddling only an inkling of a business model, instead of real top-line growth and increasing profits. Many of these Internet companies have already come up short on their business plans. They will struggle to survive or go out of business. And as these companies run out of cash, we'll see the Darwinian shake-out continue to happen right before our eyes.

# Doonesbury

# LEADERS OF THE INTERNET PACK

## Who Will Be the Winners in the Internet Market?

**A**s with America's great industrial manias of the past—railroads, the automobile industry, radio corporations, aircraft companies, and the personal computer sector—a Darwinian shakeout has beset the Internet market. And like these other industries, only a handful of Internet market leaders will emerge. Research by Morgan Stanley Dean Witter shows that 5 percent of Internet companies have yielded 68 percent of shareholder value in the Internet market, and 1 percent of companies provide 38 percent of value.

"Every time there is a new fundamental platform, there are a dozen or so businesses that become long-term *Fortune* 1000 companies," notes Jim Breyer, managing partner of Accel Partners. And within that group, the leader tends to have a sizable lead over its competitors. "The first firm, not second firm, tends to have disproportionate market share," observes Michael Mortiz, general partner with Sequoia Capital. "Pick software, pick databases, pick microprocessors, pick routers—it's Microsoft, Intel, Oracle, and Cisco. In the long run the leading company, on the whole, will be worth more than the sum of all its competitors. There's no doubt that out of all the Internet carnage some colossi will emerge."

Ultimately it's by investing in specific companies that investors prosper. "Investors will not earn superior returns by simply investing in an economy-transforming sector," states Alfred Rappaport, professor emeritus at J. L. Kellogg Graduate School of Management at Northwestern University and author of *Creating Shareholder Value* (Free Press, 1998). "Instead they must identify companies within that sector that will successfully exploit the new technology for competitive advantage."

But which companies among the current Internet businesses look like long-term winners? Identifying these can be a challenging task. "A few years ago a company needed a five-year track record and at least a couple of profitable quarters before it could go public, so you had more time to identify potential industry leaders," observes Alan Chai, managing director at Shott Capital Management, an investment firm whose illustrious clients include Stanford University and the Hewlett-Packard pension fund. "But we've seen companies go public after only seven months in business and then we get the stock distribution as early as six months after that. It's been much more difficult to identify the winners."

A sophisticated analysis of Internet companies reveals that the long-term winners ultimately will be identified by certain key characteristics, including a great core idea, a large potential market, first-rate management, sufficient capitalization, brand recognition, strong customer service and loyalty, and when applicable, a proprietary technology. Characteristically most leaders demonstrate strong positive cash flow and high gross margins relative to competitors. As a result of such qualities, such leaders are able to scale quickly, consolidate their positions in the market through acquisitions, and move fast into new markets as needed.

To the above characteristics some analysts and investment managers would also add venture capital and banking sponsorship. "The best technology companies are usually backed by the best VCs; the winners tend to come out of a pretty predictable list of venture firms," states Eric Doppstadt, director of Private Equity at the Ford Foundation who manages both the foundation's venture investments and its postventure stocks. "To this pedigree I would also add the underwriters—Goldman Sachs, Morgan Stanley Dean Witter, and the other top technology bankers," he says.

Of all these qualities, market timing is of course critical to ultimate success. It is far too costly for companies to try to educate markets. If a company is going to grow exponentially, it has to be well positioned in a large and growing market where the company can gain market share through the development and/or acquisition of more products and services.

The sine qua non for a long-term winner, however, is great management. "That's the single most important quality a company needs right now," says Lise Buyer, a former Internet analyst who is now a venture capitalist with Technology Partners. "Everyone is still trying to figure out what the best business models are for the Internet—you need a management team that can effectively navigate through the changing tides."

Thorough investment managers and analysts visit companies to make sure they are comfortable with the executives and their ability to execute their business plans in a shifting landscape. "Many public investors put management teams at the bottom of their list of criteria as the thing they think about last," says Accel's Jim Breyer. "But the fact is, if you invest in companies with preeminent teams in specific segments, over time you're going to do really well."

Closely allied with strong management is a strong company culture. If a company can recruit employees who are excited about being part of a winning team, then employee retention becomes far less of a problem, even in a volatile stock market environment— "train-hopping" does not tend to be such a problem for the best companies. "In your hiring you can weed out the people who are just searching for the next way to make a quick buck," says Bill Gurley, a general partner with Benchmark Capital. "You end up with the ability to recruit people on factors other than just salary and stock."

And beyond a company's doors, customer relationships will also become more crucial as the mere novelty of the Internet wears off and true businesses emerge. To be winners in the customer economy, businesses will have to anticipate and understand customers' needs and then beat their competitors to the delivery of the right solutions.

In this chapter we profile two leaders and putative winners in the Internet market—eBay and AOL/Time Warner. These companies show all or most of the key characteristics to win long term. The challenge will be to keep their companies on an upward trajectory in their respective markets, and do their best to grow and adapt in the postshakeout landscape.

## eBay: Auction House for the Future

eBay boasts a company culture of financial discipline and profits. And management is strong. CEO Meg Whitman was previously a general manager at toy manufacturer Hasbro, and chief operating officer Brian Swette was chief marketing officer at Pepsi-Cola Company.

Meanwhile eBay's numbers just kept improving: In the fourth quarter of 2000, for example, eBay had consolidated net revenues of more than $134 million, an increase of 81 percent over the same period in 1999. Registered users increased to 22.5 million, and those users transacted a record $1.6 billion in gross merchandise sales. For all of 2000, net revenue totaled $431.4 million, nearly twice the amount reported in 1999. Net income for 2000 was $48.3 million. CFO Gary Bengier was forecasting a doubling of operating profits and a 50 percent revenue increase in 2001, with a goal of $3 billion in revenue by 2005, in part due to an increase in users' fees.

The main reason that the company boasts such sky-high profitability is that, unlike some Internet businesses with counterparts in the brick-and-mortar world, eBay created an entirely new marketplace with its online auction community—one that appears to face no threat from the likes of Sotheby's or Christie's. "The good news for eBay," declares CEO Whitman, "is I don't think there is a land-based competitor who can compete with us." On any given day, users place 1,000 bids a minute on more than 4.5 million items for sale.

And eBay has continued to evolve from "selling stuff from someone's garage," as one analyst put it, and being largely a site for collectibles, to a broad trading platform for merchandise of all kinds including jewelry, sporting goods, appliances, musical instruments, computers, consumer electronics, office equipment, and used cars. Many users have actually set up small business exchanges on eBay, which they operate full-time. A number of e-brokers have also emerged who help sellers post, sell, and deliver merchandise via eBay in exchange for a fee and a percentage of the sale.

According to Jupiter Communications, sales in 2000 for consumer-based online auctions in the United States more than doubled to $6.4 billion, up from $3 billion in 1999. And eBay continues to increase its lead over its nearest competitors including the auction operations of Yahoo and Amazon.com. Jupiter estimated that eBay's share of the U.S. market was more than 90 percent. eBay has also continued to expand globally, with users from more than 200 countries, as well as nation-specific sites in Canada, Germany, Great Britain, Australia, and Japan, with many more to come.

"eBay doesn't have anything that's proprietary," observes Lise Buyer. "But they were the first to take the Internet in this new direction and then scale the business. Once they got big enough it was over, because buyers want to go where sellers are and sellers want to go where buyers are." Alan Chai of Shott Capital Management agrees: "As trite as it may sound, eBay is a clear example of a company that has benefited from the network effects of bringing together online so many interested parties." Not surprisingly Whitman also agrees: "We have the largest marketplace and we've built the brand that stands for person-to-person and small business-to-person commerce on the Internet."

But just as Sotheby's and Christie's have been embroiled in controversies of their own, eBay has had to cope with the attendant difficulties of ensuring clean auctions. One issue for eBay was shill bidding, not only by individuals placing bids on their own items, but also the prospect of rings working together. Such shill rings regularly bid on one another's items but rarely place the winning bid. They also pat each other on the back in user feedback postings. And although eBay employs "shill hunter" software to try to detect such collusion, tracing shills involves hours of work in sifting through and cross-referencing dozens of bidding histories and user feedback records.

Assuming that eBay can overcome such controversies, it definitely has a business model that is sustainable. "eBay is the classic consumer-to-consumer company," says Marc Klee, manager of the John Hancock Global Technology Fund. "We have owned the stock and like the company long-term."

## America Online/Time Warner: Poetic Future?

America Online is no longer just an Internet story: Instead, with its acquisition of Time Warner it creates one of the most valuable companies in the United States and provides a high-profile mix of the new and old economies.

The combined companies sport a powerful management team: AOL's CEO, Steve Case, as chairman; Time Warner's CEO, Gerald Levin, as the chief executive; and AOL's president, Robert Pittman, and Time Warner's president, Richard Parsons, as chief operating officers. Most notable in the division of executive labor is that Pittman has responsibility for all businesses—online, magazine, and television—that derive income from subscriptions and advertising. "Bob Pittman was the one at AOL who helped them leverage the industry's largest user base into high advertising rates and strong revenue," notes Lise Buyer.

It goes without saying that Pittman will take full advantage of Time Warner's entertainment and information empire, as well as its powerful advertising sales base, in order to pump up revenue for the combined company. In turn, Time Warner will enjoy direct access to AOL's cherished subscriber base to promote its magazines, television programming, movies, videos, and music titles. Time Warner's cable systems, which serve almost 13 million subscribers, or 20 percent of the cable market, will enable AOL to start offering much speedier Internet access and create a foundation for the broadband Internet era.

Some of the smartest people playing the Internet game think that combining the strengths of the old and the new is *the* poetic strategy for the future. In spite of competitors' aggressive promotion of low-cost and even free Internet access, AOL still has a total of 26.8 million subscribers. An astonishing 54 percent of Internet users in the United States access the Web through AOL.

While AOL competes with Yahoo for users, advertising, and e-commerce spending worldwide, the paths of the two companies diverge with their choice of content strategies. AOL's approach is to vertically integrate Time Warner content, whereas Yahoo has opted to partner more broadly with a variety of content suppliers in a more open system.

A common criticism of the AOL/Time Warner merger, however, is that it shackles the once high-flying AOL to Time Warner's more even-keeled (read: slow) growth. As a result, some investors bailed, causing a drop in AOL's stock; it traded for $38 a share in December 2000, well below its fifty-two-week high of $95. In fact, by the time of the FTC approval of the merger in December, AOL's market value had dropped from more than $189 billion, when the merger was originally announced in January, to $130 billion. And the value of the merger deal itself had plunged from a record $156 billion to about $110 billion. But considering that AOL traded its high-flying stock for hard assets, "the wisdom of the deal from AOL looks impeccable," says Roger McNamee.

Some see great promise in the details of the merged companies. Marc Klee thinks AOL is attractive less as a New Economy/Internet company and more as a new media company that should be viewed on a cash-flow basis. "The AOL/Time Warner combo is going to be a cash-generating powerhouse," says Klee.

Northern's George Gilbert expects continued growth in online advertising, from approximately 2 percent of overall advertising spending in 1999 to at least 10 percent of the pie in the next five years. He also expects to see significant growth in e-commerce. In fact, for advertising and e-commerce combined, Gilbert predicts that AOL's revenue will multiply by ten times in the next five years. "And this should translate into ten times total profits as well," declares Gilbert.

Kevin Landis, cofounder and chief investment officer of First-hand Funds, is also a believer in AOL. His reasoning is blunt: "A good basic question to ask about any company is, five years from now, can you imagine the Internet without it? AOL is entrenched in so many people's lives that there's no way it's going away. So the stock is a good entry point for investing in the growth of the Internet while still making a relatively safe bet."

AOL/Time Warner is also well positioned to manage through an economic downturn. "Everyone is challenged by a weaker market, but the biggest companies have the ability to cut costs and create new businesses," says Jessica Reif Cohen, an analyst with Merrill Lynch.

## Looking Ahead

In spite of the domineering prospects of AOL if past industrial manias are any guide, then some of the best Internet companies are yet to come in the post-Darwinian shakeout. This prospect is heartening to venture capitalists. "There's no doubt in my mind there are a couple of companies out there that we haven't heard of today that will be in that top tier five years from now," declares Accel's Breyer.

But will most of the Internet winners be Internet start-ups that are stand-alone, or will they largely come out of the brick-and-mortar world? "I think they'll be independent, and they'll be something that no one ever thought of before," says Benchmark's Bill Gurley. "Entrepreneurs will continue to create a few surprises coming out of the woodwork." Given Accel Partners' bet on Walmart.com, Wal-Mart's independently funded and managed Internet operation, it's not surprising, however, that Breyer is particularly optimistic about the long-term prospects of "click-and-mortar" operations. "We are fervent believers that the brick-and-mortar companies that build independent Internet companies that leverage their resources will be the huge winners on the Web," says Breyer.

Tom Wyman, an Internet analyst with JP Morgan, agrees. "Brick-and-mortar companies will take over e-tailing because they already have trusted brand names, huge buying power, and offline stores to accept returns," he says.

AMR Research noted that by fall 2000 the Internet had accounted for $29 billion in sales, only slightly more than half a percent of total retail sales. If Internet sales were to reach a projected $100 billion by 2003, that would still only be 3 percent of total retail income.

As a postmortem on the shakeout of online B2C operations, AMR lists the following reasons for the failure of the majority of these pure-play businesses:

- A deadly combination of unprofitable sales, significant upfront infrastructure costs, high customer acquisition costs, and anemic growth.

- Failure to meet or exceed customer expectations in fulfillment, value, or service.

- Insufficient motivators to attract and retain loyal customers.

- Lingering privacy and security issues.

AMR concludes that "the most likely e-commerce model for avoiding extinction is a blend of Web and store sales. The old dinosaurs will have a much easier time bringing their brands to the Web, rather than new online start-ups trying to bring their brands to the mall."

Eric Janszen, an angel investor with Osborn Capital, agrees. "We've always maintained that the brick-and-mortar retailers will eventually take the business from the e-tailers," says Janszen. "The reason is simple: Wal-Mart is successful because they figured out how to efficiently manage cash flow and distribution so that they could turn a profit in a low-margin industry. Their genius and profitability comes from solving this very difficult problem. Wal-Mart will figure out how to create a Web business way before any e-tailer figures out how to solve the distribution problem to turn a profit."

In his best-selling analysis, *The Innovator's Dilemma* (HarperBusiness, 1997/2000), Clayton Christensen qualifies what electronic commerce companies coming out of the brick-and-mortar world will have to do in order to succeed on the Web. His research shows that spin-out ventures are the best way for large, already successful brick-and-mortar companies like Wal-Mart to address or pursue the "disruptive technology" challenge of the Internet. While Wal-Mart is already known for its extraordinary logistics management processes, infrastructure, and use of information technology, for it to become a successful click-and-mortar company, Christensen believes it must manage its online operation through an independent organization. Christensen writes about Walmart.com:

> The online venture actually needs very different logistics processes than those of its bricks-and-mortar operations. Those operations transport goods by the truckload. On-line retailers need to pick individual items from inventory and ship small packages to diverse locations. The venture is not only disruptive to Wal-Mart's values, but it needs to create its own logistics processes as well. It needs to be spun out separately.

Ultimately whether an Internet company is stand-alone or a successful spin-out of a brick-and-mortar operation, assuredly it will have to show the right characteristics to be not only a survivor but a true leader in the post-Darwinian landscape.

In spite of the skepticism about B2C online commerce, John Doerr of Kleiner Perkins remains optimistic. "Lots of companies got started with no value propositions," admits Doerr. "But some business-to-consumer ideas are going to become real businesses. Homestead is getting an incredible lead in the housing and real estate market. Blue Nile's, Zagat's, and Martha Stewart's e-commerce efforts are doing well. These market leaders have a compelling proposition, in the form of unique products and over-the-top customer service."

Whatever the prospects of these companies, it's clear the days of dotcoms without clear business plans or paths to profitability are over. In sum, Morgan Stanley Internet analyst Mary Meeker writes in her *Technology & Internet IPO 2000 Yearbook*:

Investors should continue to focus on the leading names, with compelling operating models, strong cash positions, sufficient liquidity, sustainable growth, significant international opportunities, significant wireless and broadband opportunities, and strong management teams.

There could not be a better investment strategy to match what author and venture capitalist Geoffrey Moore calls the "gorilla game."

## BUYER TIPS

### *Lise Buyer on Internet Leaders*

Lise Buyer is a fifteen-year veteran of the investment research community, including a recent stint as a director of the Internet and New Media Technology Group at Crédit Suisse First Boston, focusing on strategic positioning, financial analysis, and valuation of many companies in the Internet sector. Before that, she was an equity analyst and portfolio manager for T. Rowe Price Associates, where she helped manage the top-performing Science and Technology Fund. Buyer is now a general partner with Technology Partners, a venture capital firm that specializes in early-stage investments.

**Q:** We've talked about the characteristics of Internet leaders. Are there any useful metrics to go along with this?

**A:** I've always looked for patterns on a month-by-month basis to see which way a company is going. The single-quarter "snapshot" numbers don't tell you a whole bunch. But on a month-to-month basis it's helpful to look at how much these companies are generating in profit growth and how much they are spending to get the customer; also their per customer revenue. Are companies spending more and more and getting fewer and fewer customers per dollar? Or, are they spending less and less, which is what a Yahoo is doing, and getting more users. This shows just how viable some of these businesses are such as AOL, eBay, and Broadcom.

**Q:** What about Amazon?

**A:** There are many questions about how they do things, but part of it is they're new and they were the first ones doing some of these things online. Their model is not proven. Their revenues per customer, in my opinion, ought to be going up. When you look at the Amazon customers who've been using its site for more than twelve months, shouldn't they be buying twice as much stuff today as they were last year? The amount of advertising dollars Amazon spends to generate each new dollar of revenue should go down because Amazon should have done the work already with the established customers.

**Q:** Other analysts have pointed out that the trouble with a lot of e-tailers is that they regarded Amazon as their yardstick, which was a big mistake.

**A:** Absolutely. People looked at Amazon and the huge amounts they were spending on sales and marketing. They said if Amazon can do it we can do it; that's the model. Amazon was treated differently in the market because it was young, because it kept outperforming on the top line by this huge margin. But those e-tailers that didn't pay attention to growth margins and what they were spending to attract the customer got in trouble. I think they assumed they could just keep going back to the till and filling up, that money was just coming endlessly. It didn't. The door is shut.

**Q:** How do you know what the right model is?

**A:** We don't' really know what Internet businesses are going to look like ultimately, even with an Amazon. But we can see how a Beyond.com, for example, tried to copy Amazon in terms of spend, spend, spend and get your name known, but it didn't work. The company spent all this money in advertising to sell to people who weren't really in the consumer market to buy software the way consumers were buying books on Amazon.

**Q:** Should there be then more of a brick-and-mortar comparable measure for e-tailers?

**A:** Certainly for margins. No one has convinced us that if it's a low margin business offline to begin with, that it can be a higher margin business online.

**Q:** What about the click-and-mortar strategy?

**A:** I wouldn't want to bet against Wal-Mart, for example, because of their distribution and knowledge about inventory, products, and customers. They looked at what they didn't have, which was savvy about how to do business online, and they partnered with Accel Partners, because Accel has the brain power.

**Q:** How did some of the Internet leaders get where they are today?

**A:** Yahoo, for one, got off to a fast start. It attracted money. Then it really fed on itself because advertisers knew that they wanted to be in the Internet space, but really didn't know where to go. So the easy answer was let's just go with the big one. So advertisers started advertising more aggressively on Yahoo. Then the stock started to move, partially driven by retail investors rather than just institutional investors. Those institutional investors that wanted to have a toe in the Internet water started to put their money in Yahoo, which made it go up even faster. Then a bunch of other investors said, "Well look, I don't really understand the Internet space but I'm not going to miss it altogether, so if I'm going to go down, I'm going to go down with a group. Let's put money in a business that other people have money in. That way if we screw up we're not the only ones that will look like idiots." It was a real herd mentality. So it fed on itself. I just think it was lack of information. So let's just invest in the big liquid names: AOL, Yahoo, Amazon, Ariba, Commerce One, etc.

**Q:** Speaking of Ariba and Commerce One, what's your take on the business-to-business (B2B) e-commerce market?

**A:** If you're going to do a B2B e-commerce marketplace, for heaven's sakes find one where there are eighty-seven suppliers on one side and ninety-seven end-users on the other. If you've got three suppliers and eighty-seven consumers, then guess what—the margins aren't going to the guy in the middle. That's why eBay worked, because there is an unlimited number of people on both sides and no one has pricing power.

**Q:** What's your advice to investors?

**A:** I hope we learn from the B2C (business-to-consumer) and B2B manias. Smart investors don't really care what the initials are. They stop and they analyze each individual company. Look at the company before you invest. We'll have new waves—for example, wireless devices come out and everybody is talking about them. Did we learn a lesson or are we just going to automatically invest in the new, new thing?

**Q:** Is there a way of valuing this stuff?

**A:** Let's assume that I'm a rational investor, but I want a healthy 30 percent return on any risky stock I buy. I know what the stock is going for today. I can gross it up by 30 percent for the next three years. Meanwhile, I look at Microsoft in its absolute glory days when it had a monopoly, when it was generating immense operating profits. It traded with a price/earnings (P/E) ratio that peaked at about 75. I give the benefit of the doubt to all these new companies that they will be as powerful as Microsoft, which of course is absurd, but let's give them that. Okay, now, let's see if they can have a 75 P/E in a rational market where these companies hit maturity. So now I have a price and a P/E three years out. I can try to forecast earnings and estimate shares. Companies going public always quote a target operating margin. So I can work up the profit and loss to arrive at an implied revenue level three years out. If I'm forecasting 2000 revenue of $1 billion, what is the likelihood that it could reach $9 billion by 2002?

---

## TIERS AND FEARS

### Venture Capitalist Jim Breyer Talks about the Darwinian Shakeout

Jim Breyer is widely acknowledged as one of the brightest venture capitalists in the venture industry. His firm, Accel Partners, is busier than ever: For example in 1999, 25,000 business plans were submitted to Accel and Accel made a firm-record forty new investments. We caught up with Breyer at Accel's Palo Alto offices to discuss the Darwinian shakeout among Internet companies, the state of venture capital, and how to value Internet companies.

**Q:** You always told us the reckoning was coming. Did you foresee the Darwinian shakeout happening the way it did in 2000?

**A:** Among the second- and third-tier Internet companies I did. A lot of the consumer e-commerce companies that raised $50 million or more for national advertising around the holidays in 1999 found it extraordinarily difficult to remain in business.

The other constituents that I think are getting a rude awakening are the big media companies—the Disneys, the CBSs, the Foxes. I think they have to react swiftly and directly to the AOL/Time Warner merger. Many of these companies have built phenomenal franchises, and yet have lost many of their best Internet executives. Disney is a prime example. If Disney gets proactive and serious about the Internet, it can still be an astonishing force. If they wait another year or so to get very proactive, I think they'll be in real trouble.

**Q:** But obviously, some winners will emerge in the Internet market. Not every company is necessarily overvalued.

**A:** People can overlook the fact that Yahoo, eBay, and others are profitable businesses that are scaling incredibly fast and effectively. But once you start looking at that next tier or two down, and what the losses look like, with revenue growth on one axis and the deepening losses on the other, I think the public investors should always be concerned. Stocks in that position can easily correct by 50 or 75 percent overnight. What tends to happen is that the bad news comes first. Once the correction occurs, it's just a downward spiral. And that's exactly what happened in 2000.

**Q:** How do you stay away from this as a venture investor? VCs are obviously accustomed to high mortality rates. It's normal that the majority of start-ups won't be big winners.

**A:** When we're making investment decisions on new deals, we're using an exit valuation five years from now that's 30 times earnings. If the investment doesn't stand alone on a 30X multiple—on earnings, not sales—we won't make the investment. We feel that, over a long period of time, a 30 PE is what is afforded to the very best growth companies. Meanwhile, if a start-up team can't say what the scalable business model looks like or what gross margins and operating margins look like on a very detailed level, we lose patience. Public investors should approach the investment process with the same rigor.

**Q:** But hyping Internet companies to get the big stock spike seems to be part of the game today to maximize venture returns.

**A:** The great companies, like Microsoft, really understand that you want to do everything you can to set expectations that are realistic. It's astounding to me that many of the Internet companies that went public were so consciously or unconsciously hyping their stock—hyping business deals that hold no merit, such as an affiliate deal with Amazon. Anybody can be an affiliate with Amazon. There was far too much excess around that part of the business that led to a backlash. It's much better to underpromise and overdeliver. It's the only way to come at it. Hyping companies or stocks or management teams always comes back to bite us; therefore, there's no place, and no long-term benefit, for doing that.

# Doonesbury

# *THE NEW ECONOMY*

In the lamentable era of the "New Economics"
culminating in 1929, even in the presence of dizzily
spiraling prices, if we had all continuously repeated
"two and two still make four," much of the evil
might have been averted.
—Bernard Baruch, 1932

**O**ne of the by-products of the Internet revolution and its accompanying stock bubble is a phenomenon that some industry insiders have dubbed the Venture Economy. This economy is one that operates within the New Economy and epitomizes the way in which those with the right connections and opportunities have been able to cash in big on the Internet Bubble. In previous chapters we've outlined how high-tech insiders such as venture capitalists and entrepreneurs, as well as the bankers who underwrite their companies, have made bundles of money from IPOs that bubble up fast and then are flipped into the market. Here we touch on that next ring of insiders who get pieces of these IPOs, albeit smaller ones—pieces that the average retail investor does not have access to.

In this chapter we also look at those increasingly on the wrong side of the New Economy, and the fact that the real divide may not be so much a digital one (as the high-tech elite would have us believe) as it is a good old-fashioned financial one between noninsiders and the new wealth. This applies not only to the poor but also to the skilled working class and middle class who increasingly find it difficult to make ends meet in the showcase high-tech regions that are said to epitomize the Internet revolution.

We'll also look at the claims for the larger New Economy. Was the robust U.S. economy of recent years the beginning of a Long Boom, or was it just an extended up cycle? With distinct signs of an economic slowdown, and even a possible recession in 2001, it seems that the Long Boom myth has finally come to an end.

## Getting Their Slice of the Pie

For Internet insiders the New Economy is the Venture Economy. Stock in high-tech companies is the currency that's been used to float start-ups in the public market, compensate employees, and permit overvalued companies to gobble up lesser-valued ones. In centers of the high-tech economy such as Silicon Valley, Seattle, Boston, and Austin, Texas, stock equity has been treated like gold. It's been used as collateral to finance homes, buy other big-ticket items, and pay college tuition. For many insiders, it was more important than straight cash.

The obvious beneficiaries of equity are the entrepreneurs and venture capitalists who start and take companies public. But there are a whole host of service industries that have grabbed their piece of equity pie in the Venture Economy. These service industries include executive search firms, banks, lawyers, publicists, and consultants.

Executive search firm Pierce & Crow is one example. Its brahmin-class business partners include venture capital firms Kleiner Perkins, Accel Partners, and Sequoia Capital; and its customer list features Cisco, Sun Microsystems, and Ariba. Pierce & Crow populates both established companies and a host of unknown venture-backed start-ups with senior management. But like many others serving the needs of New Economy companies, the firm has found itself eschewing cash in favor of stock in the companies it assists.

While there's nothing new about taking a stake in a company as a portion of a fee, the scope of the activity greatly expanded in the midst of the Internet Bubble. "There isn't anybody out there in the New Economy who isn't trying to get a piece of the action," said Dennis Crow, a partner with Pierce & Crow. And with more than 2,000 Internet start-ups in recent years, there's been ample opportunity.

Not surprisingly, investment banks have also gotten into the equity compensation act, primarily to attract new talent and retain experienced management. Merrill Lynch's midlevel and senior bankers can invest as much as $1 million of their own money in a private-equity fund with a focus on technology, media, and telecommunications companies. Younger bankers receive options worth as much as $100,000 on shares in the fund. Other top-tier banks such as Goldman Sachs and Crédit Suisse First Boston have put together similar compensation plans.

Surveys by VentureOne, a San Francisco–based venture research firm, showed that investment banks had put money into 305 venture-backed start-ups in 1999, up from 104 in 1998. Between 13 percent and 18 percent of Goldman Sachs's net income in 1999 came from private equity gains, primarily venture-style investments. Venture investing has proven to be a lucrative addition to underwriting and other more traditional banking services, and is in some cases more lucrative overall for banks.

Like investment banks, law firms have found the lure of the Internet start-up and a potential payoff of millions of dollars in IPO stock very strong. Many firms have set up lucrative equity pools from client companies and give a share to its lawyers. The Silicon Valley law firm Wilson Sonsini Goodrich & Rosati, for one, has been an investor in its client companies since the mid-1980s. In 1999 alone it held stock in thirty-four newly public clients, including Brocade Communications and Juniper Networks. A typical company stake was 100,000 shares.

An American Bar Association analysis of U.S. Securities and Exchange Commission records showed that one in three of the lawyers who represented the more than 500 companies that went public in 1999 held stock in these clients at the time of the offering. And these statistics reflected only publicly available data. This did not even take into account the stakes that law firms may hold in clients that have been acquired, or their investments in nonclient companies and venture capital funds.

The Venture Law Group, a combination law firm, consultancy, and venture capital fund, took this venture-economy scenario to the next logical step by purposely structuring its business model to earn more in investment returns than in fee revenues. It actively encouraged partners to take a personal stake in client companies such as Yahoo and Ventro. All of the attorneys participate and share equally in the fruits of the firm's investment program. Most of their compensation comes in equity, not salary. The equity that Venture Law takes is not only common stock but also preferred stock that is paid for with cash from a fund to which the partners contribute.

Many high-tech public relations firms have also joined the venture economy by taking equity stakes in clients. "We see our clients like VCs see their investments—they're our portfolio companies," said Pam Alexander, president and CEO of Alexander Ogilvy. "We don't take on a client that we wouldn't want to take equity in." San Francisco firm Niehaus Ryan Wong takes a similar approach, and because of a shortage of agencies that are truly expert in technology, Niehaus can pick and choose with whom it will work and how it will get paid. "For new business prospects, especially the ones in the pre-IPO stage, it's a requirement that we get a retainer plus equity," says Niehaus partner Carrie Wong, who also serves as chief operating officer and oversees the agency's equity program.

Not surprisingly, consultancies have also jumped into the act—some with both feet. McKinsey & Company used to forgo equity stakes, even as rival Bain & Company went so far as to form its own venture capital firm in the '80s, as well as a venture capital unit within the consultancy group in the '90s. In 1999–2000, however, McKinsey took stakes in more than fifty clients in exchange for lower fees. It also opened eight "business accelerators" across Europe and North America, where its consultants spend up to nine months helping start-ups in which the firm has a stake. Competitor Booz Allen & Hamilton announced it would set up its own incubators for equity start-ups. Meanwhile, Andersen Consulting (recently renamed Accenture), the world's largest consulting firm, had invested in more than 150 companies since 1996, and in early 2000 announced a new $1 billion venture capital fund.

Arthur Andersen also has its own $500 million venture fund overseen by the chief financial officer of its business consulting practice, Mathew Verghese. Arthur Andersen expects to invest the capital in select client companies over the next five years in amounts ranging from $200,000 to several million dollars a pop. The company has literally traded millions of dollars in potential fees in exchange for equity in clients. "We are partnering with client-companies so we can share in both the risks and rewards in helping them build their businesses," said Verghese.

According to SEC regulations, firms like Arthur Andersen can never invest directly in audit clients. But the fact is that auditing accounted for only 30 percent of total revenues for the larger firms in 2000, down from 70 percent in 1977. Consulting and other management advisory services—a $55 billion business—meanwhile represented more than half of total revenue, up from 12 percent in 1977. Equity stakes in consulting clients was a big reason for this spike.

## The Widening Gap

Even as the insiders of the New Economy have grown fabulously rich from the recent stock market and corporate bonanza, the gap between the haves and the have-nots has only widened. Increasingly, more people find themselves on the poor side of this widening chasm between prosperity and the lack thereof. Fifteen years of stagnant real wages have helped widen inequalities.

An article in the summer 1998 issue of *Foreign Policy* reported that the income of the poorest 20 percent of U.S. households had declined steadily since the early 1970s, while the income of the richest one-fifth had increased by 15 percent, and the income of the top 1 percent, by more than 100 percent!

The irony is that such inequality grows at a time when the triumph of democracy and open markets was supposed to usher in a new age of freedom and opportunity. Instead, asserts *Foreign Policy,* "an integrated global market has created a new divide between well-educated elite workers and their vulnerable unskilled counterparts that gives capital an apparent whip hand over labor, and pushes governments to unravel social safety nets."

Another study, "The State of Working America," published in 1998 by the Economic Policy Institute, concluded the following:

- Median family income was $1,000 less in 1996 than in 1989.

- The typical married-couple family worked 247 more hours per year in 1996 than in 1989. That was more than six weeks' worth of work just to stay even.

- The inflation-adjusted earnings of the median worker in 1997 were more than 3 percent lower than in 1989. Real hourly wages either stagnated or fell for most of the bottom 60 percent of the working population during that period.

A study titled "Shifting Fortunes: The Perils of the Growing American Wealth Gap," published in 1999, takes the trend back even further, showing that hourly wages for average workers in 1998 were 6.2 percent below those of 1973 when adjusted for inflation.

In 2000, the Center on Budget and Policy Priorities, a nonprofit group based in Washington, D.C., conducted an analysis of income in the United States and found that from 1986 through 1997 (the most recent year detailed figures were available from the Internal Revenue Service) the average income of the richest 1 percent of Americans soared 89 percent. During the same twelve-year period, the average income for the bottom 90 percent was up a scant 1.6 percent. This income gap is yet another paradox of the Information Age.

A study done by the Consumer Federation of America showed that the assets of households that earn less than $25,000 actually dropped between 1995 and 1998. The CFA found that 53 percent of U.S. families sometimes get by on a paycheck-to-paycheck basis. Mounting credit card debt and no cash reserves meant these households were particularly vulnerable to bankruptcy and impoverished retirement.

The typical American family is probably worse off at the beginning of the new millennium than it was at the end of the 1980s or the end of the 1970s. And, to the extent that the typical American family has held its ground, the most important factor has been the large increase in the hours worked by family members.

The increase in the stock market between 1989 and 2000 went to the richest 10 percent of households. Jared Bernstein, one of the authors of the "Shifting Fortunes" study, opined, "The Federal Reserve has been imbalanced. It has been overly concerned about inflation and the erosion of the assets of the wealthy."

The economy has turned harshly against unskilled workers, leaving many of their families adrift. Some estimates say that one-fifth of America's children live in poverty. The unskilled can no longer simply migrate from agricultural areas to manufacturing centers in big cities to seek their fortune like they did fifty years ago. Second Harvest Food Bank, America's largest domestic hunger relief organization, provides a snapshot of the working poor in the United States.

- There is at least one working adult in 39 percent of households receiving emergency food. Of those adults, at least 49 percent work at least forty hours a week.

- Of the 21 million needy people seeking emergency food assistance, more than 8 million are children.

- Over the past two decades, the poverty rate among working families has risen nearly 50 percent.

- Forty-three million Americans have no health insurance, even for emergencies. Nearly half of all parents in working-poor families lack health insurance.

Second Harvest also reported that demand for its services was up 18 percent in 1999. Despite increasing the amount of food distributed in 2000 to 1.5 billion pounds, from 1 billion pounds in 1999, the organization turned away a million people.

These studies show that far from being a New Economy that makes the middle class rich and the working class more comfortable, the bull market, with its overvalued stocks, has led to a new inequality from which the knowledgeable insider definitely benefited the most.

"There's a growing socioeconomic disparity," says Jim Collins, a leading business analyst and coauthor of *Built to Last*, "and, perhaps most troubling, a perceived decoupling of wealth from contribution. Not only is there an increasing sense that the social fabric is fraying, as the nation's wealth engine operates for a favored few; there is also a gnawing concern that those who are reaping more and more of today's newly created wealth are doing less and less to earn it."

In turn, the wealth gap is something that the privileged generally seem to be less aware of than in past generations. For the nouveau riche Internet elite, money often ceases to be a means to acquire more leisure opportunities or possessions, and becomes instead a scorecard used to measure their status relative to that of their peers. Meanwhile, as the writer James Fallows points out, there's a certain emotional detachment toward the less privileged. "It is the unusual social and imaginative separation between prosperous America and those still left out," writes Fallows. "Our poor are like people in Madagascar. We feel bad for them, but they live somewhere else."

## Trouble in Paradise

Even in high-tech regions such as Silicon Valley and Boston, the income and equity gap has clearly made itself felt. In these areas there's a dual economy of two classes, the haves and the have-nots. While high-tech blue chips such as Cisco and Sun Microsystems could rightfully boast that they have created a new class of employees—stock-option millionaires—alongside them has emerged another class of workers as well: the invisible toilers who earn too little to afford decent housing in a booming region.

According to an April 2000 report in the *New York Times*, janitors in Silicon Valley are still working for low wages, cleaning the well-appointed corporate buildings of high-tech companies. These janitors live in garages, rent single-family homes for four families, or sometimes share a small trailer with eight people. Most of the workers spend one-half to three-quarters of their monthly pay, often from more than one job, on housing.

But even moving up the work scale to the skilled working class and the middle class, things are still tough, especially in Silicon Valley. Many people who are vital to the health and safety of a community—teachers, police, firefighters, nurses—are having a harder and harder time living in the Bay Area. In mid-2000, in part for economic reasons, more than 1,700 nurses at Stanford University hospital were involved in a fifty-one-day strike. The nurses had asked for a 7.5 percent pay raise, were offered 4 percent, and ultimately settled for 5 percent. Many nurses were disappointed with the settlement.

The Stanford strike was only the latest in a series of high-profile labor disputes around the United States. At Nyack Hospital in New York, nurses picketed for five months before agreeing to a contract in May 2000. In Worcester, Massachusetts, it took the involvement of Senator Edward Kennedy to help settle a forty-nine-day walkout by registered nurses at St. Vincent's Hospital.

Silicon Valley in particular provides a cautionary tale. The Bay Area has often been considered the center of new wealth, but in recent years it has dramatically demonstrated the harsh results of income disparity.

"We're seeing a real resurgence of union activity in nursing, and it's really noticeable in the Bay Area," Joanne Spetz, a health economist with the California Public Policy Institute told the *San Jose Mercury News*. "A large share of nurses believe the only way they're going to get what they need is through collective bargaining." The same day that the Stanford nurses returned to the job, an additional

3,500 health-care workers began a two-day walkout at eight Bay Area regional hospitals. The disputed issues remained the same. Their union was seeking pay raises and more power to set staffing levels in hospitals, which they feel have been compromised by managed-care cutbacks.

One obvious source of financial pressure on middle- and lower-income workers in the Bay Area is the increase in rental rates for apartments. In the second quarter of 2000, the average rent for a one-bedroom apartment in San Francisco was $2,000 a month; in Palo Alto it was $1,900 and $1,400 in San Jose. The vacancy rate was down to 1.9 percent, and rents had climbed steadily for five years in a row, by 40 percent throughout the Bay Area.

This kind of inflation is one reason those in the white-collar service industries are so intent on getting their slice of the equity pie. "Professional service providers need to be able to afford a place to live," says Mark Jensen, managing director of the technology practice at Arthur Andersen. "I think what you have in Silicon Valley is younger people, the future talent, who look at the cost of the area and feel it's hopeless, so they give up and go someplace else." Douglas Henton, an economist at Collaborative Economics in Palo Alto, California, agrees. "It's very difficult for younger people to live here. We're in danger of losing our middle class."

For those at the bottom of the pay scale, the rental squeeze can be even worse. The *San Jose Mercury News* reported the case of a cafeteria worker, Katherine Robinson, sixty, who was hit with a 40 percent rent increase in May 2000 after her apartment building was sold. The price of her one-bedroom apartment rose from $895 to $1,250 a month, far more than Robinson, who earned $1,650 a month, could afford. She decided to move in with her sister. "If I hadn't, I would have been homeless," said Robinson. According to the homeless-services organization Emergency Housing Consortium of Silicon Valley, approximately one-third of all people using local shelters in 2000 were employed. It's an economic environment in which some who earn as much as $50,000 per year have found themselves homeless, and households with a combined income of $100,000 are unable to afford a house. Sunnyvale Community Services, which serves the Silicon Valley community of Sunnyvale, California, reported that the number of families in 2000 applying for help increased to 600 a month from 80 a month ten years ago.

In this kind of environment, the Silicon Valley tech boom notwithstanding, it is less a matter of New Economy/old economy (or even the so-called "digital divide"), as it is rich economy/poor economy. It was this concern over the ever greater gaps between the world's richest people and its poorest that motivated many of the protests at the World Trade Organization meeting in Seattle in December 1999. There was a sense that many workers were being left out of the corporate prosperity that was the goal of global free trade. "I think you have to be careful in an economy that everybody shares in it," says Andersen's Mark Jensen. "You can't exclude one group or another because it doesn't work long term. If most of your population is not participating in this new wealth creation, it's going to be devastating."

## The Real Estate Bubble

The rising rents in Silicon Valley are representative of another problem, a growing real estate bubble. Driven by the dotcom gold rush and the promise of lucrative stock options, housing prices were bid up some 60 percent in the San Francisco Bay Area over a three-year period into November 2000, with a resulting median price of $390,000. In Santa Clara County, the heart of Silicon Valley, the median price for a home stood at $510,000, a 70 percent increase since January 1998. North of San Francisco, Marin County reached a $600,000 median price. Only about 18 percent of Bay Area households could afford to buy a median-priced, single-family home. The market became so inflated that *San Francisco* magazine reported that staffers at real estate agency Pacific Union asked potential buyers to sign what they privately called the "Idiot Letter," which warned buyers that they were entering the market at their own risk.

"There's no guarantee that these high prices will be sustainable," the letter read.

"Real estate markets are cyclical. Anyone who suggests otherwise is drunk on his own equity," said Brad Inman, CEO of Homegain. "In the end, it is supply and demand. For now, we have more demand than supply, but things can change quickly." As a result of limited supply, bidding on homes was not unusual, and if there were equal bids for a property, sellers sometimes asked would-be owners if they had any stock they could throw in to sweeten the deal. Silicon Valley landlords, meanwhile, were demanding stock from high-tech start-ups that wanted to lease office space. Karl Case, a professor of economics at Wellesley College and an expert on real estate trends said of the Bay Area, "Few markets have an expectational bubble going like this one."

A study released in September 2000 by the Federal Reserve Bank of San Francisco corroborated the connection between rising home prices and high-tech stock prices in the Bay Area. The study reported that over the previous five years, the total market capitalization of the high-tech sector in the Bay Area had grown by 470 percent, to a staggering $2.6 trillion. Out of that growth, a definite "wealth effect" had spread to real estate prices in the Bay Area. The study concluded that each 10 percent rise in the combined market value of Bay Area high-tech firms equates roughly to a 1 percent to 2 percent increase in home prices over two years.

In the second quarter of 2000, 17 percent of Bay Area home buyers used the sale of stock or stock options as the primary source of their down payment. That was down from 24 percent in the first quarter. Even in the midst of a sinking stock market, some buyers continued with the home purchase, hoping their stock would go up, only to find themselves in a buying predicament when it did not.

Although overvalued real estate is only one piece of the puzzle in the midst of the Internet Bubble, as an inflated asset it is reminiscent of the larger asset bubble that set up the Japanese economy for a fall a decade ago. In 1990 Japan's Nikkei stock index stood at 39,000 and its property index at 20,600. Japanese companies were on top of the world, and some American companies even called for protectionist measures against Japanese imported goods and technology. However, Japan's economic miracle was based on a vast asset bubble, further inflated by leveraged speculation on the part of banks and corporations, as well as by low interest rates, an appreciating currency, and lax accounting rules.

Japan's bubble economy (called *baburu* in Japan) was first and foremost a real estate bubble. As Edward Chancellor points out in his fascinating history of financial speculation, *Devil Take the Hindmost*, land prices in Japan increased 5,000 percent between 1956 and 1986. By 1990, the total Japanese property market was valued at over 2,000 trillion yen, or four times the real estate of the entire United States. Assuming that land prices would only continue to go up, Japanese banks provided loans against real estate as collateral. This banking practice became the engine for the creation of credit in the whole economy.

Alongside the real estate boom, stocks became a national preoccupation. The massive flow of Japanese savings into the stock market combined with a scarcity of shares to drive up prices. In the second half of the 1980s, approximately 8 million new investors entered the Japanese stock market, bringing the total number to about 22 million. About a third of the private investors held their stocks in margin accounts.

This bubble economy promoted a massive increase in consumer spending, based on a wealth effect from rising land and stock prices. The Japanese took out new loans against the equity of their homes, and consumer debt per capita rose to American levels.

The Japanese began purchasing high-profile U.S. assets, such as the Exxon building in Manhattan (for a record price of $610 million), New York's Rockefeller Center, and Hollywood's Columbia Pictures. Also snapped up was the Pebble Beach resort of hotels and golf courses in California for $831 million. Japanese property developers bought most of the golf courses in Hawaii and made plans to develop more there.

The Japanese also went crazy on the international art market, beginning with the purchase in spring 1987 (by an insurance company) of van Gogh's "Sunflowers" for $40 million, a figure three times greater than had ever before been paid for a painting. Not long after, a wealthy Japanese tycoon paid $51.4 million for a Picasso. "The billion-dollar binge" continued when a few months later a paper manufacturer paid $82.5 million for van Gogh's "Portrait of Dr. Gachet" and $78 million for a Renoir.

Expensive golf club memberships became a sign of status in Japanese society. The cost of joining the exclusive Koganei Country Club in Tokyo got as high as 400 million yen (approximately $2.7 million). Over twenty clubs cost more than $1 million to join. The total value of these golf club memberships in Japan was estimated at $200 billion. Banks provided margin loans of up to 90 percent against the collateral of club membership certificates. These certificates were also used to raise money to invest in the stock market.

But not all was well in Japan's paradise even before the bubble burst. "Rising asset prices and the unevenly divided spoils of speculation created egregious disparities of wealth," writes Chancellor. "The fortunes of the richest fifth of the population quadrupled during the bubble years, while those of the poorest fifth actually declined. . . . It appeared that most of the bubble's profits accrued to insiders, while outsiders shouldered all the losses." He adds, "The bubble was seen as eroding the work ethic by severing the connection between labor and reward."

When the bubble finally popped in January of 1990, it set off a chain reaction that led to a recession in which the country is still mired. Economist Paul Ormerod calls it "the second most serious recession in capitalist history after the 1929 Crash." By late 1992 property prices in central Tokyo had fallen 60 percent from their peak. They continued falling throughout the 1990s. And despite the rise of the Japanese stock market in the 1980s, the average private investor made little money. "He remained an outsider, fodder for the brokers and their favoured clients," says Chancellor.

Not surprisingly, the sell-off of high-priced assets followed the deflation in property values and the stock market. In early 1992,

Pebble Beach was sold off at a loss of more than $300 million. Meanwhile the domestic Japanese Golf Membership Index had sunk by more than 50 percent from its peak. Many famous art pieces the Japanese had bought at auction simply disappeared.

In the first quarter of 1999, Japan's gross domestic product finally rose for the first time since 1997, gaining 1.9 percent from the last quarter of 1998, and the Nikkei index went up more than 480 points to over 17,000. But this was largely the result of a massive $800 billion spending program by the Japanese government designed to goad the economy into action. In the next twelve months Japan experienced a growth rate of 4.2 percent, with some signs of growth in consumer spending, but still most of this growth was the result of government outlays. In the second quarter of 2000 there was a 13.6 percent increase in government spending. These outlays would have to be replenished by the government through additional borrowing. Japan had already borrowed record amounts of money to finance public-works projects designed to stimulate the economy.

"When the bubble burst in Japan there were a lot of industries with 30 percent excess capacity, and not enough demand," says Robert Madsen, a financial consultant in Japan and a fellow at Stanford University's Asia/Pacific Research Center. "That's why the government's fiscal spending packages couldn't get Japan out of its recession. The government couldn't possibly spend enough over time to burn that much excess." By 2000, according to the Economist Intelligence Unit, a business and politics consultancy, Japan's national debt was equal to 120 percent of its gross domestic product. Corporate bankruptcies also continued to pile up, achieving a level of more than $100 billion in debt in the first half of fiscal 2000, which began April 1. More than 75 percent of the 9,400-plus bankruptcies were caused by factors such as weak sales and difficulties in debt collection.

Fortunately, the U.S. economy is not an exact replica of Japan's. A burst or deflated real estate bubble in the United States, especially if largely limited to high-tech regions, would not necessarily set in motion an economic depression as it has in Japan. Nevertheless, by summer 2000, largely because of high real estate prices and expensive mortgages, Silicon Valley had the highest outstanding debt per household in the nation at $96,643. Subtracting out mortgage debt put Silicon Valley at number 31, with an average outstanding balance of $14,400.

The buying binge also spread to other big-ticket items such as automobiles. The newly affluent accounted for 60 percent of the spending on cars, according to General Motors. Not surprisingly, these purchases were of larger, more expensive vehicles. These affluent buyers were also purchasing more automobiles per person. Selling third and fourth automobiles to high-income families had become one of the fastest-growth segments of the auto industry. But because high-income families are more likely to be heavily invested in stocks, this made the auto industry much more dependent on the vagaries of the stock market. David L. Littmann, the senior economist at Comerica Bank in Detroit, said a 10 percent drop in the three-month moving average of the Wilshire 5000 stock index produced a 14 percent drop in auto sales, and would continue to do so unless automakers offset the impact by offering deep discounts.

Meanwhile, some overspent Silicon Valley residents were employing devices beyond their paychecks to pay their mortgages, including using credit cards, cashing in stock, and raiding their 401(k) plans. Overall delinquency and foreclosure rates were low precisely because home prices were rising. Historically, when home prices are rising, owners do anything to hold on to their houses because they are appreciating assets. When home prices start to depreciate, the debt picture changes. "Clearly there would be a problem if there were a major recession, a decline in the stock market, or the housing market," said Lynn Reaser, chief economist for Bank of America.

John Krainer, the Federal Reserve economist who coauthored the tech stock and housing correlation study, predicts that if the Bay Area's technology market falls, then home prices will also plummet. Home prices, he said, will fall over time by the same rate as they have risen—1 percent to 2 percent for every 10 percent loss in the tech stocks' market value. This in turn might force many formerly paper-rich dotcom workers and executives, as well as others in high tech, to walk away from mortgages they can no longer afford, even as some had to in 1988–89 when Bay Area real estate prices fell with a bang. A repeat of this late '80s scenario would mean the real estate balloon will have drifted back to earth to take its place next to a deflated Internet Bubble.

## Is There a Long Boom?

In spite of the income gaps and asset bubbles, the cyber-barons of technology's Gilded Age like to talk about the Long Boom. We live in a golden era, they assert, because the old rules of business and investment no longer apply, inflation is dead, technology is boosting productivity, and the classic business cycles are less relevant, maybe even obsolete. This is the Long Boom that will last for decades to come. Every day, and in every way, things will only get better.

It is true that the business climate in the United States in recent years has been extraordinary. The economy has been unusually good, with almost no inflation and employment at a record high. Much of the credit goes to deregulation of business, increased efficiency and innovation, and effective corporate restructuring for competition in global markets. As Herb Allen Jr. of investment bank Allen & Co. says, "The streamlining and tightening up of American business over the last ten years has paid off."

But there's no reason to believe that cyclical business patterns have gone away. "I think people sometimes confuse sections of the business cycle with a new paradigm," says Allen. "We are in a cycle, probably the tail end of a bull market. To take that piece of the cycle and turn it into a standard for a new society is dangerous." Dan Case, chairman and CEO of investment bank Chase H&Q, concurs. "We don't believe business cycles have gone away, and we completely disagree with people who say they have."

So where does this notion of the Long Boom come from? In some ways it has always been part of America, usually driven by booms or manias—the building of the transcontinental railroads, the bull market of the 1920s, or the Great Society optimism of the 1960s.

"For the last five years we have been in a new industrial era in this country. We are making progress industrially and economically not even by leaps and bounds, but on a perfectly heroic scale," wrote *Forbes* magazine in June of 1929, four months before America's stock market crashed.

"As a result of what has been happening in the economy during the last decade, we are in a different—if not a new—era, and traditional thinking, the standard approach to the market, is no longer in synchronization with the real world," wrote *Forbes* in October 1968, just before the onset of a six-year decline that sliced 60 percent off stock prices in real terms.

During bull markets, Americans typically expect the market to go up and stay up, perhaps indefinitely; we like to say that the economy is simply adjusting to a new situation, a new world of greatly, even infinitely increasing returns.

It's true that stock market performance has become more heavily weighted toward technology. In the 1990s the Standard & Poor 500 stock index was increasingly dominated by technology and telecommunications stocks, as well as by stocks in areas heavily impacted by technology such as financial services. While stocks such as Gateway, Yahoo, and America Online were added to the S&P Index, older stocks such as Pennzoil–Quaker State and Safety-Kleen were dropped. In the first quarter of 1999, four stocks—Microsoft, America Online, Cisco, and MCI Worldcom—accounted for almost 50 percent of the performance of the S&P 500. From 1995, the S&P 500 stock index tripled and the tech-dominated NASDAQ composite rose fivefold.

And it's also true that much of the growth in the American economy has become increasingly technocentric. Technology enthusiasts like to point out that in 1998, U.S. technology industries generated revenues of $955 billion, and 37 percent of all new jobs were tech related. Over the last three years, technology industries contributed one-third of the growth of the gross domestic product.

Because of technology's larger role, proponents of the presumed Long Boom have argued that there's a new economic paradigm. Throughout the 1970s and 1980s, worker productivity grew at the lackluster average annual rate of about 1.3 percent. In the late 1990s, it increased to an average of about 2.5 percent annually, with a notable spike to about 5.2 percent in the last half of 1999 and first half of 2000, according to the United States Department of Labor. But the glowing 5.2 percent figure may be illusory. In doing its calculations, the Labor Department used "New Economy" accounting and decided to calculate the purchase of software as an investment rather than an expense. Otherwise the productivity increase was closer to 3.5 percent.

And even that figure is subject to debate. Economists disagree on how extensive productivity gains have been, especially as a result of information technology. Stephen Slifer (the chief U.S. economist at Lehman Brothers) believes that the U.S. economy can continue to grow at an annual rate of 4.5 percent for some years to come, without risking higher inflation, thanks to the higher productivity that has come from computing and information technology. "About every 100 years, something really big happens, and this is it," says Slifer.

Robert Gordon (an economist at Northwestern University), on the other hand, says that the productivity gains are from computer manufacturing. He argues that if one subtracts certain parts of the economy, such as the production of computers and telecommunications equipment, the productivity miracle disappears.

Productivity is calculated by adding up all the output of an economy, expressed in dollars, and then dividing by the number of labor hours spent to produce that output. The problem, according to Stephen Roach, chief economist at Morgan Stanley Dean Witter, is that recent calculations are skewed because the number of labor hours, especially for white-collar and service-industry jobs, are underreported or underestimated. For example, in making its productivity calculation, the U.S. Department of Labor assumes that people who have salaried jobs work a mere forty hours a week. But other studies have shown that white-collar workers typically labor for fifty, sixty, or even seventy hours per week.

So these shifts in the American economy and stock market do not necessarily signal a Long Boom. Venture capitalist John Shoch of Alloy Ventures terms the Long Boom "a reality-distortion field," but he also admits that "even though many of us know this is going to end, we can't help going along for the ride."

In fact by the end of 2000, it appeared that the ride was over. There were already clear signs of a slowdown, and even a possible recession in 2001. An economic study released in March 2001 by the Anderson business school at UCLA forecast a 90 percent chance of a national recession in the United States in 2001. A recession was defined as two quarters in a row of negative growth, or shrinkage. All the key factors that gave rise to earlier recessions seemed to be falling into place: rising unemployment, a tight credit environment, fewer investment opportunities, and reduced capital spending by corporations, including technology purchases. Other corporate trouble signs included missed earnings, revised growth projections, and more debt. The declining stock market, meanwhile, was discouraging companies from raising money by issuing stock. Venture capitalists had become more cautious. Consumer spending had slowed.

Economist Stephen Roach was troubled by the sudden steep nature of the economic slowdown. "As recently as the second quarter of 2000, the year-over-year growth rate of real GDP in America was 6.1 percent," Roach said in December. "That rate by the middle of 2001 will be about 1.9 percent, a 4.2-percentage-point deceleration." By March 2001, Roach noted the $5.3 trillion asset deflation over the past year. He likened the situation to the boom-bust cycles of the late 1800s and early 1900s.

## The Overworked American

In 1992 Harvard economist Juliet B. Schor published a book titled *The Overworked American*. Although her research and methods were sometimes debated, her best-seller definitely struck an emotional chord with American readers.

Not much has changed since then; Americans still experience a time squeeze, and they know it. The average worker worked 148 more hours in 1996 than his 1973 counterpart, a total of four weeks longer. The percentage of people working more than forty-nine hours per week has risen from 13 percent in 1976 to almost 19 percent in 1998, according to the U.S. Bureau of Labor Statistics. Forty-five percent of managers work more than forty-nine hours per week. And some economists, such as Stephen Roach, consider the bureau's accounting conservative—that, in fact, the percentage is probably much higher.

Venture capitalist John Doerr says, "We are experiencing extreme time famine. Everybody is short of time. And time is the most precious commodity in our connected, competitive world."

If anything, information technology has contributed to this famine rather than alleviating it. In the current information age, people are online in many parts of the information economy twenty-four hours a day, seven days a week. That's not increasing productivity; it's extending the workday.

Ironically, the white-collar professionals who most use information technology—laptop computers, cellular phones, fax machines, Internet connections, pagers—also work the longest hours. Some of these professionals end up checking electronic mail at midnight or writing memos on Sunday morning. On average, these people put in 50.8 hours per week. As one of them expressed it, "Maybe technology has put us back to an earlier era before vacations and two-day weekends came into existence." Far from being the paradise of the Long Boom scenario, the New Economy is sometimes a connected world workers can't escape. Venture capitalist Michael Moritz summarizes it best: "I think the only sure thing about technology is that it makes it harder to escape work."

## The New Growth View

Rejecting the Long Boom scenario of accelerated economic growth doesn't mean being an outright economic pessimist, especially with the view that new growth is possible.

One of the main proponents of this view is Stanford University economist Paul Romer. Some of the Long Boom enthusiasts have attempted to identify him with their position, but he eschews it. "I don't agree with the unqualified Long Boom assertion that the rate of technological change in America is permanently faster than it has been historically, or that the underlying rate of growth of the economy has increased in the last ten years," Romer says.

He points out that the Long Boomers look at indicators such as asset prices, inflation, and unemployment more than they look at productivity growth or the rate of growth per worker. He also asserts that the data doesn't support the idea that technology has automatically increased worker productivity.

Romer does believe that the American economy is driven by complexity, that the physical, social, and technological systems created are much more complicated than those we've had in the past. And that there's a corresponding demand for the education and skills necessary to cope with these higher levels of complexity. Thus, the widening income gap between haves and have-nots is in part attributable to the difference in their level of education and skill sets.

But the new complexity should not be identified with any particular technology, like the internal combustion engine, electricity, digital electronics, or the Internet. These developments are just manifestations of complexity.

Over the last 125 years in America, complexity and steady growth have gone hand in hand, as our society has learned to generate more and more value from relatively consistent amounts of physical raw material. Productivity is not necessarily in a holding pattern it can't break out of, but it's also not in the hypergrowth mode that the Long Boomers would like to believe. "I keep saying that if we make fundamental institutional innovations, we could grow faster. But the Long Boomers keep hearing that we are already growing faster," says Romer.

New Growth theory does examine the dynamics of wealth creation and the role of scientific discovery, technological change, and innovation as important factors contributing to productivity growth. Economic growth occurs whenever people discover new ways to take existing resources and make them more useful. Romer likens this process to cooking. "We develop recipes to rearrange raw materials to make them more valuable," he says. "People did that in the Bronze Age when they mixed copper and tin, and later when they learned to use interchangeable parts as well as refine iron ore and petroleum. Cooking is what Intel does when it takes silicon and makes it into a chip. That process has always been with us—it's a continuum."

The difference today is that more people-hours go into producing the recipes than into the cooking. We are steadily shifting more resources into coming up with better recipes, and the recipes now drive economic growth and improve standards of living.

New Growth identifies three special features that spur growth: first, a physical world with vastly unexplored possibilities; second, cooperation and trade among large numbers of people; third, market incentives for people to make discoveries and share information.

Nevertheless, there's a tendency to overestimate the refined, high-end part of technological change and to underestimate the grassroots benefits. Romer believes Wal-Mart is a better example of innovation than the transistor—because the discount retailer's management of inventory data represents a major technological change in the process of getting goods from the factory to the consumer. Its system allows it to chart sales precisely and keep shelves efficiently stocked at its 3,600 outlets worldwide. By gaining finely honed knowledge of inventory, distribution, and its customer base, Wal-Mart can operate its supply chain in a way that is 15 to 20 percent cheaper than before. And when a whole class of goods can be provided much more cheaply, it significantly improves the standard of living for people in the United States. This exemplifies the broad improvements in recipes that keep the whole economy going.

In terms of standards of living or output per person, the last century and a quarter shows a pretty surprisingly steady rate of growth— a ninefold increase in income per capita (see chart on page 228).

There are some peaks and dips—a big drop in the 1930s and a surge during World War II, for example. But in the larger view, those are just wiggles on the line graph, although the dips seemed like the end of the world at the time. In the long run, it matters more how fast the trend increases than whether the economy is in a bit of a downturn at the beginning of a wiggle or in an upturn coming out of a wiggle.

### U.S. GDP Per Capita

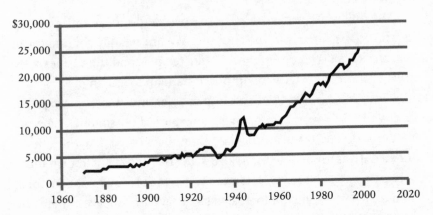

"These people who make exaggerated claims for the New Economy or the Long Boom have mistaken a positive upturn in one of those wiggles for a sign that trends have completely changed," says Romer. "If anything, in terms of growth rates, it's actually been a little bit low. I'm looking at this trend and saying: 'No sign that we've done anything better than in the last 100 years; it's just business as usual.'"

So there's actually nothing extraordinary about the most recent economic expansion, including the recent improvements in productivity since 1996. To Romer it looked like another case of an overreaction to temporary events. "In the 1980s, high inflation and a recession convinced many people that the U.S. economy had completely lost its capacity for generating growth," he says. "In the late '90s, low inflation and a recovery from a recession convinced many of these same people that the U.S. economy was generating growth in new and unprecedented ways."

He argues that the underlying trend rate of growth for the entire economy does not change from decade to decade. Superimposed on top of this steady growth in income and productivity are the temporary wiggles that economists refer to as recessions and recoveries. The slow growth of a recession and the fast growth of a recovery always converge back toward the underlying trend rate of growth. "Because asset returns and output move together, the economy can go through periods where asset returns are unusually low or unusually high, but they typically return to historical averages." If people value companies on the assumption that the slow growth of a recession will last forever, they are in for a pleasant surprise. If they value them on the assumption that the fast growth of a recovery will last forever, they are in for a shock.

Economic history shows that people make mistakes and are caught by surprise. In extreme cases these mistakes take the form of a bubble. Naturally, anything that takes a lot of air out of these bubbles poses a serious threat to the viability of concept companies not grounded on solid business fundamentals. The result has been a Darwinian shakeout. It will take a sound investment strategy to survive and prosper in the midst of the shakeout and the aftermath of the Bubble.

# Doonesbury

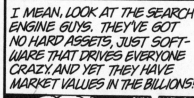

# CULT IPOS, SCAMS, AND OTHER HAZARDS OF INTERNET INVESTING

**These valuations are breathtaking. I don't recommend Internet stocks to people who don't like massive risk. People are jumping into the market like it's a gold rush.**

—**Bill Gates, chairman, Microsoft Corporation**

**B**ill Gates made the above remark to us when the Internet Bubble was at its peak. Even a seasoned tech executive and billionaire like Gates was astounded by the speculative frenzy surrounding Internet stocks. Indeed in a bubble market, greed and the herd mentality can take over, and with them comes the tendency to gamble heavily, fall prey to scams, and get burned by IPO stocks. This has never been more true than in technology's recent Gilded Age, which seemed to promise quick wealth for so many. It was easy to underestimate just how much risk was involved.

This chapter will provide some perspective on investing in technology stocks in the midst and aftermath of such massive risk, which we've called the Internet Bubble. We'll cover several investment caveats, including the pitfalls of momentum investing, the dangers of overconfidence in approaching the stock market, the growing incidence of Internet investment scams, and the pitfalls of investing in IPOs. The bottom line is that playing the Internet and high-tech investment game is not as easy as it sometimes looks. Read on and find out what to watch out for.

## The Dangers of Momentum Investing

Hot bull markets are full of momentum investing, another way of saying "buy high and sell higher." Ultimately, momentum investors are looking for the greater fool who will pay more for the stock than they did. It's really a form of gambling.

"The danger is if you're the last guy in the game and you turn out to be the greater fool," says Bruce Lupatkin, former head of research at Hambrecht & Quist and a longtime technology analyst. "I say, don't try to play the greater fool game; there's an enormous amount of risk." He adds, "It's always 'buyer beware.' Who out there says that 30 percent, 40 percent, 50 percent returns are guaranteed without risk? Nobody can say that. There's no free lunch; there never has been."

This kind of gambling makes investors particularly susceptible to torpedo stocks—the overpriced speculative issues whose prospects have been heavily hyped but are primed for a disastrous plunge that could ruin any portfolio. It's even worse when investors speculate on margin, investing with borrowed money.

Investors and day traders sometimes set each other up for this fall when hyping certain stocks themselves. Online investor message boards and chat rooms at The Motley Fool, Yahoo, and Silicon Investor were alive with the chatter of traders swapping tips. Where online investors were once caught up in supposedly hot stock issues such as Boston Chicken, The Discovery Zone, or mini-disk-drive maker Iomega, now it was any number of Internet stocks. People who didn't understand the Internet, who didn't know fundamentally what it was, gave each other investment advice.

Old-line money managers were always skeptical. Barton Biggs, chairman of Morgan Stanley Asset Management, told the *New York Times* in May 1999, "Individual investors should not be deluded by advertisements that suggest that any amateur can make money in the stock market. We are perpetuating a gambling mentality similar to the 1920s. Fifteen thousand new Internet trading accounts open every week. That is frightening." In a later interview, Biggs's colleague Byron Wien added, "People are trying too hard; they're impatient. They tend to migrate to where the action is, which is what creates the volatility."

And indeed many of these novice investors got caught up in the speculative frenzy of the last quarter of 1999 and the first quarter of 2000. It was like a grand game of musical chairs, driven by incredible momentum in the tech stock market. But when the music suddenly stopped in April, many speculators, especially those investing on margin, found themselves without a chair to sit in. The dotcom shakeout in particular wiped out almost $800 billion in Internet company stock market value, and many investors had to sell at a loss to meet margin calls.

## The Perils of Overconfidence

It's not unusual for aggressive investors to have little knowledge of what they invest in, concluded a study done at the Johnson Graduate School of Management at Cornell University. Investors given one bit of financial data about a company—the expected rate of growth for return on equity—felt just as confident in their investing as those investors who had also been given the book value and current return on equity of a company. The danger, the study stated, is that people vastly overestimate the value of what little information they have and will more likely blunder by buying stocks at high prices and then having to sell out when the stocks drop.

Such ignorant yet aggressive investing helps drive up fashionable stocks to grossly overvalued levels. Robert Bloomfield, the director of the Cornell study, states, "People are not good at figuring out how good the information is. The information keeps getting louder, but it's not more reliable."

And while self-confidence and optimism can be strong personal qualities when dealing with people, they don't necessarily help in the stock market, where investors deal with prices, not people. Overconfident investors tend to trade too much and bet too heavily on particular stocks or market sectors. Not surprisingly, trading volume tends to be higher in eras of high returns—and overconfident investors think a fatter portfolio means they are smarter.

At the height of the speculative frenzy, investors were turning over their portfolios at a rate of more than 60 percent per year. More than half of this trading was unjustified—it was just noise, not resulting in any gain for the investor and opening the way for more losses. In fact, according to a study done at the University of California at Davis, the more investors trade, the worse they do. Investors err in fairly consistent ways: (1) They react too much to short-term performance; (2) they overestimate their chances of success with long-shot investments like IPOs and risky tech stocks; (3) they think they see patterns in stock market returns where there are none; and (4) they sell winners too quickly and hold on to losers too long.

"The more you trade, the more poor decisions you potentially make," says Terrance Odean, one of the authors of the UC Davis study. "And then you pay for that privilege through trading costs." This trend is aggravated by the tendency of new online traders to trade twice as much as they did before they went online. Buying and selling in an instant, they trade too quickly and too often without understanding the risks involved.

The frequency of stock trading definitely impacted the market as a whole. "In the market's run from 3,000 to 8,000, a lot of the upward movement occurred because people were invested in mutual funds and were not apt to sell very quickly," Charles Geisst, a finance professor at Manhattan College and author of *Wall Street: A History,* told the *New York Times.* "It's no coincidence that as Internet trading became more common, the market became more volatile."

Meanwhile, according to an educational Web site, onlinetradingacademy.com, of the estimated 12.5 million online investors in the United States in 2000, only about 50,000 profited by it.

## Creative Accounting

Complicating matters for amateur investors is that many Internet start-ups have used creative accounting methods to make their top-line revenue numbers look much stronger than they really are. One common practice is the bartering or swapping of ads between online companies. With this deceptive practice, two online companies agree to run each other's ads for free, and then each company counts the other's ads as revenue. Since revenues are often the key determination of stock value, strong revenue growth usually translates into higher stock prices. "Virtually everyone who was depending on advertising support for revenue was doing it to varying degrees," says Patrick Hurley, vice president of marketing for Salon.com, a San Francisco Internet media company. Barter accounts for more than 15 percent of all Internet ad revenues, some analysts estimate. Most companies that include barter deals in their reported revenue do not mention the practice in their earnings news releases. Only by reading far into a company's quarterly report would an investor find disclosures about such transactions.

Another misleading practice is the emphasis on gross revenues rather than net revenues as the main indicator of a company's financial health. This practice shows up in the way e-tail companies account for shipping and handling costs. Although there is variation across the industry, some online merchants like Amazon.com and the now bankrupt eToys listed such costs under their marketing budgets, a practice that inflates gross margins. This is particularly telling for those companies that do not have any positive earnings, because gross margins are the main way investors have found to measure e-tailers' health. Eliminating this practice would have caused gross margins to drop to 10 percent from 20 percent at Amazon, and to negative percentages for eToys, PlanetRx, and Drugstore.com, according to Holly Becker, an Internet analyst at Lehman Brothers.

In another twist on the gross revenue measure, Priceline.com, the online travel booking company, recorded as "gross revenues" the full price of airline tickets and hotel rooms it brokered rather than just the piece they made off of each transaction. Similarly, the B2B chemical exchange Ventro reported $75 million as its "total revenue" for the four quarters ending March 31, 2000, and $25 million as the "total revenue" for one quarter ending June 30, 2000. These figures were actually gross revenue figures representing the total value of the transactions that flowed through Ventro's exchange, as opposed to the net revenue, which represents the actual fees the company collected. In the supposed $25 million revenue quarter, the net revenue was actually $1.8 million. The bottom line was that the 500-person company had in fact managed to lose $33.1 million for that quarter.

All of this means that, like analyst reports from the investment banks, financial statements from dotcoms are best taken with a grain of salt.

## THE INSIDER ADVANTAGE

In March 2000, the value of Internet stocks was a staggering $1.5 trillion, prompting famed venture capitalist John Doerr to state that we were witnessing "the greatest ever legal creation of wealth in the history of the world."

By December 2000, however, the market for Internet stocks had lost over $1 trillion from its March high. Someone was out a lot of money. And that someone was primarily the small retail investor. That's because the insiders—entrepreneurs, venture capital firms, investment banks, and large institutional investors—had pulled out their capital long before the fall, leaving mom and pop investors holding the bag.

Instead of the greatest ever legal creation of wealth, the Internet financial Bubble represented instead the greatest ever legal *transfer* of wealth—from retail investors to insiders. For example, between November 1998 and July 2000, Goldman Sachs, Morgan Stanley Dean Witter, and Crédit Suisse First Boston each pocketed more than $500 million in underwriting fees for Internet companies. According to Thomson Financial Securities Data, this was the most lucrative streak investment banks have ever seen in a single sector.

The fact is, little investors never stood a chance, because they simply don't have the same access to information as big investors. The "quiet period" mandated by the Securities and Exchange Commission, for example, requires a start-up to shun any publicity regarding its finances for at least three months before its initial public offering. The law was intended to keep a company from hyping its stock. That's a noble goal, but since a stock prospectus is issued weeks before an IPO, in reality all the law does is keep small investors in the dark.

Big institutional investors like Fidelity and Vanguard, on the other hand, are never in the dark. They're treated to what's known as a "road show" just days before an IPO. In this private meeting with company executives, institutional investors are updated on the start-up's current financial situation. So the big investors know if a stock has recently become more risky, and can pass on it. Or they may decide to buy it anyway, knowing they can resell the stock on the first day of trading before any bad news about the company is reported. This practice, known as "flipping," became very common in an era where Internet stocks were routinely tripling in value on their first day of trading.

Institutional investors weren't the only ones flipping stock during the recent hot market. Individual insiders were, too. During the Internet Bubble, investment banks would routinely give hot new IPO stocks—for free—to corporate executives, venture capitalists, and other decision makers sitting on the boards of companies whose business the banks wanted. These privileged decision makers would then flip their shares on the first day of the IPO for quick profits. And while the investment banks were giving out free stock to their favored clients, they were also giving out bad advice to their mom and pop customers. In their recent study of high-tech stocks, Roni Michaely of Cornell University and Kent Womack of Dartmouth College found that investment banks rarely downgrade a company's stock to a "sell" rating if they have a business relationship with the company. "There is a bias in brokers' recommendations when they have an underwriting affiliation with a company," says Michaely. "But the public doesn't recognize it." In fact, during the Internet Bubble, it wasn't unheard of for a bank to issue a "buy" recommendation on a stock that the bank's own fund managers were betting would drop.

But despite these shenanigans, the savvy retail investor could at least take comfort in Rule 144, the SEC regulation that bars a company's owners from selling their stock for up to two years after an IPO. (This type of stock is sometimes referred to as "locked stock.") So if the stock did tank six months after it was issued, at least the small investor could find solace knowing that the entrepreneur and his venture capital backers had taken a loss on their stock as well.

Or did they?

Actually, during the high-flying days of the dotcom bubble, few insiders were required to take risks. The investment banks devised a new financial service: they would promise to buy a venture capitalist's or tech executive's locked stock—but at the stock's higher early issue price. This special service for favored customers didn't cost the banks a thing, since they would then use a combination of sophisticated financial instruments they call a "collar" to short the stock. That is, the banks would make money if and when the stock dropped in value, which it almost always did. (During the last decade, 80 percent of new tech stocks were trading below their first day closing price within six months of their issue.)

Meanwhile *Red Herring* editor Eric Moskowitz discovered that it was not just venture capitalists and entrepreneurs who were taking advantage of clever financial instruments cooked up by ingenious bankers. High-profile CEOs and company directors were also hedging their portfolios by using zero-cost collars that enabled these insiders to save a boatload of cash while retail investors were left underwater. Such hedging actions is not a matter of public record and therefore information about them is not readily available to the average investor. The insiders wanted to use this clandestine collar method to climb out of their stock positions without drawing public attention to their financial moves and telegraphing their doubts about the current valuations of their companies' stock. Moskowitz learned that Microsoft cofounder Paul Allen, for example, collared more than 55 percent of his common Microsoft stock—over 83 million shares—from October 30, 2000, to November 17, 2000, thus saving himself $1.7 billion at the expense of other Microsoft shareholders. Others who indulged in this practice in 2000 included Dell Computer chairman and CEO Michael Dell and JDS Uniphase director William Sinclair.

The Internet Bubble and the larger tech bubble are already being compared to previous financial manias: Dutch tulips in the 1600s and U.S. railroads in the late 1800s. But what sets this most recent mania apart is its Ponzi scheme quality. Never before has so much wealth been transferred from one group of people to another in such a short time.

## Internet Scams

"In a boom, fortunes are made, individuals wax greedy, and swindlers come forward to exploit that greed. The sheep to be shorn abound," writes MIT economist Charles Kindleberger in his classic book *Manias, Panics, and Crashes.*

Some scamsters have used the Internet in the same way that con artists have used newspaper ads, the telephone, and other communication media to pitch their schemes. The old cold-calling method done from boiler rooms has given way to e-mail messages and Web sites that can reach millions of potential investors cheaply and instantly. The business of fraud has simply become more efficient.

On the Internet, it is much easier to get the word out about bogus get-rich-quick opportunities, hot stock "tips," and investments too good to be true.

One of the first online scams was Pleasure Time Inc., which in 1995 ran online advertisements promising investors that by paying $189 per share in a phantom company, they could enjoy a minimum profit of $60 a week. They were promised additional profits in return for signing up other investors. More than 20,000 investors got mixed up in this high-tech Ponzi scheme, putting a total of at least $3 million into it.

Other scamsters have engaged in the classic "pump and dump" scheme—they use online investor forums to pump up a stock by spreading positive but false information about a company, and then after fooled investors drive up the price of the stock, the scamsters and company insiders dump the inflated shares. Some have even gone so far as to create fake online magazines to promote these phony stocks. One middle manager for a telecommunications company, posing as someone else, actually created a fake news article about the takeover of the company and posted it on the Internet. The article caused the stock to spike up more than 30 percent before the announcement was exposed as a fraud.

Some online publications have been paid fees to publicize Internet companies but do not reveal that fact to investors, or the disclaimer is so far away from the stock tips that it's easy to miss. One publication, *Internet Stock Review,* published by a public relations firm, offered a list of "20 companies to watch in 1999" that included well-known names such as Borders Group and Federal Express, but also obscure companies such as Allnetservices and Dynamic Media.com, which paid the publication to promote them. The publication does publish a disclaimer on its Web site, but it is not located with the list, so even though the publication has done nothing illegal, the list could confuse investors.

Some scamsters have made a hobby out of fraudulent Internet IPOs. *Fortune* magazine reported one case of a phony high-tech start-up called Interactive Products and Services, which claimed it had revolutionary Internet devices it dubbed NetCaller and PC Remote. The company also claimed it had a partnership with Microsoft. None of these claims were true, but the phony company lured nearly 100,000 potential investors to its Web site by running at popular investor sites an online ad that read: "The next Microsoft is offering its stock to the public . . . over the Internet! . . . click here for more information."

Once at the Web site, visitors could read instructions on how to invest. Nearly 3,000 investors worldwide sent e-mail to the scamster, Matthew Bowin, and 150 people actually sent in checks. One investor from Hong Kong wired $10,000. In three months Bowin had collected $190,000 and got his ad displayed free by promising to pay for it after his IPO. He also set up the Web site so that when investors queried a search engine with the words "Internet stocks," his Web page would come up on its list of choices. Fortunately, Bowin was caught, convicted of fraud, and received a ten-year prison term.

Given this environment, it's no surprise that the SEC receives about 300 complaints a day concerning online scams, up from only 15 per day in 1996. The Federal Trade Commission said it received 18,600 consumer complaints of Internet fraud in 1999, compared with fewer than 1,000 just two years before. For the first six months of 2000, the FTC received 11,000 complaints.

## America's Most Wanted

In mid-2000, Internet fraud took a different twist when the criminal connections of two Internet start-up CEOs were exposed, demonstrating a woeful lack of due diligence on the part of the companies' founding investors. This lack of background checking ultimately hurt all the investors in the company. A third scandal involved previously successful entrepreneurs who, as it turned out, also had checkered pasts.

First there was David Kim Stanley, who founded Pixelon, a company that licenses software to play video over the Internet. But Stanley had founded the company under the assumed name of

Michael Adam Fenne in an attempt to cover up his criminal past. It turns out that Stanley was a fugitive who had spent four years on the run after fleecing elderly victims out of $1.25 million. By the time Stanley was exposed in June 2000, he had already been removed from the company after spending $11 million of Pixelon's $23 million in start-up funds on an extravagant launch party in Las Vegas that featured the rock band The Who.

In his scheme against the elderly, Stanley had promised investors a 300 percent return, but no dividends were ever paid. He was convicted in 1989 on fifty-three counts of fraud. In 1996, he suddenly stopped paying restitution and fled.

Pixelon investors had no idea about Stanley's background. "They didn't check Stanley out. That's all there is to it," said Ian Sitren, an Orange County–based private investigator with nineteen years' experience in corporate investigations.

Pixelon was forced into bankruptcy proceedings just after Stanley's arrest. Layoffs had cut the number of employees from more than 100 to 15. The news of the arrest also raised questions over the video software Stanley said he had invented. Advanced Equities Inc., a Chicago venture-capital firm that sank about $40 million into Pixelon, was trying to save the company and recoup its money.

Around the same time as the Pixelon scandal, an online security firm called Cyberbuck was also exposed to infamy because of a founder with a criminal past. Tony Mazzamuto, the cofounder and president of Cyberbuck Corp., had served three years in prison for possessing three pounds of cocaine for sale, and for carrying a gun when he had a prior felony conviction. He was paroled in 1994. The board of directors and the investors who had funneled nearly $1 million into Cyberbuck apparently knew nothing of Mazzamuto's checkered past. Mazzamuto had also manufactured his educational history, saying he had college degrees he didn't possess. He initially said he had master's degrees from UCLA and the University of Colorado at Greeley. Neither school has a record of his attendance. In fact, there is no University of Colorado at Greeley.

When Mazzamuto's criminal record finally came to light, the board of directors forced him to resign. Cyberbuck was considering an initial public offering in 2001, an event that would have forced the company to disclose the chief executive's criminal convictions.

A third scandal involved Digital Entertainment Network (DEN), an Internet video company that burned through $60 million of investor money in two years, under the management of former chairman Marc Collins-Rector and cofounders Chad Shackley and Brock Pierce. The company ended up in bankruptcy.

At its peak, DEN had more than 300 employees and boasted of investments by Microsoft, Dell Computer, NBC, and other major technology and entertainment companies. The company won national attention for its pioneering and ambitious strategy of putting youth-oriented video programming on its Web site.

But turnover at the company was high, and a number of staffers felt uncomfortable because of the overlapping business and social lives of the three founders, who lived together on a multimillion-dollar southern California estate. Some employees were asked to work at the mansion instead of at DEN's main offices, and others were asked to accompany the three on vacations.

The three founders left the company in fall 1999 after Collins-Rector settled a sex molestation suit by a teen who had worked at his previous company, Concentric Research. (Longtime partners Collins-Rector and Shackley cofounded Concentric in 1991 and made millions when they sold control to other investors.) Then in July 2000, a former employee of DEN sued the bankrupt company and its three founders, accusing them of inducing him into sexual relationships after hiring him as a fifteen-year-old actor.

In early 2001 the FBI had Collins-Rector, Shackley, and Pierce under surveillance overseas in connection with further allegations of drugging, molesting, raping, and issuing death threats against both adults and minors, according to the FBI and two private attorneys representing the victims. Meanwhile a California court had entered a $4.5 million default judgment against the DEN founders and the company following their failure to contest a civil suit making claims on behalf of three former DEN employees, one of whom was the fifteen-year-old boy.

Even more shocking was the announcement in late July that the doors of another Internet start-up, ClickMed.com, had to be shut because its founder and CEO, Boston-area cosmetic surgeon Dr. Richard Sharpe, could no longer run the company. Sharpe had just been convicted of brutally murdering his wife.

In fact, a study done by Kroll Associates, a corporate securities company, found that executives at Internet firms were four times more likely to have "unsavory backgrounds" than executives at traditional companies. Kroll researched the backgrounds of seventy U.S., European, and Asian Internet executives and board members over a six-month period in 2000. Past misdemeanors included problems with the U.S. Securities and Exchange Commission, insurance fraud, bankruptcies, and even links to organized crime.

All of these cases and studies are sobering reminders of how the lack of due diligence on the part of venture capitalists can backfire on all the investors in a company. When a company founder or CEO goes to jail, investors are often left with worthless stock.

## IPOs and Retail Cult Stocks

While most Internet speculators have not been victims of fraud or put money into scandalous companies, many have still been caught up in a big part of Internet mania—the purchase of hot initial public offerings. The problem, however, is that IPOs are generally not good investments for noninsiders. "The long-term performance of IPOs is bad," says Harvard business professor Bill Sahlman. "This has always been the case. The public always ends up holding the bag." Roger McNamee of Integral Capital Partners agrees: "High attrition rates are natural; it's the Darwinian process. If ever there was a caveat emptor of business, it's the IPO market." Steve Forbes, editor in chief of *Forbes* magazine, chimes in: "It's normal—most new businesses do not make it past their fifth year. The mortality rate is very high. So it's not a great surprise that the vast majority of IPOs would end in disappointment."

Data from investment bank Broadview International shows that of the 1,259 high-technology companies that went public from 1992 through mid-2000, 51 percent traded below their IPO values by the end of May 2000. And this assumes investors bought the IPOs at the initial offering price, something individuals rarely do. If the performance of these stocks is measured from the share price after the first day of trading, when most individuals can buy such stocks, then 70 to 80 percent of IPOs were underwater.

Paradoxically, this weak IPO performance came during a bull market. In fact, the safest time to buy high-technology IPOs is during years when fewer technology companies tap the equity market for capital. In other words, when the market is bearish on tech stocks, only the highest-quality stocks go public; these stocks are generally not as susceptible to momentum buying and therefore to extreme price volatility during these periods.

But no matter what the environment—good, bad, or indifferent—IPOs are a bad place for investors to focus their energy. "The real money in tech investing comes from correctly identifying the long-term winners, something much easier to do over the course of time than at the time of an IPO," says Integral's McNamee.

Nevertheless, during frothy bull markets, overvalued IPOs can evolve into what one investor calls "retail cult stocks." These are the go-go stocks, often with a small float, that get lots of publicity and experience heavy trading volume inside the Bubble. Unfortunately, since only 10 percent of Internet companies have any real long-term future, the Darwinian scenario means that the other Internet stocks were destined for serious devaluation or extinction. "High mortality rates are typical when you have missionary market building," says Harvard's Bill Sahlman.

In the midst of the Internet market froth, some were so eager to get in on hyped-up IPOs that they made the mistake of putting in market orders for these stocks at whatever price the market dic-

## Post-IPO Value Creation?

Median Annualized Returns Post-IPO

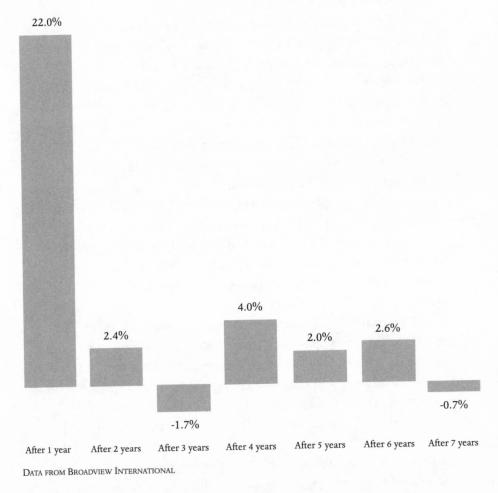

DATA FROM BROADVIEW INTERNATIONAL

tated. In most cases, these investors' buy orders got stacked up on the first day of trading, and when they were finally executed, it was generally at a price far above the initial issue price.

Many investors had this happen with the IPO for Theglobe.com. The issue price was $9 per share, but by midday it had risen to $90 per share. A number of first-time buyers got locked into this higher price, only to see the price slip to $63.50 per share by the end of the day. Two months after the IPO, the price was $37 per share. Some investors lost thousands of dollars on buy orders as low as 500 shares. One investor even racked up a bill of $200,000 for a buy order of 2,500 shares.

"Everybody has to remember that markets typically change direction when it's most inconvenient for the largest number of people," says Integral's McNamee. "In bubble markets, the most dangerous words for these overvalued stocks are, 'Look, I'm a long-term investor,' because if something structural changes in the market and stock prices drop, the amount of time it's going to take for gigastocks to get back to their peak valuations could be years or even a decade."

An overvalued company might be a great company, but it's still not a great investment until the industry settles in and the valuations are based on business fundamentals.

"If you look at the PC wave, the last time we saw a bubble like this, retail investors were largely absent," observes Frank Quattrone, managing director and head of the technology group at investment bank CS First Boston. "Retail investors have become more interested in the Internet because everybody thinks this is the next television or the next radio. And some investors feel in their heart of hearts that one or two or three of these companies will end up being the next Microsoft or Intel or Cisco. But nobody knows for sure who those companies are."

It was much the same situation when the first radio companies came along. In the first two decades of the twentieth century, investors who had missed out on the telephone felt they could still invest in radio, confident that, as an investment ad for a radio company pointed out, "all great discoveries which have brought civilized communities into close touch have made millions for those who attained an interest in them in the early stages of development." So investors bought anything involving radio. New radio companies offered what became the retail cult stocks of their day.

The radio industry's revenues jumped from $60 million in 1922 to $850 million in 1929—a 1,400 percent increase. At the same time, the value of a share of stock of Radio Corporation of America (RCA) increased from $5 per share to $500 per share. Nearly a third of American homes had radios in them, and the car radio had come along as well.

As with the wreckage of the PC boom, the majority of the hot radio manufacturers of the 1920s failed and are now forgotten. RCA was one of the few that actually turned a profit and survived, even as it branched into phonograph records and movies. Even so, investors who bought RCA stock in the summer of 1929 lost almost all their investment in the stock market crash. It was three decades before RCA got back to its precrash high in the midst of a new mania over television. The more things change, the more they stay the same.

# Doonesbury

# INVESTING IN THE TECHNOLOGY MARKET

> **There is no reason to believe that we need to throw out the fundamentals. Rather, we need to do a better job of applying the fundamentals more than anything else.**
> —James Collins, coauthor, *Built to Last*

**D**espite the pitfalls of public high-tech investing, many experts remain bullish on its prospects for the future. "The United States does two things better than the rest of the world—grow food and make technology products," says technology banker Sandy Robertson. "Our economy has transformed itself magnificently from a manufacturing economy to an information-technology-based economy. And with this transition comes a lot of new investment opportunities."

And the markets for technology have only grown. Twenty-five years ago, the largest buyer of technology was the government. Fifteen years ago, business became the biggest buyer. Eventually, consumers will pull ahead of both of them, even as the government and businesses continue to buy. The end markets will just keep getting bigger. Today, high technology accounts for about 25 to 30 percent of the growth in the American economy, the way the auto industry drove growth in the 1920s.

But experience matters when it comes to investing in technology. A lot of technologies and trends come and go; there are cycles, ups and downs, bull markets, bear markets, bubbles and recessions, loose capital, tight capital, and all kinds of changing conditions—some of them unexpected and certainly not always predictable. Two firms that have posted great results from navigating the high seas of technology investing are venture capital firm Sequoia Capital and Integral Capital Partners, which invests in both private and public companies. We thought these two firms' approaches to investing were so thoughtful and intelligent that we would share them with our readers. We'll also get some perspective from Jim Collins, a leading business analyst and coauthor of the best-selling *Built to Last: Successful Habits of Visionary Companies.* Finally, we'll wrap up with some basic advice on how to ride out the market storm and come out ahead long term.

## Sequoia Capital

Founded in 1972 and led by the venerable curmudgeon Don Valentine, Sequoia Capital is one of the premier venture capital firms. It has invested in over 350 companies, of which 100 have gone public and numerous others have been sold successfully. Sequoia's investments include Cisco Systems, Yahoo, Apple Computer, Oracle, Electronic Arts, Cypress Semiconductor, 3Com, and Arbor Software. It has raised more than $1.3 billion and provided the original financing for companies together worth more than $300 billion.

Don Valentine, known as one of the toughest and smartest venture capitalists in Silicon Valley, is a cool and rational thinker when it comes to analyzing companies and different industry situations. His rules for venture investments include: (1) find "monster" markets that can get really big, (2) find good technology and technologists who can stay ahead of competitive threats, (3) find outstanding leaders and management teams that can drive these technologies forward into the monster markets, and (4) invest in and build companies, not just products.

Sequoia is also known for the financial discipline it brings to its companies. The firm considers frugality a virtue. It encourages its portfolio companies to "bootstrap" themselves so they can learn how to effectively manage their capital resources for the long term. Preferring to start companies with less money than other venture capitalists invest, Sequoia expects those companies to become profitable quickly. "We like to get companies off the ground with a small amount of fuel," says general partner Michael Moritz, Sequoia's lead investor in Yahoo. "We like to start wicked infernos with a single match rather than with two million gallons of kerosene."

As Sequoia's Internet guy, Moritz is more involved in the firm's sexiest investments these days than even Don Valentine. Yet Moritz doesn't have the typical tech VC background—engineering degree, requisite stint at Hewlett-Packard, Intel, or some other high-tech blue-chip company. Instead, Moritz came to venture capital by way of the unusual route of journalism. A business correspondent for *Time* magazine before joining Sequoia in 1986, he also wrote two books—one about Chrysler, and closer to home, one titled *The Little Kingdom: The Private Story of Apple Computer*. Sequoia was willing to bet on Moritz as someone a little different from the stereotype and mentor him in the ways of the venture capital business.

"People have come into the venture business with blue-chip, gold-plated, platinum-tipped résumés who have flamed out," says Moritz. "It's like Woody Allen says—the secret to life is showing up every day. In the venture business it's showing up, working pretty darn hard, not getting arrogant or complacent, and realizing that you're only as good as your next investment, not your last one."

Moritz decided that it was better for a venture capitalist to invest in Internet mania rather than to ignore it. For insiders, Barton Biggs of Morgan Stanley says about the mania: "The fools are dancing, but the greater fools are still watching." Moritz agrees. "The biggest expense is not to be an investor in the Internet," he says. "It's costly for a venture firm to sit out the Internet, just as it would have been costly to sit out the PC business or the semiconductor business. There are some venture firms that have not participated in the Internet, and they have lost their positions in the venture industry."

In order to fund great companies, Sequoia's top priority—and the hallmark of its investment philosophy—is its focus on markets. Sequoia's objective is to identify and support the companies it thinks will ultimately dominate rapidly expanding new markets.

The firm wants to gain the largest market share in large markets. Capturing these markets means that a company needs either a product difficult to duplicate or a first-mover's advantage that lets the company roll out very quickly to garner large market share and turn that position into a powerful competitive weapon.

Sequoia's market focus is well known in both the venture capital community and in the technology finance community at large. "They look for huge markets; everything else is secondary to that," says Geoff Yang of Redpoint Ventures. Joel Romines of Knightsbridge Partners, a fund of funds that invests in venture capital partnerships and young companies in the public market, adds, "In real estate it's location, location, location, and to many venture capitalists, it's management, management, management. For Sequoia, the first thing is market, market, market."

A company can have a great product or brilliant management, but it won't matter if there is no market for the product. For one thing, the best technology doesn't always win. Two classic examples are the triumph of VHS over Betamax as the standard for VCRs and the huge market-share advantage Microsoft Windows has over the Macintosh operating system.

And while it's always nice to invest in a company with superior technology, Sequoia has helped build companies that have a good but not enormous technology advantage. These companies have gotten to market early and have built a formidable sales-and-distribution machine that becomes a difficult barrier for competitors to overcome. Cisco Systems is a classic example of this.

Sequoia also believes that while good management is always in short supply, it's still easier to find new managers than to sell into markets that don't exist. "We cannot afford to wait for markets to develop," says Valentine. "And we don't have the money or the inclination to educate customers to buy products they don't know they need."

Nonetheless, finding great managers can also be tough. "The great imponderable is to judge accurately and predict how well a president will run the business. It's easy to mistake the facade for reality," says Moritz. "The qualities we look for are frugality, competitiveness, confidence, and paranoia."

Because experienced management is scarce, Sequoia will step in and run a company if necessary. For example, the firm had to intervene during the early stages of Cisco. Sequoia general partner Pierre Lamond spent a tremendous amount of time at the company, working behind the scenes to make sure the engineering department was designing and getting new products to market. "Pierre is the great unsung hero of Cisco," says Moritz. "People don't realize the significant contribution he made because Don Valentine's name is on the hubcaps as the chairman of the company."

But for Sequoia, ultimate success is still possible only if there's a true market for the product or service. For the lay investor, the nonspecialist, Sequoia's market focus is a great insight. It is difficult to assess the viability of many technologies or the caliber of company management, but if a big market exists for what a company offers, the potential is certainly there.

The lay investor cannot and should not try to play the venture capital game—it is far too complicated and risky for nonspecialists. The required due-diligence process is time-consuming and complex, and the passive investor does not have the power of a venture capitalist to change management or help companies forge the strategic partnerships that will let them prevail in the market.

Another caveat for the lay investor to remember is the 2:6:2 rule. If you take ten companies in a typical venture portfolio, there might be one or two big winners, six mediocrities (including the aptly named "living dead"), and one or two partial or total losers. And even among the winners, a Sun Microsystems, Cisco, or Microsoft is extremely rare.

In a bubble market in particular, the buyer should beware. "In a bull market, everyone is invincible," says Valentine. "Over the last ten years, the stock index funds have continued to go up, way up. People think, 'If Vanguard can do it, I can do it, I can pick these goddamn Internet stocks.' That is a traditional mistake made at the peak of a bull market. People become convinced that the world is so simple, and that you don't have to be careful or deliberate. They think that because these companies have so much publicity, they must be good."

In fact, in what many regarded as the post-Valentine era at Sequoia Capital, the venerable firm itself was not immune to the dotcom frenzy. In 1999, the firm raised a late-stage (aka mezzanine) venture fund that they dubbed the Franchise Fund. It was designed to put some serious cash into what Sequoia thought would be some big-time Internet winners, perhaps as spectacular as their biggest dotcom success to date, Yahoo. The Franchise Fund raised $440 million overall in 1999. In July 1999, the firm put $45 million of that fund into online grocery concern WebVan, at a valuation of $12 per share. WebVan ultimately went public on November 5, 1999, at $15 per share. The business rationalization was that WebVan was going to be the big winner in the race to provide the "last mile" for the delivery of online goods to customers. By March of 2001, WebVan's stock stood at 20 cents per share, and it still remained to be seen if its business model was going to work out.

Sequoia also put a big chunk of Franchise change—$10 million at $10 per share—into eToys, an online toy shop. By March 2001, eToys was going out of business. Similarly, online luxury goods site Ashford.com got $6 million of Franchise money at a valuation of a little over $4.50 per share, and its stock was down to 75 cents per share by March 2001. All told, some $61 million of the $440 million—almost 14 percent—had gone into just three companies that had no guarantee of living up to their mezzanine-level valuations. Meanwhile one of Sequoia's other late-stage investments was to put almost $8 million into Scient, an Internet consulting-services business, at $6.75 per share. This was just before the company's IPO in the second quarter of 1999 at $20 per share. Scient did a secondary offering in January 2000 at $88 per share. By March 2001, Scient's stock price was down to $2.70 per share. The reality distortion field had proven so strong that even a top venture firm like Sequoia had been drawn into it.

In the midst of this kind of mania and market distortion, what should the average investor do? "Buy a mutual fund, don't try to buy Amazon or C/Net or any other Internet example that you want to name," says Valentine.

There's a danger of getting too caught up in the phenomenon, investing blindly in a category of companies perceived as able to do no wrong because they are on the Internet. "These companies are so overreported," says Valentine. "They have a level of emergence that is scary."

And at the peak of bubbles, many institutional investors exit their Internet holdings, leaving them mostly to the retail market where the Aunt Millies start to place their bets and set themselves up for a loss. "It's greed," says Valentine. "The retail investors buy things they don't understand."

According to Sequoia's partners, the best alternative, especially if investing in high technology, is a reasonably diversified technology fund exposed to a select cross section of companies coming out of the high-tech market—at least 60 to 70 percent of the fund. Diversifying instead of gambling is a word to the wise from these experienced investors, who have had to learn from their own mistakes.

## Integral Capital Partners

In the mid-1980s, when Roger McNamee was a manager of the Science & Technology Fund for T. Rowe Price, someone very smart suggested to him that he get to know a rising young partner at the venture capital firm Kleiner Perkins Caufield & Byers. This venture capitalist had a dynamic and innovative approach to private technology investing that McNamee's friend thought could work just as well with the public investing McNamee was doing at T. Rowe Price. The venture capitalist's name was John Doerr. After getting to know Doerr, McNamee realized he had found his role model and mentor.

"I followed John around and began imitating some things he was doing, particularly his practice of participative investment," says McNamee. "He taught me that the role of the investor was not to sit in your office with the money and wait for people to come to you. Instead, you had to actually get involved in the industry and interact with the people as peers and exchange insights with them."

This approach, widely practiced today, seems obvious, but it was not typical of fund managers at the time. The technology industry generates hundreds of press releases a week, and there are scads of trade journals and newsletters. This makes trying to stay informed like sipping water from a fire hose. If the investor sits in one place, he spends his time reacting and never sees the big picture. Putting details into a spreadsheet only creates an illusion of precision. "Life takes place to the left of the decimal point," says McNamee.

McNamee started attending trade shows and conferences to become part of the industry network and gain insights that he could barter in exchange for other insights. Fortunately, the industry was young, so it was easier to get to know people. "Folks who today are totally unapproachable were still looking for an audience in those days," says McNamee. "To some extent, all I did was show up." McNamee also had over 400 face-to-face meetings with company executives every year—basically two every business day, compared, at that time, to an average of about 23 face-to-face meetings annually by the typical industry analyst.

Not surprisingly, the Science & Technology Fund did well. It had an annual internal rate of return of 17 percent, compared with an industry average of 6 percent for similar funds and 9 percent for the Standard & Poor 500 Index. It was consistently ranked number one of the seventeen science and technology funds tracked by Morningstar.

By 1990, even as Japan's bubble burst, America was on the brink of a tremendous technology bull market. Sensing this, McNamee and his partner, John Powell, began working on a business plan that was to become Integral Capital Partners. McNamee wanted to invite John Doerr to become a partner but feared it would spoil their relationship if Doerr said no. This changed at a big party thrown by Will Hearst III at the Comdex electronics trade show in 1990. "I went to the party and John walks up to me and says, 'Roger, we ought to create a fund that does both later-stage venture and public-incentive pool investing, and you ought to run it. What do you think?' " exclaims McNamee, still in awe. "I said, 'When do we start?' I was proud of myself for not just standing there with my tongue hanging out."

After almost a year of further research and incubation, and several more iterations of the business plan, they launched Integral Capital Partners as a private investment partnership that invested in the securities of expansion-stage private companies and growth-stage public companies in the information and life-sciences industries.

Kleiner Perkins Caufield & Byers joined Integral as its "insight partner" but without any fiduciary control. Investment bank Morgan Stanley also became an institutional partner and acted as a placement agent. McNamee and Powell would make all the investment decisions and manage the fund, and they planned to raise most of the money from senior executives within the technology industry.

Integral benefited tremendously from the insights of John Doerr and the other Kleiner Perkins partners. Integral was invited to Kleiner Perkins's frequent off-sites, where the Kleiner Perkins partners had detailed discussions about strategy and the future of the technology industry. "At least twice a year, John Doerr or somebody else at Kleiner Perkins hits me with an insight that's a bolt of lightning," says McNamee. "This gives Integral a gigantic competitive advantage." In turn, Integral helps Kleiner Perkins with its companies' road shows and with decisions concerning post-IPO stock distribution.

These lightning bolts and Integral's industry networking helped the partnership enjoy an internal rate of return of 25 percent for Integral Capital L.P. Fund I. Integral also learned to focus on a carefully defined set of investment opportunities. This focus is based on specific investment themes. They are: (1) *Connectivity*—the push for improved communication flows within and between corporations; (2) *Interactivity*—real-time information exchange; and (3) *Mobility*—products that support mobile lifestyles and workstyles.

A larger theme overlaying all of these is "the real-time economy" based on real-time models of computing. In practice it means that the old models of control-oriented data processing are giving way to a model in which businesses use technology more and more to be in touch with the customer in real time, in the here and now. The Internet explosion is an obvious expression of this real-time model.

Integral has some even more specific guidelines that can benefit anyone interested in investing in the technology market. "Our rules to live by represent the collective scar tissue of almost eighteen years of investing in technology stocks," says McNamee.

- *Rule one: Information is a commodity, but insight is precious.* Insight is much more valuable because it is a filtering of information. Sometimes too much detail clouds your investment vision, but insight allows you to operate at a higher level of understanding and see what's actually going on.

- *Rule two: Product cycles are the only cycles that matter.* On Wall Street, there is a tremendous focus on the economic cycle, interest rates, and politics. But for technology companies, product cycles are the real drivers. These product cycles have not only upswings but downswings, and the ability to tell the difference is critical. These swings are natural, and technology businesses are not made obsolete because they are in a product transition, even though they are often priced on Wall Street as if they are. Never confuse an upswing with greatness or a downswing with the end.

- *Rule three: Favor products that are bought, not sold.* If a company sells tens of millions of its products, it will not sell them all on the last day of the quarter. They will sell continuously through the quarter. Wall Street loves predictability, and it will give a higher valuation to a company if it sells 10 million items at a dollar apiece than if it sells just one big item for $10 million.

- *Rule four: In making investment decisions, do not rely on guidance from company management alone.* The vast majority of the industry analysts get all their information about companies from the company itself. But when it comes to the company's own business, management is often the last to know what the problems are. The customers, however, always know, and competitors will also have a lot of insights. "You need to get beyond a company's 'story' and into a realistic understanding of the business issues involved," says McNamee.

- *Rule five: Balance research insights with opportunism.* Research determines what should be done, but the market determines what can be done today.

- *Rule six: A perfectly diversified technology stock portfolio is bound to underperform the market.* You want to diversify away the risk of execution problems without diversifying away the opportunities. Stick to two or three major investment themes, and use diversification within those themes to minimize risk. Never put all your bets on one company, but find three or four of the best-positioned companies to invest in. Avoiding losers is every bit as important as picking winners.

- Also keep in mind that there is only one Microsoft. If you spend all your time looking for the next Microsoft, you will probably find it only after it is too late. If you invest in the best-positioned companies in the major themes, and the next Microsoft emerges, it will already be in your portfolio. Meanwhile, don't forget that every stock must eventually be sold, and when the time comes to sell it, don't hesitate. You have to do it.

So what about Internet mania? "The essence of a mania is that its pace became so frenetic that people stopped thinking clearly, and it only ended when some element of economic reality disrupted the fantasy and brought the mania to an end," says McNamee.

In the midst of the mania, Integral continued to invest in private Internet companies, but it only rarely bought Internet companies in the public market. Integral held on to its Internet stocks but counseled its clients to move away from Internet stocks in their other investing. In essence, Integral's clients paid Integral to hold on to Internet stocks as long as Integral's managers thought it was feasible, even as Integral's clients were off-loading much of their own risk.

"Common sense tells you that the Internet is going to be a huge business," says McNamee. "That said, it has been subject to all the forces that affect any industry during its land-rush period." Now after the land rush, there will be a series of consolidations before market shares stabilize and the industry becomes more predictable.

And what's next for McNamee and his colleagues post–Internet mania? They've realized that much of the high-technology market has matured or is maturing. Integral has ridden the bull market and benefited from Internet mania, but given the overabundance of capital and the consequent overvaluation of companies, it's challenging to find good investments that generate the same returns Integral enjoyed throughout the 1990s. It has become more time-consuming to find investments at good valuations.

"Integral got into the game in 1991 at the end of a long bear market in the technology sector," says McNamee. "Technology stocks were so significantly undervalued that it was easy to find good investments. All you had to do was buy all the big-cap stocks and just hang on. You could buy Microsoft, Intel, Applied Materials, Dell, and Cisco, and go to sleep, and still have 40 percent price appreciation per year out of a portfolio of those core holdings."

Now that the Internet market is beginning to mature, McNamee has launched a technology buyout fund called Silver Lake Partners. The fund seeks out technologies and divisions within mature companies that are grossly undervalued (or even ignored) because they are not part of the companies' core competencies. Wall Street has failed to recognize the value of these businesses because it focuses on hypergrowth and the sizzle of the hottest stories on a quarterly basis. Yet many of these undervalued businesses may actually be growing at rates of 15 to 20 percent annually.

"You've got 80 percent of technology companies effectively being ignored by Wall Street. Within them, there are thousands of divisions, really successful businesses, with no home, that are basically undermanaged and underinvested in, and which get no analyst coverage," says McNamee.

One of Silver Lake's first deals was to lead an investor group that acquired the disk drive businesses of Seagate Technology in 2000 for approximately $2 billion. This deal was part of a nearly $20 billion management buyout that involved taking the company private. Other investors in the group included Texas Pacific, Chase Capital Partners, August Capital, Goldman Sachs, and Integral Capital Partners. Seagate's remaining assets—including its 128 million shares in Veritas Software—would be merged into Veritas itself, with Seagate stockholders receiving cash and Veritas shares. Meanwhile Seagate would have the opportunity to go public again in the future, offering another opportunity to make its owners wealthier.

With Silver Lake, McNamee and company are ready to move on to the next opportunity, even as Internet mania and the success of the tech sector as a whole have spurred other investment managers to create Integral-like structures and investment businesses.

"They say that generals are always prepared for the last war, the war they just finished," says McNamee. "Well, just as each war is different, so is each market cycle. The great irony is that you know it's getting late in the cycle when people are creating a gazillion new investment vehicles optimized to do whatever has worked for the last decade, rather than thinking about what comes next."

## Built to Last

In 1994, James Collins and Jerry Porras published *Built to Last: Successful Habits of Visionary Companies*, which has been a business bestseller ever since—and with good reason. In it, Collins and Porras distill what has enabled great companies to adapt, grow, prosper, and therefore last. The companies they profile, such as Hewlett-Packard, General Electric, IBM, and Wal-Mart, are the envy of the world.

Along the way, Collins also worked with senior executives and CEOs at over 100 major corporations, received numerous awards, including the Distinguished Teaching Award while on the faculty of Stanford University Graduate School of Business. More recently he founded a research and teaching lab in Boulder, Colorado.

Collins has always believed that the "Silicon Valley Paradigm" does not create companies that are built to last or that will become classic blue-chip investments. His definition of the paradigm as "Have a good idea, raise venture capital, grow fast, go public, and generate vast liquid wealth quickly" describes perfectly what happened with most Internet start-up companies. This approach would have been alien to some of America's greatest entrepreneurs. In an article for *Fast Company* magazine titled "Built to Flip," Collins writes:

> Imagine Hewlett and Packard sitting in their garage, sipping lattes, and saying to each other, "If we do this right, we can sell this thing off and cash out in twelve months." Now that's an altogether different version of the HP Way! Or picture [Sam] Walton collecting a wheelbarrow full of cash from flipping his first [Wal-Mart] store after 18 months, rather than building a company whose annual revenues now exceed $130 billion.

Later in the article, Collins adds, "The entrepreneurial mindset has degenerated from one of risk, contribution, and reward to one of wealth entitlement. . . . By fostering a culture of entitlement, Built to Flip debases the very concept of meaningful work."

In contrast, *built to last* means that the most important creation is the company itself and what it stands for. Such companies will generate numerous ideas and transcend any one business life cycle. Thomas Edison's greatest invention is arguably not the light bulb, the phonograph, or the motion-picture machine, but rather the General Electric Company that ticks along decades after his death. GE contrasts sharply with many of today's start-ups that are built around one product or idea and try to cash in on that alone.

An older technology company that has struggled with being a one-trick pony is Xerox. The company focused on one product—

the photocopier—rather than on building the company. As a result, it missed out on numerous revolutionary ideas and products discovered at its own Palo Alto Research Center. These include the laser printer, desktop publishing, electronic mail, mouse pointers, and the graphical user interface that became the basis of the Macintosh operating system. Xerox simply did not have the organizational capability to capitalize on these ideas and run with them, and the company has struggled to reposition itself ever since.

While there is a great sense of urgency in recent years associated with "Internet time" and "Web weeks" and the need to be first to market, there are certain built-to-last principles that transcend the current mania and create long-term successful companies and investments. One is the supreme value of the entrepreneur.

Collins says, "From an investor standpoint, I would ask, 'Which entrepreneurs could I invest in with the confidence that they would succeed no matter what?'" Collins' list of examples includes Bill Gates, Bill Hewlett and David Packard, Henry Ford, and even Howard Schultz, founder of Starbucks coffee.

If it had not been automobiles, Henry Ford would have taken the concept of mass-production technology and applied it to something else that would have been just as successful. Hewlett and Packard didn't even know what their company was going to be when they brought together some very capable people. At one point, they discarded their original area of focus and finally got into an unrelated product arena that fueled the growth and success of the company.

"I'd invest not because something is an Internet company, or because the Internet's the play, but because the people doing this company are the kind that if the whole Internet crashed, they'd figure out something else to do and they'd make that successful," says Collins. "The whole idea that something is an Internet company is no more reason to invest in that company than investing in any one of the 508 automobile companies in business around 1910. Only a few of them will be there when the whole thing settles out."

The real question is: What can someone create that will produce a change in people's lives in a profitable and sustainable way? If the entrepreneur can't answer that question, there's no reason to invest. "Unless you want to play the shell game, in which you're not really investing, but instead playing the 'I hope I get in and out in time' game, which I can't condone," says Collins.

Business fundamentals don't change. A company's earnings are a function of the economic and social contributions it makes. Unless a company can demonstrate how it will create that sustained flow based upon its contribution, there is nothing to invest in. If the entrepreneur has a single idea or a single insight that is not sustainable, the advantage of it will dissipate. The company has to have the ability to generate new insights and build new economic engines.

Collins compares the relationship of business fundamentals and sustained growth to the relationship of physics and engineering. Physics is physics; its laws don't change. So, too, with business fundamentals. But the way they are applied always changes, the way engineering constantly evolves.

"The way you design products will continually evolve," says Collins. "You used to use blueprints and pencil diagrams, and now you can use design software to go through multiple iterations of a Triple 7 jet before you actually build anything with metal. You're changing the form of engineering, but the underlying physics are still the same; they don't change."

And just as there is no way to ignore physics when you are engineering a real product, you also can't ignore business fundamentals if you are to have a real company. "There is no reason to believe that we need to throw out the fundamentals. No. We need to do a better job of applying the fundamentals more than anything else," Collins concludes.

## Final Advice

"Professional investors measure themselves against the market every day, because that's how they get paid," says Bruce Lupatkin, former head of research at Hambrecht & Quist and a longtime technology analyst. "But most nonprofessionals do not have time to do that. Yet if you have patience and discipline, you can still do well. Stocks will go up and they will go down. Just take your time and be patient."

How do you pick the best stocks? "You ought to find industry leaders, companies that are causing structural change in a given industry," says Lupatkin.

In the Internet realm, Lupatkin points to America Online and Yahoo as companies to watch, but quickly adds, "The issue is what you should pay for them." This, of course, gets back to the whole issue of valuation, as well as diversification.

One solution is to approach the public market the way venture capitalists approach their privately held portfolios. "A venture capitalist is more than happy to see a single holding increase to 80 or 90 percent of the value of his portfolio," says Brad Kelly, general partner at Knightsbridge Partners, a fund of funds that invests in both venture partnerships and the public market. In other words, you should hold a wide range of potential winners, not just one stock. One way to do this is to hold substantial positions in a basket of the putative long-term winners and recognize that it would cost a lot more to sell a big winner than to hold some losers. "You make a lot of money from holding these stocks," agrees Eric Doppstadt, director of Private Equity at the Ford Foundation, who manages both the foundation's venture investments and its postventure stocks.

A company's leadership status indeed gives investors a certain measure of safety. But not everyone wants to put their money in the perceived leaders. "When you're investing in a leader, you're talking about a company that already has a large market cap," says Kevin Landis, cofounder and chief investment officer of Firsthand Funds. "We feel this puts some limits to the percentage gains you are going to get on the stock. Obviously those who invested before these companies attained leadership status made all the easy money and got all the gaudy numbers. But in terms of current valuation, these stocks will always look expensive and the upside will always be limited." Firsthand tends to dig down into the industry food chain to buy companies that people haven't heard of yet—harder to understand, less well-known companies. "We don't feel as if sophisticated investors in high-tech have to buy the household names," says Landis. For example, Landis is very excited about wireless and the optical space.

Alberto Vilar, manager of Amerindo Technology Fund, reports that his fund, in addition to its investments in the consumer Internet (represented by its holdings in eBay and Yahoo) has four other areas of Internet-related investing: (1) broadband and telecommunications networks; (2) software infrastructure and application companies (ASPs); (3) some business-to-business (B2B) companies; and (4) international tech companies.

Meanwhile, how are the pros navigating through all the stock market volatility? "It's important to recognize that in the market environment of the last couple of years, cycles happen much faster than they used to," says Ford Foundation's Doppstadt. From January 1, 1998, through the first quarter of 2000, for example, there were four declines of 30 percent or more in the Morgan Stanley Internet Index. "Consequently, you have to pick your spots for buying and selling pretty carefully," says Doppstadt. "And there are some clear mistakes to avoid such as emotion-based panic selling or automatically selling around lockup expirations."

"You don't have to put all your money into stock," cautions George Shott of Shott Capital Management. "Instead, you should invest slowly and over time." Joel Romines of Knightsbridge Partners adds, "If you are interested in investing in high technology, look for mutual funds that specialize and have a good record in young high-technology companies."

For most investors, it comes back to the need for a long-term investment strategy and with it an appropriate long-term portfolio. Meanwhile, bear in mind that in recent years, the financial community has successfully convinced individuals to invest directly in stocks while steering investors away from normal asset allocation. "The American populace doesn't really understand equity risk," Bill Gurley, a onetime Wall Street analyst and now a venture capitalist with Benchmark Partners, told us in early 1999. "And it's highly unlikely that the financial returns awarded to the entire market, and certainly to these Internet stocks over the past three to five years, are sustainable." And indeed Gurley proved right.

Perhaps no other generation in American history has taken on the stock market risks the baby boomer group has. New investors didn't always realize that the S&P could lose 50 percent over a mere three-year period—as it did in 1972 through 1974—or that there have been other booms and busts, like oil stocks in the early 1980s. Some investors, meanwhile, have loaded up exclusively on their employer's stock, leaving them doubly vulnerable if their company falters.

By contrast, asset allocation and a diversified portfolio are still the safest way to go over the long term. This approach lets you weather all kinds of market conditions. Your money should be spread out among different asset classes, not only stocks but also some bonds and money market funds. Diversification might mean holding both large- and small-company stocks, as well as some international investments. Some investment managers also recommend breaking your portfolio out into growth stocks (shares of fast-growing companies) and value stocks (neglected stocks that trade at bargain prices). A typical portfolio might be 30 to 40 percent bonds; 30 percent big U.S. stocks; 20 percent smaller U.S. stocks; and 10 to 20 percent internationals, including 5 percent in emerging markets.

Remember that investing in individual stocks is risky, especially if you don't have a lot of time to research individual companies or the stomach to ride the ups and downs of a portfolio of limited stock holdings. Even investing too much in blue chips does not guarantee a great return, especially if we go into a recession or a bear market.

Be careful about lining up behind supposed investment gurus. There may be a level of risk that is far from clear, and their success to date could be more a matter of luck, especially in a bull market, than anything else. Supposed financial innovations are usually variations on something that's been done before, and it's important to look below the surface.

Also realize that in a post-Bubble aftermath, bottom fishing can backfire. When stock prices sink to single digits, the odds are that they are sunk for good. This was demonstrated in a study published in 2001 by Thomas Watts, an Internet analyst at Merrill Lynch. Going back to 1985, Watts studied the trading of 1,900 publicly held companies spanning the technology sector. He found that of those companies whose stocks had fallen to single digits, only 3.4 percent rebounded to $15 or higher within the next year. Most of those that didn't bounce back in the first year never did.

It's always dangerous to be too greedy—remember the old Wall Street adage: "Bulls make money, bears make money, but pigs get slaughtered."

# Doonesbury

I'M SORRY, MIKE — I NEVER DREAMED BERNIE WOULD BAIL ON US. I'LL RETURN THE CAR IN THE MORNING.

I DON'T KNOW. MAYBE WE SHOULD KEEP IT...

WHAT DO YOU MEAN?

WELL, BERNIE THINKS WE OUGHT TO TRY TO TAKE THE COMPANY PUBLIC...

9-4

OUR ONLY HOPE OF ACTUALLY PULLING THAT OFF MAY LIE IN **APPEARING** TO BE SUCCESSFUL. A LUXURY CAR MIGHT HELP...

POPPA? I COULD START WEARING RALPH LAUREN.

THAT'S OKAY, SWEETHEART. THE CAR SHOULD COVER IT.

# EPILOGUE: *AN OPEN LETTER*

To: Internet Company Investors
From: The Authors
Re: Bet on real-time computing (but make sure it's at the right price)

The day we wrote this open letter (April 4, 2001), NASDAQ hit a new fifty-two-week low of 1,619, after reaching a high on March 10, 2000 of 5,132. When you look back on this speculative bubble, it almost seems too impossible to have been real. Bill Joy has sarcastically referred to this era as an "upside panic," a time when most people were afraid of missing out.

The great fallacy of the Internet Bubble era was the idea that you could make a lot of money by starting a company that simply replicated a physical world practice in cyberspace. Most of these companies had no compelling value proposition; they merely got their hands on a URL and figured that this put them in business.

But Internet investors shouldn't despair. In fall 2000, John Doerr of Kleiner Perkins told the Churchill Club (a Silicon Valley speaker's forum) that he doesn't feel the least bit disheartened with the decline in the technology stock market because he believes that there is still a massive opportunity to build out the next generation of the Web. We agree with him.

The multibillion-dollar investment made during the first phase of the Internet has had at least one very positive result. It has created a completely new computing and networking architecture, and this architecture is now ready to be exploited. While it's true that this new platform still needs to be integrated with the older systems that many companies are still using, the PC and the database are basically over as investment opportunities. As Roger McNamee of Integral Capital Partners contends, every company that is interesting in the marketplace today derives from the emergence of the new, real-time computing.

The emergence of this new computing and communications platform has created a whole slew of interesting growth investment opportunities. It is important to note that while some technology titans such as Cisco, and perhaps Oracle, will play more than a peripheral role in establishing the new computing architecture, we think the long-term technology winners will come from the new guard.

On the networking equipment side, Corvis, Sycamore, and Extreme Networks all look like they are positioned well. There are also new applications like Zaplet that are turning electronic mail into a powerful new collaborative software platform for employees and customers. Finally, in the network semiconductor space, we continue to think Broadcom, PMC Sierra, and Applied Micro Circuits appear to be the most promising.

Smart investors will focus on these emerging technology sectors, applying the analysis techniques and making use of the insider information that we discuss elsewhere in this book. Keep in mind that there will be winning companies that aren't even on the horizon yet.

We learned another simple rule when we listened to Bill Joy explain how he tried to sidestep the Internet Bubble. "Anything with a P/E ratio over 100, or that was losing lots of money, I sold. I was completely indiscriminate," he explained. We think this is good advice. Realistically, as big an opportunity as the so-called "Evernet" is—where literally billions of devices will be always on, enabled by a high-speed, broadband, multiformat Web—there are only so many half-trillion-dollar, Cisco-like companies that can be built in a generation. Investing in a company with a 600 P/E ratio means assuming that company will grow 100 percent annually for some incredible number of years.

Jeremy Siegel, a professor of finance at the Wharton School and author of the classic investment tome *Stocks for the Long Run*, agrees with us that the excitement generated by the technology and communications revolution is fully justified. He also thinks there's no question that the firms leading the way are superior enterprises. But he also corroborates Joy's investment practice by noting the failure of any large-cap stock to justify, by its subsequent record, a P/E ratio anywhere near 100. In fact, Siegel takes it a little further. "History has shown that whenever companies, no matter how great, get priced above 50 to 60 times earnings, buyer beware," declares Siegel. "Once a firm reaches big-cap status—ranked in the top fifty by market value—its ability to generate long-term double-digit earnings growth slows dramatically," he warns.

In the final analysis, the quality that will determine your investment success or failure is your ability to be dispassionate, to remember the differences between companies and stocks, to recognize as early as possible when you have made a mistake and get out.

Taking all the above into consideration, we believe that the investment future in technology is brighter than at any time in history. One story to remember is that Microsoft's value didn't spike until after its Windows-installed base had matured and its applications business took off. The good news for Internet investors is that it's still early in the game, so the big money for the greatest number of investors is still in front of us.

# APPENDIX A: *CALCULATING THE BUBBLE'S DEFLATION*

**I**n the first edition of *The Internet Bubble,* we postulated that public-market investors had overbid the stock prices of many Internet-related companies based on hype and overly aggressive expectations. In order to demonstrate that these stocks were over-valued, we chose 133 companies in Internet-related businesses and created a methodology to quantify the expectations of the market (see Appendix B for that methodology). We found that for almost all of these companies, investor expectations of future growth were entirely unrealistic, even considering the huge opportunity pre-sented by the Internet. Eighteen months later, we have looked back at these 133 companies to determine how well they have fared.

If we had created a portfolio of all 133 companies and invested equally in each company at the end of June 1999, then held that portfolio until December 15, 2000, we would have lost much more than half of our invested capital. In fact, this portfolio would have lost 65 percent (yes, almost two-thirds) of its value during that period, which is very poor compared to the broader markets. The NASDAQ Composite Index only lost 1 percent of its value during the same period (and one could argue that the Internet stocks above helped to drag down the NASDAQ) and the S&P 500 Index lost 4 percent. (A portfolio created by weighting our investment in each company according to that company's market capitalization— that is, if we had invested more heavily in larger companies—would have still lost 44 percent of its value during the same time frame).

Of the 133 companies that we originally examined, 123 lost value during the course of the eighteen-month time period, and investors in 110 of them (7 out of 8 of the companies) lost more than 50 percent of their invested capital in those investments. Even more alarming is the fact that the stock prices of eighty-six of the companies (almost two-thirds) fell below 25 percent of their original value. This is particularly disturbing for retail investors, who typically invest in a relatively small number of stocks. If a retail investor had chosen only a handful of Internet stocks to invest in, he/she would have been over twenty times as likely to choose stocks that lost more than half of their value than to find one of the few stocks that more than doubled in value. These are staggering results considering the "can't lose" attitude of Internet investors up until March 2000. (See Chart A for the distribution of return of the 133 Internet stocks.)

Examining these results more closely, we find that while certain segments fared better than others, every segment lost value. The companies involved in e-commerce, content, and enabling services lost an average of 82 percent, 68 percent, and 81 percent of their value, respectively, during the period. In each of these segments, investors in every single company lost money. Enabling telecommunications-service-provider stocks lost an average of 68 percent of their value during the same period, although 10 percent of the companies did gain value. The only "bright spot" during the period that we examined was in the enabling software segment of the market, which only lost 26 percent during the period. Almost three-quarters of the companies lost value in this segment, so one could only expect the best stock pickers to have made any money in this segment.

---

### Average Loss of Internet Industry Sectors
### (6/30/99 through 12/15/00)

| | | |
|---|---|---|
| **Commerce** | −82% | (100% of the companies lost value—32 out of 32) |
| **Content** | −68% | (100% of the companies lost value—27 out of 27) |
| **Services** | −81% | (100% of the companies lost value—18 out of 18) |
| **Software** | −26% | (74% of the companies lost value—20 out of 27) |
| **Telecom service** | −68% | (90% of the companies lost value—26 out of 29) |

---

Since we wrote the first edition of *The Internet Bubble,* a number of additional companies have found their way into the public markets (most before the first signs of a market correction in April 2000). Venture capitalists and bankers had continued to push unproven companies into the IPO queue in order to force the inordinately high risk of small, loss-driven technology companies onto retail investors. This has happened with Internet-related segments, as well as with other technology companies (like optical components and equipment companies). While many retail investors consider new IPOs to be great opportunities for aggressive returns, it is important to remember that historically more than half of all IPOs trade below their IPO price within six months after issue. (Also note that most individual investors typically cannot buy at the IPO price and therefore pay more for the stock.)

Looking at the broader market, we have seen Internet stocks and a number of other market segments collapse as the investor community realized that valuations were unrealistic (see Appendix C). Some companies lost more than half of their value in a matter of days. These corrections in valuation should be viewed as just that—corrections, and healthy ones at that. But savvy investors should not assume that stock prices will automatically rebound to previously astronomical levels. At the same time, neither should investors assume that a company that has lost value in a significant correction is a fundamentally bad company; it may just be that expectations were out of whack with reality, due to the frothier attitude of the market.

In many ways, it's a good thing that commonsense valuations have returned to the market. By doing their homework and investing in fundamentally sound companies, investors now have the opportunity to generate reasonable returns.

## Chart A
### DISTRIBUTION OF INTERNET COMPANY RETURNS

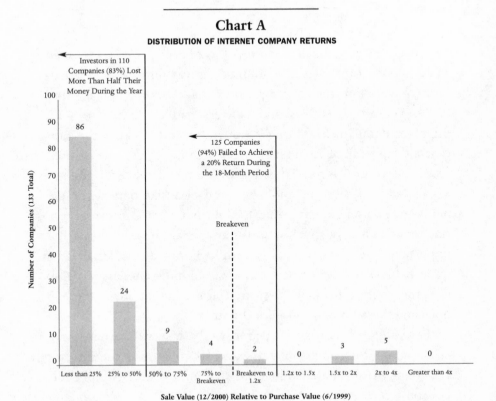

Sale Value (12/2000) Relative to Purchase Value (6/1999)

# APPENDIX B: *BUBBLE CALCULATION METHODOLOGY*

**T**he Internet Bubble calculations referenced in this book are based on several key assumptions. The general model was developed with help from analysts, investment bankers, and venture capitalists with years of experience valuing technology companies. Traditional valuation methodologies such as P/E ratios and discounted cash flows were not thought to be applicable to Internet companies because of the high expectations and the uncertainty of future growth, as well as the lack of historical earnings.

The primary assumption we relied upon is that during a finite time period, the hypergrowth expected by Internet investors will be at least partially realized and future growth will be more easily quantifiable from that point onward. At that time in the future, valuations will be based on more traditional methodologies similar to those used for other technology-focused companies. For simplicity's sake, we have chosen a five-year time horizon (beginning in June 1999 when our first Bubble calculation was done), which means that by June 2004, we expect that Internet valuations will be based more on realistic financial metrics and less on expectations of short-term hypergrowth. To illustrate the methodology, we will use Amazon (AMZN) as example.

## Calculating Future Market Capitalization

We have estimated that the return required by investors given the risk born by investing in a particular Internet-related stock to be 20 percent. The 20 percent figure was chosen by examining more traditional technology companies and using a Capital Asset Pricing Model (which calculates a discount rate by comparing the volatility of stock prices to market volatility). When examining established technology companies like Microsoft, IBM, Cisco, Nokia, and Hewlett-Packard, the required rate of return tends to be about 15 percent. We have added a premium to this figure because Internet companies tend to be less established and more volatile—and therefore more risky to the investor.

We feel that an appropriate range of forward-looking discount rates is 15 percent to 25 percent. By applying this required rate of return to the current market capitalization, we can calculate the future market capitalization for the company in question. To use our example, the market capitalization for AMZN on June 11, 1999, was $17.1 billion. If you assume a 20 percent required rate of return, AMZN would have needed to grow to a market capitalization of $42.6 billion by June 2004 in order to satisfy investors, given the risk of the investment.

In addition to generating return for current investors, many technology and Internet companies lure top engineering, marketing, and management talent by granting employees stock options. For the set of Internet companies, we have assumed that current investors will be diluted by 5 percent through the future exercise of employee options. While future potential dilution from option issuance varies from company to company, experience tells us that this number is representative for IPO-stage technology companies. Returning to our example, this assumption implies that AMZN actually needed to achieve a market capitalization of $44.7 billion in order to satisfy investor risk, given future employee-option dilution.

## Calculating Operating Figures Implied by Future Market Capitalization

A standard valuation methodology for more established technology companies is the price-to-historical-earnings (P/E) multiple, determined by dividing the market capitalization by the earnings generated over the last twelve months by the company. The assumptions that earnings are a quantifiable proxy for future potential cash flows and that a group of companies with similar growth trajectories and market opportunities will trade at similar P/E ratios underpin the theory that justifies using P/E ratios.

We have assumed a P/E of 40 for the set of Internet companies we are analyzing by examining a set of successful and established technology companies. Examples include Computer Associates (40X), Oracle (37X), Intel (33X), Nokia (41X), Ericsson (32X), IBM (30X), and Sun Microsystems (50X). This ratio could change depending on the future growth opportunities of the company as well as on the execution history of management and many other factors. Most of the Internet companies could realistically range anywhere from 20 to 60X. Using the P/E assumption, we can calculate the earnings the future valuation implies. In our example, based on the assumption of a P/E ratio of 40, the future market capitalization of $44.7 billion implies future earnings of $1.1 billion.

We have assumed that as the Internet becomes more established, competition will drive net margins to become aligned with those of more traditional companies in similar subsegments. These net margins vary according to subsegment, but, for example, a number of online retail stores will emerge and drive net margins to those similar to today's traditional retail stores. More value-added or differentiated services such as financial services will continue to command higher net margins. The assumed margins for each segment are listed in the following table.

Once we have assumed a certain future margin, we can calculate the future expected revenues implied by the current market valuation. In our example, we apply the assumed margin of 5 percent to AMZN's future earnings of $1.1 billion, which would yield future revenues of $22.3 billion.

## Examining Implied Revenue Growth Rates

By comparing this future revenue number to the company's revenues for the previous twelve months, we could calculate an implied future growth rate. You could make the case that this calculation be used to determine whether the company in question is undervalued or overvalued. If you believe the company will grow faster than this growth rate over the next five years, the company would be undervalued. On the other hand, if you don't believe the company can generate that sort of growth (or the industry in general cannot generate that growth year over year), that company (or industry) is overvalued.

In our example, AMZN generated revenues of $813.3 million in the twelve months ending in March 1999. AMZN would have to grow its revenues at 94 percent year over year (or almost double in revenues every year) for the next five years in order to justify its June 1999 market capitalization. We can compare this growth to selected equity analyst projections, which indicate that AMZN will grow at a compounded annual growth rate (CAGR) of 46 percent over the next four years. Using the assumptions listed above, this methodology implied that AMZN was overvalued.

## Using Estimated Growth Rates to Determine Implied Current Value

This same methodology can be used in reverse in order to determine an implied value of a company today. If you assume a set growth rate for any particular company or group of companies, you can calculate the future revenues. For our example, AMZN's revenues for the given twelve months were $813.3 million. If you assume a CAGR for the next five years of 46 percent, AMZN would need to achieve revenues of $5.4 billion within five years. With the revenues and assumed net margin, you can calculate the future implied earnings.

For the retail space we have assumed a net margin of 5 percent, which indicates that AMZN should generate earnings in five years of $270 million. With the earnings, assumed P/E ratio, and option dilution, you can calculate what the expected future market capitalization, excluding option dilution, would be. When we use the same P/E and option-dilution assumptions as above (40× and 5 percent), the implied future equity market capitalization is $10.3 billion. Then, by discounting that market capitalization back to the present by the required rate of return, we can calculate what the actual valuation for this company or set of companies should be. Using the 20 percent assumption for the required rate of return, we find that according to this methodology, AMZN should actually have had a market capitalization in 1999 of $4.1 billion. When compared to the market capitalization of $17.1 billion on June 11, 1999, these assumptions and valuation model indicate that AMZN was overvalued by approximately $13.0 billion, or over 75 percent of its value at the time.

# APPENDIX C: *THE INTERNET WASTELAND*

*(Information as of March 1, 2001;
www.vtoreport.com/other/wasteland.htm)*

| Company | Symbol | Industry | 52-Wk High | Price | Change |
|---|---|---|---|---|---|
| 24/7 Media, Inc. | TFSM | Internet Software & Services | 61.25 | 0.78 | −98.7% |
| 3dshopping.Com | THD | Internet Software & Services | 14.00 | | −100.0% |
| 724 Solutions Inc. | SVNX | Internet Software & Services | 240.00 | 14.25 | −94.1% |
| Accrue Software, Inc. | ACRU | Internet Software & Services | 57.38 | 1.03 | −98.2% |
| adam.com Inc. | ADAM | Internet Information Providers | 15.63 | 2.06 | −86.8% |
| AdStar.com, Inc. | ADST | Internet Service Providers | 11.00 | 0.94 | −91.5% |
| AGENCY.COM Ltd. | ACOM | Internet Software & Services | 35.94 | 1.94 | −94.6% |
| Allaire Corporation | ALLR | Internet Software & Services | 92.59 | 8.75 | −90.5% |
| Allied Riser Communications | ARCC | Internet Software & Services | 48.75 | 2.31 | −95.3% |
| Allscripts Healthcare Solutions | MDRX | Internet Software & Services | 89.63 | 5.63 | −93.7% |

| Company | Symbol | Industry | 52-Wk High | Price | Change |
|---------|--------|----------|-----------|-------|--------|
| Amazon.com, Inc. | AMZN | Internet Software & Services | 75.25 | 10.44 | −86.1% |
| AppliedTheory Corporation | ATHY | Internet Software & Services | 37.00 | 1.22 | −96.7% |
| Apropos Technology, Inc. | APRS | Internet Software & Services | 69.00 | 5.19 | −92.5% |
| Aptimus, Inc. | APTM | Internet Information Providers | 36.00 | 0.50 | −98.6% |
| Ariba, Inc. | ARBA | Internet Software & Services | 242.00 | 17.06 | −93.0% |
| ARTISTdirect, Inc. | ARTD | Internet Software & Services | 12.75 | 0.78 | −93.9% |
| AsiaContent.com, Ltd. | IASIA | Internet Software & Services | 15.94 | 0.50 | −96.9% |
| AsiaInfo Holdings, Inc. | ASIA | Internet Service Providers | 100.81 | 12.06 | −88.0% |
| At Home Corporation | ATHM | Internet Information Providers | 50.00 | 5.88 | −88.2% |
| Audible, Inc. | ADBL | Internet Software & Services | 15.31 | 1.38 | −91.0% |
| Authoriszor Inc. | AUTH | Internet Service Providers | 40.50 | 1.44 | −96.4% |
| autobytel.com inc. | ABTL | Internet Software & Services | 11.50 | 2.00 | −82.6% |
| Autoweb.com, Inc. | AWEB | Internet Software & Services | 10.56 | 0.34 | −96.8% |
| Avenue A, Inc. | AVEA | Internet Service Providers | 67.69 | 1.31 | −98.1% |
| BackWeb Technologies Ltd. | BWEB | Internet Software & Services | 59.13 | 3.22 | −94.6% |
| Baltimore Technologies plc | BALT | Internet Software & Services | 44.00 | 7.56 | −82.8% |
| barnesandnoble.com inc. | BNBN | Internet Software & Services | 11.25 | 1.38 | −87.7% |
| BarPoint.com, Inc. | BPNT | Internet Software & Services | 28.00 | 0.94 | −96.6% |
| Be Free, Inc. | BFRE | Internet Software & Services | 50.63 | 2.06 | −95.9% |
| BID.COM International Inc. | BIDS | Internet Software & Services | 10.06 | 0.72 | −92.8% |
| Blue Zone, Inc. | BLZN | Internet Software & Services | 15.38 | 0.38 | −97.5% |
| Braun Consulting, Inc. | BRNC | Internet Software & Services | 63.31 | 6.06 | −90.4% |
| Broadbase Software, Inc. | BBSW | Internet Software & Services | 82.31 | 3.47 | −95.8% |
| BroadVision, Inc. | BVSN | Internet Software & Services | 93.20 | 7.47 | −92.0% |
| BUY.COM INC. | BUYX | Internet Software & Services | 16.81 | 0.41 | −97.6% |
| CacheFlow Inc. | CFLO | Internet Software & Services | 161.38 | 7.00 | −95.7% |
| Caldera Systems, Inc. | CALD | Internet Software & Services | 33.00 | 2.00 | −93.9% |
| CareScience, Inc. | CARE | Internet Service Providers | 12.13 | 1.13 | −90.7% |
| C-bridge Internet Solutions, Inc. | CBIS | Internet Software & Services | 60.00 | 2.94 | −95.1% |
| chinadotcom corporation | CHINA | Internet Information Providers | 78.00 | 4.25 | −94.6% |
| CMGI, Inc. | CMGI | Internet Software & Services | 154.00 | 4.22 | −97.3% |
| CNET Networks, Inc. | CNET | Internet Information Providers | 75.00 | 11.50 | −84.7% |
| Cobalt Group, Inc. | CBLT | Internet Software & Services | 15.50 | 3.06 | −80.3% |
| Crayfish Co., Ltd. | CRFH | Internet Software & Services | 1,660.00 | 13.00 | −99.2% |
| CUseeMe Networks | CUSM | Internet Software & Services | 49.63 | 1.31 | −97.4% |
| CyberCash, Inc. | CYCH | Internet Software & Services | 16.00 | 0.78 | −95.1% |
| Cyberian Outpost, Inc. | COOL | Internet Software & Services | 11.81 | 0.88 | −92.5% |
| Daleen Technologies, Inc. | DALN | Internet Software & Services | 35.25 | 2.00 | −94.3% |
| Data Return Corporation | DRTN | Internet Software & Services | 94.25 | 3.66 | −96.1% |

| Company | Symbol | Industry | 52-Wk High | Price | Change |
|---|---|---|---|---|---|
| Delano Technology Corporation | DTEC | Internet Software & Services | 54.13 | 2.50 | −95.4% |
| deltathree inc. | DDDC | Internet Software & Services | 50.38 | 1.50 | −97.0% |
| Digex, Incorporated | DIGX | Internet Software & Services | 184.00 | 18.19 | −90.1% |
| Digital Impact, Inc. | DIGI | Internet Software & Services | 47.25 | 2.16 | −95.4% |
| DigitalThink, Inc. | DTHK | Internet Software & Services | 62.00 | 8.56 | −86.2% |
| Digitas Inc. | DTAS | Internet Software & Services | 40.00 | 4.94 | −87.7% |
| divine interVentures, Inc. | DVIN | Internet Service Providers | 12.44 | 1.75 | −85.9% |
| DoubleClick Inc. | DCLK | Internet Software & Services | 119.00 | 13.75 | −88.4% |
| drkoop.com, Inc. | KOOP | Internet Information Providers | 10.94 | 0.22 | −98.0% |
| drugstore.com, inc. | DSCM | Internet Software & Services | 24.50 | 1.31 | −94.7% |
| e.spire Communications, Inc. | ESPI | Internet Service Providers | 16.81 | 0.66 | −96.1% |
| eBenX, Inc. | EBNX | Internet Software & Services | 62.00 | 5.75 | −90.7% |
| ebookers.com plc | EBKR | Internet Software & Services | 43.00 | 2.50 | −94.2% |
| EDGAR Online, Inc. | EDGR | Internet Information Providers | 16.00 | 2.06 | −87.1% |
| Egghead.com, Inc. | EGGS | Internet Software & Services | 10.50 | 0.75 | −92.9% |
| El Sitio, Inc. | LCTO | Internet Software & Services | 24.25 | 1.16 | −95.2% |
| Eloquent, Inc. | ELOQ | Internet Software & Services | 40.00 | 1.06 | −97.4% |
| eLoyalty Corporation | ELOY | Internet Software & Services | 34.75 | 3.47 | −90.0% |
| e-MedSoft.com | MED | Internet Software & Services | 24.25 | 1.05 | −95.7% |
| eMerge Interactive, Inc. | EMRG | Internet Service Providers | 68.00 | 4.63 | −93.2% |
| Engage, Inc. | ENGA | Internet Software & Services | 95.00 | 1.03 | −98.9% |
| eOn Communications Corporation | EONC | Internet Service Providers | 25.88 | 1.41 | −94.6% |
| Eprise Corporation | EPRS | Internet Software & Services | 27.44 | 1.31 | −95.2% |
| Equinix, Inc. | EQIX | Internet Service Providers | 16.75 | 3.16 | −81.1% |
| e-SIM Ltd. | ESIM | Internet Software & Services | 41.00 | 1.88 | −95.4% |
| E-Stamp Corporation | ESTM | Internet Software & Services | 13.88 | 0.13 | −99.1% |
| E-Sync Networks, Inc. | ESNI | Internet Service Providers | 16.00 | 0.91 | -94.3% |
| euro909.com A/S | ENON | Internet Service Providers | 25.50 | 2.31 | −90.9% |
| eXcelon Corporation | EXLN | Internet Software & Services | 27.50 | 3.00 | −89.1% |
| Exodus Communications, Inc. | EXDS | Internet Software & Services | 89.81 | 15.25 | −83.0% |
| Extensity, Inc. | EXTN | Internet Service Providers | 75.50 | 8.59 | −88.6% |
| Extreme Networks, Inc. | EXTR | Internet Software & Services | 128.88 | 23.31 | −81.9% |
| F5 Networks, Inc. | FFIV | Internet Software & Services | 119.00 | 7.75 | −93.5% |
| FASTNET Corporation | FSST | Internet Software & Services | 20.00 | 1.13 | −94.4% |
| FiNet.com, Inc. | FNCCD | Internet Software & Services | 29.25 | 1.31 | −95.5% |
| FreeMarkets, Inc. | FMKT | Internet Software & Services | 215.50 | 18.25 | −91.5% |
| Freeserve plc | FREE | Internet Information Providers | 144.38 | 14.00 | −90.3% |
| GigaMedia Limited | GIGM | Internet Service Providers | 86.25 | 2.50 | −97.1% |
| Global Sources Ltd. | GSOL | Internet Software & Services | 99.88 | 10.50 | −89.5% |
| GlobalNetFinancial.com, Inc. | GLBN | Internet Service Providers | 57.50 | 0.94 | −98.4% |
| Globix Corporation | GBIX | Internet Software & Services | 64.00 | 3.56 | −94.4% |
| GoTo.com, Inc. | GOTO | Internet Information Providers | 62.44 | 8.09 | −87.0% |
| GRIC Communications, Inc. | GRIC | Internet Service Providers | 62.00 | 2.00 | −96.8% |

| Company | Symbol | Industry | 52-Wk High | Price | Change |
|---|---|---|---|---|---|
| GSV, Inc. | GSVIC | Internet Software & Services | 18.05 | 0.31 | −98.3% |
| HealthAxis Inc. | HAXS | Internet Software & Services | 27.75 | 1.16 | −95.8% |
| HealthStream, Inc. | HSTM | Internet Service Providers | 11.00 | 1.63 | −85.2% |
| HearMe | HEAR | Internet Software & Services | 29.38 | 0.94 | −96.8% |
| High Speed Access Corp. | HSAC | Internet Software & Services | 21.25 | 1.38 | −93.5% |
| HomeSeekers. com, Inc. | HMSK | Internet Information Providers | 23.88 | 0.34 | −98.6% |
| HotJobs.com, Ltd. | HOTJ | Internet Information Providers | 32.75 | 4.22 | −87.1% |
| iBasis, Inc. | IBAS | Internet Software & Services | 86.00 | 4.69 | −94.5% |
| iBEAM Broadcasting Corporation | IBEM | Internet Service Providers | 29.44 | 1.34 | −95.4% |
| IFX Corporation | FUTR | Internet Software & Services | 37.94 | 3.25 | −91.4% |
| imageX.com, Inc. | IMGX | Internet Software & Services | 29.38 | 2.09 | −92.9% |
| iManage, Inc. | IMAN | Internet Software & Services | 27.38 | 3.53 | −87.1% |
| ImproveNet, Inc. | IMPV | Internet Software & Services | 20.00 | 0.69 | −96.6% |
| Infonautics, Inc. | INFO | Internet Information Providers | 13.50 | 0.81 | −94.0% |
| InfoNow Corporation | INOW | Internet Service Providers | 24.13 | 2.06 | −91.5% |
| InfoSpace, Inc. | INSP | Internet Information Providers | 135.44 | 3.72 | −97.3% |
| Inktomi Corporation | INKT | Internet Software & Services | 241.50 | 11.44 | −95.3% |
| Integrated Information Systems | IISX | Internet Software & Services | 28.00 | 1.19 | −95.8% |
| interactive investor international | IINV | Internet Information Providers | 65.38 | 3.75 | −94.3% |
| INTERLAND, INC. | ILND | Internet Software & Services | 12.00 | 1.81 | −84.9% |
| Interliant, Inc. | INIT | Internet Software & Services | 49.50 | 2.94 | −94.1% |
| InterNAP Network Services | INAP | Internet Service Providers | 101.50 | 4.16 | −95.9% |
| Internet America, Inc. | GEEK | Internet Service Providers | 15.25 | 0.81 | −94.7% |
| Internet Capital Group, Inc. | ICGE | Internet Software & Services | 156.06 | 3.50 | −97.8% |
| Internet Commerce & Comm. | ICCX | Internet Service Providers | 11.94 | 0.50 | −95.8% |
| Internet Commerce Corporation | ICCA | Internet Service Providers | 96.00 | 3.22 | −96.6% |
| Internet Gold—Golden Lines Ltd. | IGLD | Internet Information Providers | 33.00 | 1.81 | −94.5% |
| Internet Initiative Japan Inc. | IIJI | Internet Service Providers | 111.69 | 7.13 | −93.6% |
| Internet Pictures Corporation | IPIX | Internet Software & Services | 46.25 | 0.59 | −98.7% |
| Internet.com Corporation | INTM | Internet Information Providers | 66.13 | 7.75 | −88.3% |
| Intershop Communic Ads | ISHP | Internet Service Providers | 34.88 | 2.63 | −92.5% |
| InterWorld Corporation | INTW | Internet Software & Services | 88.88 | 0.53 | −99.4% |
| Intraware, Inc. | ITRA | Internet Software & Services | 77.88 | 2.09 | −97.3% |
| iPrint.com, inc. | IPRT | Internet Software & Services | 28.50 | 0.41 | −98.6% |
| ITXC Corp. | ITXC | Internet Software & Services | 96.00 | 6.13 | −93.6% |
| iVillage Inc. | IVIL | Internet Information Providers | 27.31 | 1.28 | −95.3% |

| Company | Symbol | Industry | 52-Wk High | Price | Change |
|---------|--------|----------|-----------|-------|--------|
| iXL Enterprises, Inc. | IIXL | Internet Software & Services | 40.38 | 1.38 | −96.6% |
| j2 Global Communications, Inc. | JCOMD | Internet Software & Services | 27.00 | 2.63 | −90.3% |
| Juno Online Services, Inc. | JWEB | Internet Service Providers | 25.69 | 1.44 | −94.4% |
| Kana Communications, Inc. | KANA | Internet Software & Services | 175.50 | 3.22 | −98.2% |
| Keynote Systems, Inc. | KEYN | Internet Software & Services | 164.50 | 12.94 | −92.1% |
| Korea Thrunet Co., Ltd. | KOREA | Internet Service Providers | 69.50 | 3.19 | −95.4% |
| L90, Inc. | LNTY | Internet Software & Services | 25.69 | 3.25 | −87.3% |
| Landacorp, Inc. | LCOR | Internet Software & Services | 17.25 | 2.03 | −88.2% |
| Lante Corporation | LNTE | Internet Service Providers | 80.88 | 1.88 | −97.7% |
| lastminute.com plc | LMIN | Internet Software & Services | 46.50 | 3.88 | −91.7% |
| Liberate Technologies | LBRT | Internet Software & Services | 110.00 | 9.63 | −91.2% |
| LifeMinders, Inc. | LFMN | Internet Software & Services | 94.81 | 2.00 | −97.9% |
| Liquid Audio, Inc. | LQID | Internet Software & Services | 31.13 | 2.75 | −91.2% |
| LookSmart, Ltd. | LOOK | Internet Information Providers | 72.00 | 2.09 | −97.1% |
| Loudeye Technologies, Inc. | LOUD | Internet Software & Services | 54.00 | 1.28 | −97.6% |
| Mail.com, Inc. | MAIL | Internet Software & Services | 21.00 | 1.13 | −94.6% |
| Mainspring, Inc. | MSPR | Internet Information Providers | 19.38 | 2.38 | −87.7% |
| Marex.com, Inc. | MRXX | Internet Software & Services | 37.00 | 2.00 | −94.6% |
| Marimba, Inc. | MRBA | Internet Software & Services | 62.00 | 5.25 | −91.5% |
| MarketWatch.com, Inc. | MKTW | Internet Information Providers | 45.19 | 4.88 | −89.2% |
| McAfee.com Corporation | MCAF | Internet Software & Services | 58.50 | 8.72 | −85.1% |
| Mediaplex, Inc. | MPLX | Internet Software & Services | 81.00 | 0.88 | −98.9% |
| MedicaLogic/ Medscape, Inc. | MDLI | Internet Software & Services | 41.38 | 2.56 | −93.8% |
| MessageMedia, Inc. | MESG | Internet Software & Services | 17.50 | 0.84 | −95.2% |
| Micro General Corporation | MGEN | Internet Service Providers | 45.00 | 8.63 | −80.8% |
| MP3.com, Inc. | MPPP | Internet Software & Services | 29.94 | 2.75 | −90.8% |
| musicmaker.com, Inc. | HITS | Internet Software & Services | 47.50 | 5.38 | −88.7% |
| MyPoints.com, Inc. | MYPT | Internet Software & Services | 70.50 | 1.13 | −98.4% |
| MyWeb Inc.com | MWB | Internet Software & Services | 18.13 | 0.35 | −98.1% |
| N2H2, Inc. | NTWO | Internet Software & Services | 25.25 | 0.50 | −98.0% |
| National Information Consortium | EGOV | Internet Software & Services | 78.00 | 3.03 | −96.1% |
| NaviSite, Inc. | NAVI | Internet Service Providers | 164.94 | 1.84 | −98.9% |
| Neoforma.com, Inc. | NEOF | Internet Software & Services | 59.00 | 1.16 | −98.0% |
| net.Genesis Corp. | NTGX | Internet Software & Services | 53.25 | 3.31 | −93.8% |
| Netease.com, Inc. | NTES | Internet Information Providers | 17.25 | 1.97 | −88.6% |
| Netopia, Inc. | NTPA | Internet Software & Services | 86.63 | 6.03 | −93.0% |
| Netplex Group, Inc. | NTPL | Internet Software & Services | 19.50 | 0.13 | −99.3% |
| Netpliance, Inc. | NPLI | Internet Software & Services | 26.13 | 0.38 | −98.5% |
| Network Commerce Inc. | NWKC | Internet Software & Services | 21.81 | 0.25 | −98.9% |
| Network Engines, Inc. | NENG | Internet Service Providers | 48.50 | 1.72 | −96.5% |
| Netzee, Inc. | NETZ | Internet Software & Services | 25.38 | 0.50 | −98.0% |

| Company | Symbol | Industry | 52-Wk High | Price | Change |
|---|---|---|---|---|---|
| NetZero, Inc. | NZRO | Internet Software & Services | 27.00 | 0.81 | −97.0% |
| Niku Corporation | NIKU | Internet Service Providers | 101.25 | 5.13 | −94.9% |
| Novo Networks | NVNW | Internet Software & Services | 35.00 | 4.25 | −87.9% |
| NQL Inc. | NQLI | Internet Software & Services | 11.38 | 2.03 | −82.2% |
| On2.com Inc. | ONT | Internet Software & Services | 23.75 | 1.04 | −95.6% |
| Online Resources & Comm. | ORCC | Internet Software & Services | 24.50 | 2.69 | −89.0% |
| Onvia.com, Inc. | ONVI | Internet Software & Services | 59.00 | 0.66 | −98.9% |
| Open Market, Inc. | OMKT | Internet Software & Services | 66.00 | 2.16 | −96.7% |
| Openwave Systems Inc. | OPWV | Internet Software & Services | 208.00 | 33.81 | −83.7% |
| Opus360 Corporation | OPUS | Internet Software & Services | 15.78 | 0.34 | −97.8% |
| Organic, Inc. | OGNC | Internet Software & Services | 37.50 | 0.69 | −98.2% |
| OTG Software, Inc. | OTGS | Internet Software & Services | 61.44 | 10.75 | −82.5% |
| Pacific Internet Limited | PCNTF | Internet Service Providers | 67.00 | 3.31 | −95.1% |
| PacificNet.com Inc. | PACT | Internet Software & Services | 25.88 | 0.78 | −97.0% |
| PartsBase.com, Inc. | PRTS | Internet Software & Services | 14.88 | 1.63 | −89.0% |
| PASW, Inc. | PASW | Internet Software & Services | 12.63 | 0.53 | −95.8% |
| PeoplePC Inc. | PEOP | Internet Service Providers | 10.38 | 0.78 | −92.5% |
| Pilot Network Services, Inc. | PILT | Internet Software & Services | 55.13 | 1.31 | −97.6% |
| Preview Systems, Inc. | PRVW | Internet Software & Services | 72.00 | 2.97 | −95.9% |
| priceline.com Incorporated | PCLN | Internet Software & Services | 104.25 | 2.56 | −97.5% |
| Primix Solutions Inc. | PMIX | Internet Software & Services | 14.75 | 2.00 | −86.4% |
| Primus Knowledge Solutions, Inc. | PKSI | Internet Software & Services | 137.25 | 6.19 | −95.5% |
| Promotions.com, Inc. | PRMO | Internet Software & Services | 17.31 | 0.38 | −97.8% |
| PSINet Inc. | PSIX | Internet Service Providers | 60.94 | 1.34 | −97.8% |
| PurchasePro.com, Inc. | PPRO | Internet Software & Services | 82.00 | 12.13 | −85.2% |
| QXL ricardo plc | QXLC | Internet Software & Services | 586.88 | 2.81 | −99.5% |
| Rare Medium Group Inc. | RRRR | Internet Software & Services | 94.75 | 2.09 | −97.8% |
| RealNetworks, Inc. | RNWK | Internet Software & Services | 84.75 | 7.78 | −90.8% |
| Red Hat, Inc. | RHAT | Internet Software & Services | 79.56 | 6.25 | −92.1% |
| Rediff.com India Limited | REDF | Internet Information Providers | 27.63 | 3.25 | −88.2% |
| Register.com, Inc. | RCOM | Internet Service Providers | 116.00 | 5.88 | −94.9% |
| Resonate Inc. | RSNT | Internet Service Providers | 50.56 | 3.75 | −92.6% |
| Rhythms NetConnections Inc. | RTHM | Internet Software & Services | 45.25 | 0.97 | −97.9% |
| S1 Corporation | SONE | Internet Software & Services | 120.00 | 7.25 | −94.0% |
| Safeguard Scientifics, Inc. | SFE | Internet Software & Services | 98.90 | 7.00 | −92.9% |
| Satyam Infoway Limited | SIFY | Internet Service Providers | 97.50 | 4.06 | −95.8% |
| SAVVIS Communications Corp. | SVVS | Internet Software & Services | 24.00 | 1.13 | −95.3% |
| Scient Corporation | SCNT | Internet Software & Services | 133.75 | 2.53 | −98.1% |
| SciQuest.com, Inc. | SQST | Internet Software & Services | 84.50 | 1.84 | −97.8% |
| Scoot.com plc | SCOP | Internet Information Providers | 111.50 | 13.25 | −88.1% |

| Company | Symbol | Industry | 52-Wk High | Price | Change |
|---|---|---|---|---|---|
| ScreamingMedia, Inc. | SCRM | Internet Service Providers | 15.75 | 2.06 | −86.9% |
| Selectica, Inc. | SLTC | Internet Software & Services | 154.44 | 7.69 | −95.0% |
| Sequoia Software Corporation | SQSW | Internet Software & Services | 21.75 | 3.25 | −85.1% |
| ServiceWare Technologies, Inc. | SVCW | Internet Service Providers | 10.50 | 1.19 | −88.7% |
| SignalSoft Corporation | SGSF | Internet Software & Services | 50.88 | 7.94 | −84.4% |
| SimPlayer.com Ltd. | SMPL | Internet Software & Services | 14.00 | 0.31 | −97.8% |
| SINA.com | SINA | Internet Software & Services | 58.56 | 2.47 | −95.8% |
| Snowball.com, Inc. | SNOW | Internet Software & Services | 20.00 | 0.47 | −97.7% |
| SoftLock.com, Inc. | DIGS | Internet Service Providers | 24.00 | 1.47 | −93.9% |
| SoftNet Systems, Inc. | SOFN | Internet Service Providers | 39.00 | 1.38 | −96.5% |
| Sohu.com Inc. | SOHU | Internet Information Providers | 13.78 | 1.09 | −92.1% |
| SonicWALL, Inc. | SNWL | Internet Software & Services | 66.69 | 11.00 | −83.5% |
| SportsLine.com, Inc. | SPLN | Internet Information Providers | 60.50 | 5.19 | −91.4% |
| Stamps.com Inc. | STMP | Internet Software & Services | 35.00 | 2.78 | −92.1% |
| Stockwalk Group, Inc. | STOK | Internet Software & Services | 17.13 | 2.50 | −85.4% |
| Styleclick Inc. | IBUY | Internet Software & Services | 12.50 | 2.00 | −84.0% |
| Sunhawk.com Corporation | SNHK | Internet Service Providers | 28.50 | 4.13 | −85.5% |
| Take to Auction.com, Inc. | TTA | Internet Service Providers | 10.38 | 0.80 | −92.3% |
| Talk City, Inc. | TCTY | Internet Software & Services | 13.50 | 0.13 | −99.0% |
| Talk.com Inc. | TALK | Internet Software & Services | 18.00 | 1.50 | −91.7% |
| Telemate.Net Software, Inc. | TMNT | Internet Software & Services | 16.56 | 1.13 | −93.2% |
| Terra Lycos, Inc. | TRLY | Internet Service Providers | 121.00 | 11.81 | −90.2% |
| TheStreet.com, Inc. | TSCM | Internet Information Providers | 14.25 | 2.81 | −80.3% |
| topjobs.net plc | TJOB | Internet Software & Services | 20.00 | 1.47 | −92.7% |
| Tumbleweed Communications | TMWD | Internet Software & Services | 136.00 | 3.41 | −97.5% |
| Universal Access, Inc. | UAXS | Internet Software & Services | 63.00 | 6.81 | −89.2% |
| Uproar Inc. | UPRO | Internet Software & Services | 35.00 | 2.97 | −91.5% |
| USABancShares.com, Inc. | USAB | Internet Software & Services | 12.44 | 1.50 | −87.9% |
| USinternetworking, Inc. | USIX | Internet Software & Services | 71.70 | 2.00 | −97.2% |
| Ventro Corporation | VNTR | Internet Software & Services | 228.00 | 1.09 | −99.5% |
| Venture Catalyst Inc. | VCAT | Internet Software & Services | 12.75 | 1.19 | −90.7% |
| VerticalNet, Inc. | VERT | Internet Information Providers | 148.38 | 3.06 | −97.9% |
| VIA NET.WORKS, Inc. | VNWI | Internet Service Providers | 70.00 | 5.25 | −92.5% |
| Viant Corporation | VIAN | Internet Software & Services | 44.63 | 3.03 | −93.2% |
| Vicinity Corporation | VCNT | Internet Service Providers | 76.25 | 2.34 | −96.9% |
| Vignette Corporation | VIGN | Internet Software & Services | 100.57 | 6.38 | −93.7% |
| VINA Technologies, Inc. | VINA | Internet Software & Services | 24.00 | 2.00 | −91.7% |
| VocalTec Communications Ltd. | VOCL | Internet Software & Services | 52.13 | 4.47 | −91.4% |
| WatchGuard Technologies, Inc. | WGRD | Internet Software & Services | 125.36 | 10.81 | −91.4% |

| Company | Symbol | Industry | 52-Wk High | Price | Change |
|---|---|---|---|---|---|
| Web Street, Inc. | WEBS | Internet Software & Services | 11.94 | 0.91 | −92.4% |
| Webb Interactive Services, Inc. | WEBB | Internet Software & Services | 54.50 | 2.81 | −94.8% |
| WebTrends Corporation | WEBT | Internet Software & Services | 86.63 | 15.00 | −82.7% |
| Women.com Networks, Inc. | WOMN | Internet Information Providers | 15.00 | 0.31 | −97.9% |
| Xpedior Incorporated | XPDR | Internet Software & Services | 25.69 | 0.66 | −97.4% |
| Yahoo! Inc. | YHOO | Internet Information Providers | 205.63 | 24.44 | −88.1% |
| ZapMe! Corporation | IZAP | Internet Information Providers | 11.63 | 0.63 | −94.6% |
| Zixit Corporation | ZIXI | Internet Software & Services | 96.50 | 8.75 | −90.9% |

These tables published with the permission of VTO Report. For further information, see www.vtoreport.com/other/wasteland.htm.

# BIBLIOGRAPHY

## Books

Allen, Frederick Lewis. *Only Yesterday: An Informal History of the 1920s*. New York: Harper & Row, 1931/1964.

Baldwin, Neil. *Edison: Inventing the Century*. New York: Hyperion, 1995.

Boorstin, Daniel J. *The Americans: The Democratic Experience*. New York: Random House, 1973.

Bygrave, William D., and Jeffry A. Timmons. *Venture Capital at the Crossroads*. Boston: Harvard Business School Press, 1992.

Bylinsky, Gene. *The Innovation Millionaires: How They Succeed*. New York: Charles Scribner's Sons, 1976.

Carlton, Jim. *Apple: The Inside Story of Intrigue, Egomania, and Business Blunders*. New York: Times Books/Random House, 1997/1998.

Chancellor, Edward. *Devil Take the Hindmost: A History of Financial Speculation*. New York: Plume/Penguin Putnam, 1999.

Chandler, Alfred D., Jr. *The Visible Hand: The Managerial Revolution in American Business*. Cambridge, Mass.: Harvard University Press, 1977.

Chopsky, James, and Ted Leonsis. *Blue Magic: The People, Power, and Politics Behind the IBM Personal Computer.* New York, Oxford: Facts on File Publications, 1988.

Christensen, Clayton M. *The Innovator's Dilemma.* New York: Harper-Business, 1997/2000.

Collier, Peter, and David Horowitz. *The Fords: An American Epic.* New York: Simon & Schuster, 1987.

Collins, James C., and Jerry I. Porras. *Built to Last: Successful Habits of Visionary Companies.* New York: HarperBusiness, 1994.

Cringely, Robert X. *Accidental Empires: How the Boys of Silicon Valley Make Their Millions, Battle Foreign Competition, and Still Can't Get a Date.* Reading, Mass.: Addison-Wesley Publishing, 1992.

Cusumano, Michael, and David B. Yoffie. *Competing on Internet Time: Lessons from Netscape and Its Battle with Microsoft.* New York: The Free Press, 1998.

Davidow, William H. *Marketing High Technology: An Insider's View.* New York, London: Free Press, 1986.

DeNovo, John, ed. *The Gilded Age and After.* New York: Charles Scribner's Sons, 1972.

Doerflinger, Thomas M., and Jack L. Rivkin. *Risk and Reward: Venture Capital and the Making of America's Great Industries.* New York: Random House, 1987.

Edstrom, Jennifer, and Marlin Eller. *Barbarians Led by Bill Gates: Microsoft from the Inside.* New York: Henry Holt and Company, 1998.

Galbraith, John Kenneth. *The Great Crash: 1929.* New York: Houghton Mifflin, 1954/1997.

Galbraith, John Kenneth. *A Short History of Financial Euphoria.* New York: Whittle Books/Viking Penguin, 1990.

Geisst, Charles R. *Wall Street: A History.* New York: Oxford University Press, 1997.

Gordon, John Steele. *The Scarlet Woman of Wall Street: Jay Gould, Jim Fisk, Cornelius Vanderbilt, The Erie Railway Wars and the Birth of Wall Street.* New York: Weidenfeld & Nicolson, 1988.

Grove, Andrew S. *Only the Paranoid Survive.* New York: Doubleday, 1996.

Gupta, Udayan, ed. *Done Deals: Venture Capitalists Tell Their Stories.* Boston: Harvard Business School Press, 2000.

Hooke, Jeffrey C. *Security Analysis on Wall Street.* New York: John Wiley & Sons, 1998.

Ichbiah, Daniel, and Susan L. Knepper. *The Making of Microsoft: How Bill Gates and His Team Created the World's Most Successful Software Company.* Rocklin, Calif.: Prima Publishing, 1991.

Jackson, Tim. *Inside Intel: Andrew Grove and the Rise of the World's Most Powerful Chip Company.* New York: Dutton Books, 1997.

Kaplan, Jerry. *Startup: A Silicon Valley Adventure Story.* New York: Houghton Mifflin, 1995.

Kelly, Kevin. *New Rules for the New Economy.* New York: Viking Penguin, 1998.

Kindelberger, Charles P. *Manias, Panics, and Crashes: A History of Financial Crises.* New York: John Wiley & Sons, 1996.

Kornberg, Arthur. *The Golden Helix: Inside Biotech Ventures.* Sausalito, Calif.: University Science Books, 1995.

Krugman, Paul. *The Return of Depression Economics.* New York: W. W. Norton & Company, 1999.

Lewis, Oscar. *The Big Four.* New York: Alfred A. Knopf, 1938.

———. *The Silver Kings.* New York: Ballantine Books, 1947.

Mackay, Charles. *Extraordinary Popular Delusions & the Madness of Crowds.* New York: Three Rivers Press, 1980.

Malone, Michael S. *The Big Score: The Billion Dollar Story of Silicon Valley.* New York: Doubleday, 1985.

———. *Going Public: MIPS Computer and the Entrepreneurial Dream.* New York: E. Burlingame Books, 1991.

Manes, Stephen, and Paul Andrews. *Gates: How Microsoft's Mogul Reinvented an Industry—and Made Himself the Richest Man in America.* New York: Doubleday, 1993.

Meeker, Mary, and the Morgan Stanley Technology Team. *The Technology & Internet IPO Yearbook*, 6th ed. New York: Morgan Stanley Dean Witter, 2000.

Moore, Geoffrey A. *Crossing the Chasm: Marketing and Selling Technology Products to Mainstream Customers.* New York: HarperBusiness, 1991.

Moore, Geoffrey A., et al. *The Gorilla Game: An Investor's Guide to Picking Winners in High Technology*. New York: HarperBusiness, 1998.

Moritz, Michael. *The Little Kingdom: The Private Story of Apple Computer*. New York: William Morrow and Company, 1984.

Myers, Gustavus. *History of the Great American Fortunes*. Charles H. Kerr Publishing Co., 1982.

Perkins, Michael C. *The Red Herring Guide to the Digital Universe: The Inside Look at Technology Business from Silicon Valley to Hollywood*. New York: Warner Books, 1996.

Perkins, Michael C., and Celia Núñez. *A Cool Billion*. Campbell, Calif.: iUniverse.com, 2000.

Quittner, Joshua, and Michelle Slatalla. *Speeding the Net: The Inside Story of Netscape and How It Challenged Microsoft*. New York: Atlantic Monthly Press, 1998.

Reid, Robert H. *Architects of the Web: 1,000 Days That Built the Future of Business*. New York: John Wiley & Sons, 1997.

Rogers, Everett M., and Judith K. Larsen. *Silicon Valley Fever*. New York: Basic Books, 1984.

Rolm, Wendy Goldman. *The Microsoft File: The Secret Case Against Bill Gates*. New York: Times Business Books/Random House, 1998.

Saxenian, AnnaLee. *Regional Advantage: Culture and Competition in Silicon Valley and Route 128*. Cambridge, Mass.: Harvard University Press, 1996.

Schama, Simon. *The Embarrassment of Riches: An Interpretation of Dutch Culture in the Golden Age*. Berkeley: University of California Press, 1988.

Schiller, Robert. *Irrational Exuberance*. Princeton, N.J.: Princeton University Press, 2000.

Schilt, W. Keith. *Dream Makers & Deal Breakers: Inside the Venture Capital Industry*. Englewood Cliffs, N.J.: Prentice Hall, 1991.

Schor, Juliet B. *The Overworked American*. New York: Basic Books, 1992.

Schwartz, Peter, Peter Leyden, and Joel Hyatt. *The Long Boom*. New York: Perseus Press, 1999.

Siegel, Jeremy J. *Stocks for the Long Run*. New York: McGraw Hill, 1998.

Stewart, James B. *Den of Thieves*. New York: Simon & Schuster, 1991.

Stross, Randall E. *The Microsoft Way: The Real Story of the How the Com-*

*pany Outsmarts Its Competition.* Reading, Mass.: Addison-Wesley Publishing, 1996.

Swisher, Kara. *aol.com.* New York: Times Business Books/Random House, 1998.

Wallace, James. *Overdrive: Bill Gates and the Race to Control Cyberspace.* New York: John Wiley & Sons, 1997.

Wallace, James, and Jim Erickson. *Hard Drive: Bill Gates and the Making of the Microsoft Empire.* New York: John Wiley & Sons, 1992.

Wilson, John W. *The New Venturers: Inside the High-Stakes World of Venture Capital.* Reading, Mass.: Addison-Wesley Publishing, 1985.

Wilson, Mike. *The Difference Between God and Larry Ellison: Inside Oracle Corporation.* New York: William Morrow and Company, 1997.

Wolff, Michael. *Burn Rate: How I Survived the Gold Rush Years on the Internet.* New York: Simon & Schuster, 1998.

## Articles

Aragon, Larry. "CMGI Creates Confusion by Clarifying." *Redherring. com,* September 8, 2000.

Barack, Lauren. "The Underdogs of Underwriting." *Red Herring,* Going Public: 1999.

Barboza, David. "Loving a Stock Not Wisely but Too Well: The Price of Obsession with a Promising Startup." *New York Times,* September 20, 1998.

Birdsall, Nancy. "Life Is Unfair: Inequality in the World." *Foreign Policy,* Summer 1998.

Bousquin, Joe. "Ventro's Numbers Just Don't Add Up." *TheStreet.com,* July 21, 2000.

Brooker, Katrina. "The Scary Rise of Internet Stock Scams." *Fortune,* October 26, 1998.

Byron, Christopher. "Was the Dot-com Gold Rush Worth It?" *MSNBC.com,* July 5, 2000.

Carvajal, Doreen. "Trying to Read a Hazy Future." *New York Times,* April 18, 1999.

Cassidy, John. "The Woman in the Bubble." *The New Yorker,* April 26/May 3, 1999.

Caulkin, Simon. "The Trouble with Bubbles." *Worldlink: The Magazine of the World Economic Forum*, March/April 1999.

Clements, Jonathan. "In the Field of Investing, Self-Confidence Can Sometimes Come Back to Haunt You." *Wall Street Journal*, September 23, 1998.

Collins, James C. "It's Time to Rethink the Silicon Valley Paradigm." *Red Herring*, July 1993.

———. "Built to Flip." *Fast Company,* March 2000.

Darwell, Christina, and Michael J. Roberts. "The Band of Angels." *Harvard Business School*, March 11, 1998.

Fallows, James. "The Invisible Poor." *New York Times Magazine*, March 19, 2000.

Fisher, Larry. "Money Walks: VCs Are Bailing on Biotech." *Forbes ASAP*, May 31, 1999.

Fishman, Ted C. "Up in Smoke." *Harper's Magazine*, December 1998.

Foust, Dean, and Linda Himelstein. "Time to Buy Net Stocks?" *Business Week*, May 17, 1999.

Gove, Alex. "Sendmail Pits Angel Investors Against VCs." *Red Herring*, November 1998.

Gurley, Bill. "A Dell for Every Industry." *Fortune*, October 12, 1998.

———. "Internet Investors: Beware." *Fortune*, August 17, 1998.

Hamilton, Andrea M. "Japan, Heal Thyself." *Red Herring*, October 2000.

Hansell, Saul. "New Breeds of Investors, All Beguiled by the Web." *New York Times*, May 16, 1999.

———. "Cnet Is Singed by the Offbeat Logic of the Internet Investor." *New York Times*, July 6, 1999.

Hatlestad, Luc. "Free Mail Explosion." *Red Herring*, July 1998.

Heilemann, John. "The Networker." *The New Yorker*, August 11, 1997.

Henig, Peter D. "And Now, EcoNets." *Red Herring*, February 2000.

Himelstein, Linda. "Crunch Time for VCs." *Business Week*, February 19, 2001.

Hof, Robert D. "Amazon.com: The Wild World of E-Commerce." *Business Week*, December 14, 1998.

Holson, Laura M. "Still Feeding an Internet Frenzy." *New York Times*, June 6, 1999.

Hwang, Suein, and Mylene Mangalindan. "Yahoo's Grand Vision for Web Advertising Takes Some Hard Hits." *Wall Street Journal*, September 1, 2000.

Ip, Greg, Susan Pulliam, Scott Thurm, and Ruth Simon. "The Color Green: The Internet Bubble Broke Records, Rules, and Bank Accounts." *Wall Street Journal*, July 14, 2000.

Johnson, Franklin "Pitch." "The Application of Venture Capital and the Entrepreneurial Revolution in Russia." Center for International Security and Cooperation, Stanford University, August 1998.

Johnston, David Cay. "On a New Map, the Income Gap Grows." *New York Times*, September 17, 2000.

Krainer, John, and Fred Furlong. "Tech Stocks and House Prices in California." Federal Reserve Bank of San Francisco Economic Letter, Number 2000–27, September 15, 2000.

Krantz, Matt. "What Is Just an Optical Illusion?" *USA Today*, October 25, 2000.

Laderman, Jeffrey. "Wall Street's Spin Game." *Business Week*, October 5, 1998.

Laderman, Jeffrey, and Geoffrey Smith. "Internet Stocks: What's Their Real Worth?" *Business Week*, December 14, 1998.

Land, Anne Adams. "Behind the Prosperity, Working People in Trouble." *New York Times*, November 20, 2000.

Lardner, James. "Ask Radio Historians About the Internet." *U.S. News & World Report*, January 23, 1999.

Lawlor, Julia. "Book Cookery." *Red Herring*, December 4, 2000.

Leibovich, Mark. "Assembling a Brain Trust to Retail to the Masses." *The Washington Post*, September 2, 2000.

Lohr, Steve. "Computer Age Gains Respect of Economists," *New York Times*, April 14, 1999.

Lucchetti, Aaron. "Internet Public Offerings Aren't the Same in Era of Internet Stock Mania." *Wall Street Journal*, January 19, 1999.

Malik, Om. "Why Vinod Khosla May Be the Best Venture Capitalist on the Planet." *Red Herring*, February 13, 2001.

Maremont, Mark. "Raising the Stakes: As Wall Street Seeks Pre-IPO Investments, Conflicts May Arise." *Wall Street Journal*, July 24, 2000.

McNamee, Roger. "Welcome to Technology's Gilded Age." *Forbes ASAP*, October 5, 1998.

Morgenson, Gretchen. "Just Another Round of Technology Delusion." *New York Times*, April 25, 1999.

Moskowitz, Eric. "Choke Hold: Collars Can Cloak Insider Bearishness." *Red Herring*, March 6, 2001.

Mullarkey, Markus F., and André F. Perold. "Integral Capital Partners." Harvard Business School Case 9-298-171, September 1998.

Nolan, Chris. "It Pays to Be a Friend of Frank." *New York Post*, January 11, 2001.

Peltz, Michael. "High Tech's Premier Venture Capitalist." *Institutional Investor*, June 1996.

Perkins, Anthony B. "Have the Rules Really Changed?" *Red Herring*, October 1997.

———. "Navigating the Amazon." *Red Herring*, June 1997.

———. "Now Watch Out for the Incubator Bubble." *Red Herring*, July 2000.

———. "Open Letter to Trip Hawkins." *Red Herring*, April 1993.

———. "The Thinker." *Red Herring*, March 1995.

———. "Venture Pioneers." *Red Herring*, March 1994.

———. "Bill Joy on Sun's Long Road from Java to Jini—and Where Microsoft Comes In." *Red Herring*, January 1999.

Perkins, Michael C. "Angels on High." *Red Herring*, Going Public: 1997.

———. "Burn, Baby, Burn." *Red Herring*, June 2000.

———. "Cash Is for Dummies." *Red Herring*, August 2000.

———. "Leaders of the Pack." *Red Herring*, August 2000.

Perkins, Michael C., and Anthony B. Perkins. "3DO's New Trip." *Red Herring*, May 1996.

———. "Case by Case: A Conversation with Steve Case." *Red Herring*, June 1996.

Perkins, Michael C., and Celia Núñez. "Insiders Pull the Rug from under Small Investors." *Milwaukee Journal Sentinel*, February 4, 2001.

———. "Why Insiders Don't Feel Your Pain." *Washington Post,* March 15, 2001.

Pollack, Andrew. "It Sliced, It Sentimentalized, but Now Can It Surf?" *New York Times,* November 23, 1998.

———. "Weed-out Time in Biotechnology." *New York Times,* December 16, 1998.

Richtel, Matt. "Stock Option Blues: Slide Leaves Little but a Big Tax Bill." *New York Times,* February 18, 2001.

Romer, Paul. "It's All in Your Head." *Outlook Magazine,* no. 1, 1998.

Sahlman, William A. "The Race Between Capital and Opportunity." Harvard Business School, July 1998.

Sahlman, William A., and Dimitri V. d'Arbeloff. "Sense and Nonsense in the Capital Markets." Harvard Business School, 1998.

Sahlman, William A., and Howard H. Stevenson. "Capital Market Myopia." *Journal of Business Venturing,* Winter 1985.

Schifrin, Matthew, and Om Malik. "Amateur Hour on Wall Street." *Forbes,* January 25, 1999.

Siconolfi, Michael. "The Spin Desk: Underwriters Set Aside IPO Stock for Officials of Potential Customers." *Wall Street Journal,* November 12, 1997.

Siegel, Jeremy J. "Big-Cap Stocks Are a Sucker's Bet." *Wall Street Journal,* March 14, 2000.

Smith, Randall, and Susan Pullman. "U.S. Probes Inflated Commissions for Hot IPOs." *Wall Street Journal,* December 7, 2000.

Stein, Tom. "Who Wants to be a Venture Capitalist?" *Red Herring,* May 2000.

Streitfeld, David. "In Silicon Valley, No Time to Be Jolly." *Washington Post,* December 17, 2000

Taptich, Brian E. "The New Startup." *Red Herring,* October 1998.

———. "Pop Goes the Weisel." *Red Herring,* August 1999.

Thomas, Landon Jr., "Amazon Board Member, in a Fury, Tried to Suppress Lehman Report." *New York Observer,* February 14, 2001.

Uchitelle, Louis. "Reviving the Economics of Fear." *New York Times,* July 2, 1999.

Warner, Melanie. "Inside the Silicon Valley Money Machine." *Fortune,* October 26, 1998.

———. "Seduced by the Internet." *Fortune*, March 5, 2001.

Wyatt, Edward. "Feasting on a Banquet of Internet Offerings." *New York Times*, April 12, 1999.

———. "Old Stocks, New Technology, More Questions." *New York Times*, February 16, 1999.

# ACKNOWLEDGMENTS

*T*he *Internet Bubble* would not be comfortably resting in your hands right now if we had not received the active and enlightening participation of the following list of people.

For the revised edition of *The Internet Bubble* we once again must give our effusive thanks to Cameron Hyzer, associate of Broadview Capital Partners, a private equity affiliate of Broadview International Bank. As with the first edition of the book, Cameron's help analyzing the financial data, as well as calculating the Bubble, was absolutely essential. Neither edition of the book would have been complete without his assistance. We must also acknowledge Vinnee Tong, research specialist at *Red Herring,* whose help with the data was also essential to the second edition. Finally, we must tip our hats to Celia Núñez, who did a brilliant job of editing the entire revised edition.

Writing a pointed analysis of the technology investment market was obviously a Herculean task. It was accomplished by seeking the insights and perspectives of only the most insightful and powerful insiders in technology, and ruthlessly selecting what we felt were the most logical and best supported arguments and analysis. The book has new and often trenchant things to say about venture capital and public company investing. In the tradition of *Red Herring* magazine, we do not conceal our opinions, and we anticipate that these opinions will unsettle many important players in the technology community.

Our most gracious thanks goes to Roger McNamee, cofounder and partner at Integral Capital Partners, the person who spent the most time with us, initially helping us develop the book's general thesis, and later poring over and editing many of the different sections in the book as they were drafted. It will become clear to the readers as they delve into the book that we, along with the rest of the industry and the media that covers technology, believe that Roger is one of the brightest and most forward-thinking commentators in the business.

Other industry titans who were also generous with their time and observations include: Herb Allen Jr.; Marc Andreessen, cofounder of Netscape and LoudCloud; Andy Bechtolsheim; Jeff Bezos, CEO of Amazon.com; Bill Brady at CS First Boston; Jim Breyer, managing partner at Accel Partners; Lise Buyer, general partner at Technology Partners; Bandel Carano, general partner at Oak Investment Partners; Dan Case, chairman and CEO of investment bank Chase H&Q; Jim Clark; Sandy Climan, managing director of Entertainment Media Ventures LLC.; Sam Colella, general partner at Institutional Venture Partners and Versant; Jim Collins; Ron Conway general partner and founder of Angel Investors; Dennis Crow, partner at Pierce & Crow; Yogen Dalal and Kevin Fong, general partners at the Mayfield Fund; Paul Deninger, chairman and CEO of technology investment bank Broadview International; Mark Diocioccio, vice president at Lehman Brothers; John Doerr, general partner at Kleiner Perkins Caufield & Byers; Eric Doppstadt, director of Private Equity at the Ford Foundation; Bill Draper and Robin Richards Donohoe of Draper Richards; Tim Draper, general partner at Draper Fisher Jurvetson; Ira Ehrenpreis, general partner at Technology Partners; Steve Forbes; Stu Francis, managing director at Lehman Brothers; Bill Gates, chairman and CEO of Microsoft; George Gilbert, comanager of the Northern Technology Fund; Eric Greenberg, CEO of Scient; Michael Grimes, managing partner at Morgan Stanley Dean Witter; Bill Gurley, general partner at Benchmark Partners; Will Hearst III, general partner at Kleiner Perkins Caufield & Byers; David Henderson, economist and research fellow at the Hoover Institution; Phil Horsley, managing director of Horsley Bridge Partners; Mark Jensen, managing director of the technology practice at Arthur Andersen; Franklin "Pitch" Johnson, general partner at Asset Management; Bill Joy, cofounder and chief scientist at Sun Microsystems; Steve Jurvetson, general partner at Draper Fisher Jurvetson; Eric Janszen, general partner at Osborn Capital; Robert Kagle, general partner at Benchmark Partners; Andy Kessler at Velocity Capital; Vinod Khosla, general partner at Kleiner Perkins Caufield & Byers; Marc Klee, manager of the John Hancock Global Technology Fund; Brad Koenig, managing director and head of the technology banking practice at Goldman Sachs; Tim Koogle, Chairman of Yahoo; Mark Kvamme, general partner at Sequoia Capital; Kevin Landis, cofounder and chief investment officer of Firsthand Funds; Bruce Lupatkin, former director of research at Hambrecht & Quist; Donald Luskin; Jeff Mallett, president at Yahoo; Arthur Marks, general partner at New Enterprise Associates; Mary Meeker, Internet analyst at Morgan Stanley Dean Witter; Bob Metcalfe; Cristina Morgan, managing director at Chase H&Q; Michael Moritz, general partner at Sequoia Capital; John Mumford, general partner at Crosspoint Venture Partners; Elizabeth Obershaw, vice president and chief investment officer for Hewlett-Packard pension fund; Tom Perkins; Frank Quattrone, managing director and head of technology banking at CS First Boston; Dan Reeve of Horsley Bridge Partners; Stephen Roach, chief economist at Morgan Stanley Dean Witter; Sandy Robertson; Arthur Rock; Paul Romer, economist at Stanford University; Joel Romines and Brad Kelly, partners at Knightsbridge Advisors; Phil Rotner, managing director in the Office of the Treasurer at MIT; William Sahlman, professor at Harvard Business School; George Shott and Alan Chai at Shott Capital Management; Roger Siboni, CEO at E.piphany; Don Valentine, general partner at Sequoia Capital; Andrew Verhalen, general partner at Matrix Partners; Alberto Vilar, manager of the Amerindo Technology Fund; Meg Whitman, CEO of eBay; Ann Winblad, general partner at Hummer Winblad Partners; Carrie Wong, partner at Niehaus Ryan Wong; Geoff Yang, general partner at Redpoint Ventures; Jerry Yang, cofounder and chief Yahoo at Yahoo; and Edward Yardeni, chief economist at Deutsche Grenfell Morgan.

For extensive help in data collection, financial analysis, and our Bubble calculation we would like to acknowledge the entire Broadview International organization for their tireless work and quick turnaround. In addition, Broadview was very helpful in producing extensive strategic insight into the Internet market and its various segments.

Dave Witherow and Jean Yaremchuk of VentureOne and Roydel Stewart at Hambrecht & Quist also deserve kudos for their help and support in the data-collection area.

The first edition never would have been in the kind of shape it needed to be without the highly intelligent and invaluable work of our developmental editors, Nina Davis and Shirley Tokheim. Nina was particularly helpful in bringing to bear on the book her extensive knowledge of the industry and technical insight, as well as her unfailing logic. She saved us from many potential mistakes. Shirley was especially helpful in editing the book for style and giving us the constant perspective of an intelligent reader living outside the industry.

We can't forget Ellen Anderson and her transcription service Anderson Typefast for timely and precise rendition of our numerous interview tapes. Their work helped assure that we would accurately quote the numerous on-the-record interviews we did for the book. A special thanks to many *Red Herring* staff members, including Charlotte Dicke, Danielle Unis, and Pam Dabney, who helped us arrange and coordinate a grueling schedule of meetings and interviews. And, finally, Chris Alden, cofounder and editorial director at *Red Herring* for his general support for the project.

At Harper: Adrian Zackheim, publisher, who provided us with the original inspiration for the book and believed in us all the way, and David Conti, executive editor, who patiently put up with our many broken deadlines and the management of what became a very complex task. At International Creative Management: Esther Newberg, the queen of literary agents, who successfully banged on Harper and doubled our advance, and John De Laney of the ICM legal department, who provided extensive help with the contract.

Special affection is reserved for Georganne Perkins, wife of Michael, who though offering no advice or information due to professional confidentiality issues, nevertheless provided continual moral support throughout this project.

Also many thanks to Anthony's new wife, Nicole, for her faith and prayers.

# INDEX